Watergate Summer

Watergate Summer

Allie McNeil

authorHOUSE

AuthorHouse™
1663 Liberty Drive
Bloomington, IN 47403
www.authorhouse.com
Phone: 1-800-839-8640

© *2012 by Allie McNeil. All rights reserved.*

No part of this book may be reproduced, stored in a retrieval system, or transmitted by any means without the written permission of the author.

Published by AuthorHouse   03/29/2012

ISBN: 978-1-4685-3215-9 (sc)
ISBN: 978-1-4685-3214-2 (e)

Library of Congress Control Number: 2012905870

Any people depicted in stock imagery provided by Thinkstock are models, and such images are being used for illustrative purposes only.
Certain stock imagery © Thinkstock.

This book is printed on acid-free paper.

Because of the dynamic nature of the Internet, any web addresses or links contained in this book may have changed since publication and may no longer be valid. The views expressed in this work are solely those of the author and do not necessarily reflect the views of the publisher, and the publisher hereby disclaims any responsibility for them.

DEDICATION . . . .

I dedicate this Book to 6-6 my son, my lovely Critters, the the 99 Percenters and to all Bloggers and Independent Media who speak Truth to Power . . . .

And an huge thank you to my son who would always ask "What are you blogging today?"

He made me think, he made me pay attention, he made me care more.

INTRODUCTION: LETTER TO THE READER ABOUT WATERGATE SUMMER... THE BEST AND WORST OF 6 YEARS OF BLOGGING...

I originally started this Blog as a place to rant about the Bush White House. I like thousands of others during the Bush years took to blogging. In many ways Citizen Journalism started right after Bush took the White House in 2001. You will notice that I don't ever name the President in my posts, I call him Mr.Bush and occasionally I call him the King. Much of the early part of my blog has snark, anger,disgust, and yes, some cursing. Over time the blog evolved and my foul mouth was tamed and I became more concerned with reporting what our MSM was not reporting. I also began to research and report What MSM was not reporting from Disasters to Health Crisis Statistics to Housing /Homelessness and VET issues.

I also blogged much that is not in this book, months on the Oilspill in the Gulf 2010, thousands of us documenting and blogging the Horrors of that Disaster.

We researched health issues, concerns for the Shrimpers, and we tried to guess-estimate the true expelled volume of the Gusher at the bottom of the Sea. We tried to track and write about the effects on the ecosystem, and document the damage to the Sea, the Coasts, the sea life.

I blogged and tweeted Uprisings, Egypt to Libya to

Iran. The Summer of 2009 I even had a blog dedicated to The Iran Uprising, and another blog that was just for medical assistance, (wound care to head wounds to Tear gas remedies). Over time that very information began to be helpful not just for Iran, but for Egypt and then finally for the OWS protests here in the states. And on twitter in the middle of the night when USTREAM would show some occupy settlement facing police brutality I would tweet more medical aid.

Being a Nurse and Blogging also I meant I blogged and tweeted over the years many Disasters and Health Crisises. From Haiti to Japan the Tsunami and Fukushima. I partly did this to try to help get help to these regions, but it was also done in an effort to get keep alive a certain level of Humanity and Compassion, Especially under the Bush Regime who was known for sleeping through Disasters or doing Flyovers.

In some ways that first summer of 2005 living in Downtown Cleveland would shape the Blog, I was living in a place where the Effects of a Country recklessly throwing money into two wars was being seen. Homeless Iraq Vets with PTSD were living on the streets by our Loft. I would take them food, water and do Pet Therapy with my dog. (Truth be told it is now 2011 and I am still doing all those things, I still drive downtown to check on them and take them what they need). And now as of 2011 Finally all of the things that I blogged about are being covered in the Mainstream Media and the OCCUPY Movement has brought them attention long overdue, from the Foreclosure Crisis to the Vet homelessness and unemployment crisis).

So yes much of my early Blogging was me venting, ranting, cursing. I was going to edit that out, but then I thought about it, why should I edit out my anger?

Our country was thrown upside down, and in public maybe people were not talking, but Blogs were on fire with the disgust and dismay. In public people didn't talk.

When Bush or Cheney would come to Cleveland they would shut off whole blocks from the public so their motorcade could race through downtown. There was no waving to the masses. And the first time I saw Cheney's motorcade come through Downtown Cleveland whipping corners at 80 mph, it struck me that if it moved that fast it didn't have to see us The People either.

Most of the MSM media from small broadcasting stations to bigger print media empires all began to shift their reporting as soon as Bush became President. The actual mess of that election did not receive the coverage and investigation it should have. (Which is also unfortunate as even in 2000/2001 it highlighted that our Government needed to make reforms to the system, not to work on issues of "Voter fraud" as the Republicans like to rant, but to prevent Voter Manipulation. And yes, I write about Caged Voting and Purging in this Book. Which is another reason I never really accepted Bush as President, as my Vote was purged in 2000. Yet here it is 2011 and now the Tea Party and Republicans are finding ways to limit People's abilities to Vote, which is Voter Suppression.

Blogs began in earnest in 2003, and by the time the War was cranked up Blogs were flourishing. The First two blogs I starting reading daily were "Crooks and Liars" and "Skippy "and then Truthout, and by 2005 I was hooked. I ended up going to read blogs to search for some Truth. It's very odd because even early on Blogs and Bloggers were ridiculed by Mainstream Media and Journalists. Yet then some very fine online News Magazines and Blogs and Internet News Sites began to absorb some topnotch journalists, and that changed the landscape. And by 2005 many papers were laying off fine journalists and Investigative Writers as well, and independent Media were on the rise. In time when History remembers this era I hope the honesty and angst and the integrity of Bloggers speaking Truth to Power during a dark time is somehow honored.

And there were people like me, Moms, and Dads and college students and even old political activists who were frustrated by Our Country and what was happening. First it started with Bush being put into the White House in 2001, with none of us sure what had happened with the Election, and then witnessing 2004 another possible Stolen Election. And yet the MSM did not investigate either incident or series of events, they remained silent. And then there other events that the MSM seemed to handle with great apathy? The Elections, 911, and then the War and the Build Up to the War, and the Lies and Propaganda that was peddled. And then came Gitmo and Torture and Abu Gahrib and still no real reporting or follow up. Some

Issues were explored, but then quickly the conversation would change and issues such as the Patriot Act or Torture would move below the fold in the Papers. And all of us that felt concern, rage, outrage and horror had nowhere to get our Information, our Data. The Media was inconsistent and labile. Blogs began to flourish because MainStream Media failed to provide the needed "news" and information and investigative reporting that was so needed.

Blogs also had a feature that Newspapers did not, they had a way to interact, to connect and to share. The Comment Sections began to be a place where people could share and talk and stay connected. People were not really meeting in groups or in public during the Bush years. The Military and Other groups including Security Entities that were spying on citizens, infiltrating Granny Knitting Groups and Quakers against the War, and even Vegan groups. Yet Online there were thousands of people talking and sharing information and talking about what was happening to our Country, from the Illegal War to Gitmo to Torture.

Yet I also ended up reporting, covering in detail so much more, from the Haiti earthquake, to the Health care Crisis in America, to Homelessness, the 2008 Economic Meltdown, to the Vets Crisis of PTSD to suicide rates, to Japan Fukushima and Tsunami Disasters. I covered Disasters in detail, sometimes daily logging the latest information and links, especially for Haiti and Japan, and the Gulf Oil Disaster, covering for many months.

But I also covered other situations, like Iran and their uprising over Voting. I realized over time I had this idea that if disasters are reported and people can help, then compassion is spread just by sharing information. And that in some way people still feel connected, even though under Bush that was often lost or damaged.

I had started reading blogs in 2003, by the Summer of 2005 I personally was living in Cleveland, transplanted by my own miserable Whistleblower Circumstances and battling for my health, while trying to still take care of my son. I was in a strange city, and I was also living again for a time with my Ex. He had moved and traveled with us to Cleveland as I was pretty sick, with muscle and heart issues. We were living in Downtown Cleveland in a Loft. It was a hot steamy summer. My Ex had come to help take care of me and help with my son, but it was also fairly obvious as we had been seperated for 2 years that we should not be living together . . . But what my Ex did that spring and summer helping us relocate was a noble admirable thing. He also bought me a laptop and it was truly needed and appreciated, it was truly my very own first Computer that I did not have to share with him or with my son. (More of what happened in the previous 5 years and led to the Cleveland Transplantation is in "Silent Fallout" my other book).

So that summer while being sick, I taught myself how to blog and my son gave me the Handle "Enigma4ever" which I had been using as my persona to visit other blogs and leave comments since 2003. (Actually my son came up with the Enigma4ever handle long ago, and I love it, it suits me.) I like that no one really knew who I was and that I did not have to have a name or face, I could just share thoughts, concerns. After writing letters for years about Contamination in a small town it was nice to be faceless and nameless. (You can read more about the Whistleblower Story in Silent Fallout.). And yes, in other ways since I had had dealings already with the the Bush EPA and other agencies I was more than jaded, I was worried about how the American people really were being taken care of.

So summer of 2005 true story, I had nightmares all summer about a Bad Hurricane. And my ex was really sick of me complaining about this issue, and ironically enough we had a few hurricanes that summer. And he kept saying, "See it was not that bad Allie, it 's ok" And I kept telling him that it hadn't happened yet, and finally I shut up about it as really it was annoying to him and me. And then Bush spent the summer doing other horrible things like ratting out a CIA agent, and calling her "Fair Game", and documents came forward showing the Iraq War as a Sham ("The Downing Street Documents") And for a time a core group of liberals were convinced that said documents would help to unravel the Illegal Iraq war for what it was and also produce Criminal charges against the Administration for lying to the People.

And so that July 2005 I started Blogging. And yes, I named it Watergate Summer, because as nerdy 12 year old I had followed the Nixon Era with great interest. I had watched and read everything from the Break In and even the Hearings that famous summer. And in my heart I always thought that Summer tested us as a Nation, made us scrutinize Our Leaders, Our Justice, and our Journalists. It was a turning point in our History. And in many ways I was hoping, praying for another Such Summer, a Summer of Unraveling of Crimes, A Watergate Summer. And yes, in many ways, I kept blogging and hoping for such a Summer all these years.

So by August 2005 Bush went on Vacation and we now all remember his long extended Vacations, and how every time he went away for a long time Things Would Happen and he would remain Silent, Invisible. The First time this happened was the Christmas Tsunami. I was in California then, and I worked with Travel Agents doing Lost and Found Work (For Missing Persons) Online. It was one of those moments when having online skills paid off, I taught myself a smidge of Thai and worked reading Hospital and Temple Lists of Dead and Missing and helped relay information to Foreign families and other families' agents. I even had some contacts with some State Department Workers and NGO's and Relief Agencies that Christmas, as well as Social Workers at the Thai Hospitals. It was the first time I can ever remember being mortified by our Government's pathetic response to such a huge Disaster. It took Bush 5 days to respond. Some of the foreigners I met during that Situation responded, "Your President was slow, maybe it is because the people are not white? are foreign? Non Christian?" I had no response to their concerns, but it did strike me as worrisome. People in California said something that shook me, "I am sure if there was an American Disaster he would handle it better, we all knew he lacked Diplomacy Skills when he came to DC". That statement left me wondering, how would he handle Disasters at Home?

So by summer of 2005 I started blogging, and the first posts were of course political, I did not share any of my Life that first year. No One knew I was sick or even where I lived or what I had been through, they knew I was a mom and a nurse and that was it. And so Bush went on Vacation and I ranted and raved about that, and Cindy Sheehan went and camped by his ranch and I thought that was astounding. And then his vacation went on and on and then we knew that Katrina was coming. The Weather and NASA maps were stunning, and still no word of Federal Warnings or Involvement. It seemed all the states in the Eye were on their own (and they were).

Watergate Summer

So Watergate Summer, the Blog began by focusing on Katrina and Bush's Long Silent Vacation that First Summer. And for some reason the July Posts have vanished from my Blog, but the August ones remain, so I am sharing them, exactly as they are, raw and real. And they are written in Capitals, partly out of anger, and partly because that August I had a bad eye Bleed, so typing was hard. I never went back and re-read those posts until now. It is rather shocking to read how alarming it was that the President let a Major City Drown. (There would be many posts by me on Katrina, over 100 over the next 3 years.) I wrote letters to Bush, I wrote scathing posts about Brownie and his lack of FEMA skills, and even about people that died. When Anderson Cooper found a woman dead sitting in her wheelchair, I was determined to find out WHO she was, I could not rest until I knew her name and what happened. So that story is also shared here. I searched Phone Records and reports trying to assess the Total Dead and I even searched Obituaries.

What people don't know is that I was relentless that August and September. I sent Medical Supplies to the Vets for Peace and I called Liquor and Beer Companies ordered /begged for Water for the different shelters in Alabama, NOLA, and even Houston. And I even contacted the Disaster Refugee Rapporteur for the UN, I spoke with two, one in London and another from Geneva. I taped 50 hours of Katrina and the tapes I sent to the UN. And the UN said that a Team would be sent to investigate. And I wrote a letter to Al Gore about the Hospitals that could not evacuate and that were stranded with their patients. As a Nurse I think that was what horrified me the most that the Bush Administration with one of the largest Militaries in the world would not send help to so many there, it would have been so easy to send the Navy or Air Force. He did not even air drop water or MRE's until after Day 5, and by then bodies were floating in the streets and on roofs. I will never forget his silence, and then the "Show" that followed it.

And all I could think was, this is the same President and Administration that would not respond to concerns about Drinking Water for 90,000 people in the NW, am I really shocked that he would turn his back on his Own People. The Answer is No. And now I knew that more people would see what a disaster this President and his inept Administration really were.

Allie McNeil

So the Bush years were Blogged, all of it, Torture, Loss of Rights, Bad Decisions, Lies, PTSD, all of it. And then I also blogged other aspects of Life. I have always felt that Politics does impact our Lives, so it is woven into the blog. I also blogged funny stories and happenings living in Cleveland, from Burnt Cornbread to Getting Mugged to Pet Therapy with Iraq War Vets to Homeless living on the Grates, to Memories of growing up in Baltimore, to Working as an AIDS Nurse, it is all here . . . Shared. Along the way I blogged Funerals (Ford, James Brown to Coretta Scott King). and shared videos and music. I shared stories that are in a way my History, of who I am, or how I came to be so "damn political". It's all here, the good, the bad, the ugly, but also what matters during the Bush years up through 2011 and a new Administration. I have tried to pick the Posts that are the most important from those years, and why I blogged them. And I admit some of the posts were just for me, and some for my teenage son, and some were for Readers. In an odd way they are my History, but also Our History during a very difficult time.

And for those that say that Bloggers aren't Journalists I can live with that, but I also know that we did change History and we did raise important questions and the ugly Truth when Real Journalists were not. I am proud I was a Blogger during the Bush years, I am proud that I blogged what mattered during an ugly time in our History. I blogged what Mattered.

AUGUST 18, 2005, THURSDAY

BUSH'S AUGUST NUMBERS IN THE DITCH

Friends-

Before you read the numbers in the Ditch . . . .

Pass on Elizabeth Edwards letter . . . pass on to the Red Blogs as well if you can . . . it is something to stir Every mom: http://theimmoralminority.blogspot.com/2005/08/elizabeth-e

So I was trolling the internet and there are alot of polls coming out for August—and what is amazing, is that they are actually only for the First week—Aug 5 & 6, which is only a few days into the Camp Casey Vigil (and the King's Vacation).

(So we really bet they must Really Suck now?!)

This poll is of all States and compares numbers falling in Red States and Blue States.

* * * Be Sure to read this with the Google Game PartI: Bush there are some interesting overlaps with these numbers* * *

Go to the August 5th survey that just came out August 16th: http://www.democrats.org/blog

Bottom Line:

Weighted Average:

Approval of President's Bush's job as president: 41%

Dissapproval: 55%

Lowest 29 %: Rhode Island

Highest: Idaho 58%

RED STATES that are now Below 50% Approval: (This includes 50% and below)

ALASKA (46), ARIZONA (45), ARKANSAS (40), COLORADO (45), FLORIDA (44), GEORGIA (47),INDIANA (48), IOWA (42),

KANSAS (46), KENTUCKY (42), LOUISIANA (48), MISSISSIPPI (49), MISSOURI (38), MONTANA (50), NEW MEXICO (41), NEBRASKA (55), NEVADA (40), NORTH CAROLINA (47), OHIO (37), OKLAHOMA (50), PENNSYLVANIA (40), SOUTH CAROLINA (45), SOUTH DAKOTA (45), TENNESSEE (43), WEST VIRGINA (45), VIRGINIA (42) . . . .

Blue States that Have below 50% rating:

Delaware (32), California (32), Hawaii (43), Illinois (38), New Hampshire (42), New Jersey (35), New York (34),Connecticut (?), Massachusetts (?), Oregon (41),Vermont (33), Washington(40), Wisconsin (41), And so WHAT does this mean? Here is a List of States that are above 50% in Approving King George's handling of his job as President (and by the way 50 % is Proud of . . . .)

The States that nothing to be still Approve: (Damn Short list): Idaho(59), Utah (57), Alabama (52), North Dakota (51), Texas (54), Nebraska (55), Wyoming (58). Yup KIng George is still "approved" above 50%—by a slim margin in some—In SEVEN STATES . . . SEVEN.

AND on another level it shows ALOT of Americans are Very Unhappy with the King . . . . Republicans too?

AUGUST 30, 2005, TUESDAY

KING GEORGE GET OFF YOUR ASS— YOUR VACATION IS LONG OVER

FIRST I HAVE TO APOLOGIZE THIS WHOLE POST WILL BE IN A LARGE LETTERS. I HAVE A BLOWN EYEBALL—SO IT WILL BE THIS SIZE SO I CAN READ IT.

HERE'S THE THING GEORGE, YOUR VACATION ACTUALLY ENDED WEEKS AGO—BUT WHEN KATRINA HIT—IT ACTUALLY ENDED FOR GOOD—6:50 AM VERY EARLY MONDAY MORNING. TRUTHFULLY YOU SHOULD HAVE GONE BACK TO DC ON SATURDAY MORNING EARLY WHEN EVERY WEATHERMAN WORTH HIS SALT WAS PERDICTING DEVASTATION FOR THE GULF COAST.

(I AM AGAIN NOT GOING TO BE NICE HERE—RAISED BY SOUTHERN WOMEN AND ALSO HAVING RIDDEN OUT A FEW HURRICANES DOWN SOUTH—I FEEL I MIGHT KNOW MORE THAN KING CHICKEN SHIT ABOUT THIS. I ALSO HAVE FEMA AND RED CROSS TRAINING ABOUT THIS, AND AS A NURSE I KNOW 1000'S ARE NOW ENDANGERED BECAUSE OF THE KING'S INCOMPETENCE).

AND WE KNOW IT TOOK FIVE DAYS FOR THE KING TO ACKNOWLEDGE THE TSUNAMI IN INDONESIA . . . BUT HELL THIS IS RIGHT HERE, RIGHT NOW, IN HIS BACKYARD, AND MILLIONS ARE EFFECTED.

FIRST OFF THE GUARD—ALL GUARD SHOULD HAVE BEEN PLACED ON ALERT ON SATURDAY—READYING ALL FLIGHT VEHICLES, AND AMPHIBIAN VEHICLES, BOATS. ALL MEDIC TEAMS AND RESCUE TEAMS SHOULD HAVE BEEN MADE READY AND PUT IN PLACE IN TENNESSEE. READY TO MOBILIZE TO THE GULF STATES. NATIONAL GUARD—HALF THAT ARE IN IRAQ—WHEN THEY SHOULD BE HERE DOING WHAT THEY WERE TRAINED TO DO= TAKING CARE OF THEIR NEIGHBORS AT HOME. IT IS NOW 6PM TUESDAY—AND YOU MADE A LITTLE PEEVISH SPEECH FROM YOUR "PARTY"/ CELEBRATION OUT ON NAVY SHIP IN SAN DIEGO—YOU HAD PLANNED TO GIVE A BIG "AXIS OF EVIL SPEECH" BUT INSTEAD THE STORM SEEMS TO HAVE RAINED ON YOUR PARADE.

SO IN YOUR SPEECH ON THE SHIP YOU GAVE OUT SOME IRRITATED ADVICE—BUT REALLY DID NOT OFFER YOUR CONDOLENCES OR SUPPORT TO THE POOR FOLKS DOWN SOUTH. YOU ONCE AGAIN SEEM IRRITATED THAT THEY WERE NEEDING TO BE RESCUED. THOUSANDS NEED WATER, FOOD, SHELTER, HEALTHCARE. THEY NEEDED YOU TO STATE THAT THE GUARD IS ON THE WAY. HERE IT IS 36 HOURS INTO THIS CATOSTOPHRE, AND NOT A PEEP FROM DHHS, HOMELAND SECURITY, EPA, DEPT OF ENERGY, YES WE HAVE HEARD FROM FEMA—BUT AGAIN JUST LIKE AFTER 911 WE LEFT SURFING THE CHANNELS TO ATTEMPT TO FIND OUT IF PEOPLE ARE BEING CARED FOR.

THOUSANDS—25,000 IN THE DOME WITH A SHREDDED ROOF—AND MINIMAL POWER . . . . AND MINIMAL MANPOWER, WATER RSING OUTSIDE—WAIST HIGH BY 6PM, ONE SUICIDE, 1000'S BROUGHT THERE . . . PLUCKED OFF ROOFS . . . AND BROUGHT TO THE HELL OF THE DOME. 1000'S SITTING IN THE DARK WONDERING HOW THEIR HOMES ARE, THEIR FAMILIES, THEIR NEIGHBORS. AND SOME ARE SICK, SOME POOR, SOME WITH PETS, OR RELATIVES THAT THEY COULD NOT LEAVE . . . . THEY HAD NO CHOICE.

13% OF THE U.S. LIVES BELOW POVERTY LEVEL, SO YEAH, ATLEAST ONE THIRD OF THE 37 MILLION OF OUR POOR LIVE IN THE SOUTH, AND SO NOW 1000'S THAT WERE ALREADY POOR ARE NOW IN MORE DANGEROUS STRAIGHTS NEED THE GUARD TO ARRIVE WITH C5S', CHINOOKS, AND AMPHIBIAN VEHICLES TO BRING FOOD AND WATER AND SHELTER, AND YEAH HOPE.

SEE HERE IS THE THING GEORGE THAT IS YOUR JOB—GO SIT AT THE WHITE HOUSE AND ORGANIZE, OR ATELAST ACT LIKE IT. AND GO ON THE AIR AND SAY THAT HELP IS ON THE WAY AND THE GUARD IS ON THE WAY. I MEAN I KNOW ATLEAST HALF TO THE GUARD IS OVER IN IRAQ, BUT YOU COULD OFFER THE GUARD HERE. NINETEEN STATES AND GOVERNORS HAVE OFFERED THEIR GUARD. (THERE IS 31,000 AVAILABLE IN THE GULF STATES ALONE—ALTHOUGH WE DON'T KNOW IF DUE TO DOWN LINES AND COMMUNICATION PROBLEMS THOSE GUARD CAN BE REACHED) AND YET YOUR SILENCE AND ABSENCE IS PALPABLE . . . . ;.ONCE AGAIN MISSING IN ACTION.

I DON'T WANT TO HEAR "I WAS SO SHOCKED—I DIDN'T KNOW HOW BAD IT WAS"

HURRICANE SEASON PEAKS EVERY YEAR AT THIS TIME—EVERY YEAR ON YOUR VACATION. IF YOU DON'T REMEMBER—TALK TO JEB—HE WOULD REMEMBER LAST YEAR.

1000'S WITH CHILDREN SICK RELATIVE, ELDERLY, THANK GOD FOR THE COAST GUARD HELPING PEOPLE BUST HOLES IN THEIR ROOFS . . . . WHERE ARE YOU TONIGHT? DINING AT THE WEST WHITE HOUSE OR AT SOME PARTY IN SAN DIEGO?

TO MY POOR READERS, PLEASE CALL THE RED CROSS AND SALVATION ARMY AND OFFER MONEY . . . .

CHECK CRAIGLIST.COM IF YOU WANT TO OFFER SERVICES AND YOU LIVE IN THAT AREA.

VACATION IS OVER GEORGE, GET OFF YOUR ASS AND SIGN THE EXECUTIVE ORDERS THAT ARE NEEDED TO SAVE LIVES NOW, AND ALLOW THE GOVERNORS OF THESE STATES TO GET THE HELP AND THE GUARD THERE NOW, THEY NEED HELP—NOW

AUGUST 31, 2005, WEDNESDAY

THE KATRINA MESS IN A NUTSHELL: BUSH'S GOAT MOMENT

IT IS NOW 3PM WEDNESDAY WE ARE IN HOUR 84 OF THIS CRISIS.

ANOTHER GREAT GOAT MOMENT FOR BUSH—AND UNCLE DICK AND RUMMY ARE MIA.?????

(1) CHERTOFF GAVE A CONFERENCE AT 2PM EST WITH HIS "COLLEGUES", WITH ALL THE KEY DISASTER PEOPLE ADDRESSING THE NATION AND HOW THIS CRISIS WILL BE DEALT WITH—EPA, NTA, DHHS, AND FEMA, AND ENERGY—BUSH'S CABINET—NO WH LEADERSHIP PRESENT—WHAT THE F IS GOING ON FOLKS THIS IS CRITICAL....
(2) SUSPOSEDLY WHILE THIS CONFERENCE WAS GOING ON BUSH WAS FLYING OVER THE REGION IN AIRFORCE ONE—THAT IS NOT ACCEPTABLE OR GOOD ENOUGH. HE NEEDS TO FLY OVER IN HIS MARINE HELICOPTERS AND SEE UP CLOSE AND PERSONAL HOW BAD THIS DEVASTATION IS, AND NOW WE ARE TOLD BY MEDIA THAT KING CHICKENSHIT WILL BE GIVING A PRESS CONFERENCE IN THE ROSE GARDEN AT 5PM HIS TIME. WHERE IS DICK? OR RUMMY?
(3) THE NATIONAL GUARD QUESTIONS REMAIN VERY BLURRY AS TO WHAT THE PENTAGON CAN AND

WILL SPARE TO THE REGION—KEEP AN EYE ON THIS FOLKS . . . . THERE ARE ONLY 8300 GUARD ON GROUND IN THE REGION RIGHT HERE AND NOW—WITH MILLIONS IN DANGEROUS SITUATION—UNACCEPTABLE, BUSH AND RUMMY COULD FREE UP 1000'S RIGHT NOW—BUT THEY WON'T ASK WHY???!!! . . . .

(4) GO TO FEMA WEBSITE AND READ TRANSCRIPT ON THE CONFERENCE—IT SEEMS TO ME THAT THESE FOLKS AT THE CONFERENCE WORKED ALL WEEKEND PROBLEM-SOLVING AND TRYING TO STRATEGIZE WHAT TO DO . . . . BUT NO EXECUTIVE ORDERS HAVE BEEN SIGNED—AND THAT CHERTOFF IS TRYING AS BEST HE CAN TO WORK WITH FEMA TO GET WHAT THESE PEOPLE NEED. CHERTOFF AND THOSE PRESENT I ACTUALLY THINK ARE TRYING TO ORGANIZE AND COORDINATE . . . . BUT MISSING LEADERSHIP IS A PROBLEM . . . ESP. WHEN MILITARY RESOURCES ARE SO BADLY NEEDED. THIS IS WHY WE HAVE A NATIONAL GUARD FOLKS—19 GOVERNORS FROM OTHER STATES AHVE OFFERED THEIR GUARD—ONLY ONE THING STANDS IN THE WAY—THE KING . . . . HE WOULD HAVE TO ALLOW GUARD FROM OTHER STATES TO GO TO THE REGION AND HE SEEMS VERY RELUCTANT TO DO THAT . . . ASK WHY??? AND WHERE ARE DICK AND RUMMY? I MEAN AFTER RIAQ WAS INVADED THEY WERE ON THE MIC WITH ON HOURS OFFERING HEALTHCARE, REBULDING, AND MORE . . . WHY THE SILENCE? HAVE THEY EMPTIED THE PENATGON COFFERS? ASK WHY? SOMETHING SMELLS—AND IT AIN'T JUST THE FUMES FROM THE DOME AND THINGS FLOATING IN THE FLOOD WATERS . . .

(5) MAYOR OF NEW ORLEANS FINALLY HAS SAID WHAT WE ALL FEARED/KNEW THAT HE FEARS HUNDREDS IF NOT 1000'S ARE DEAD . . . . THERE ARE DEAD FLOATING IN THOSE WATERS FOLKS . . . . WE ALL KNOW IT. 1000'S COULD NOT LEAVE BECAUSE THEY WERE TOO POOR

OR INFIRMED AND DO NOT HAVE A CAR OR COULD NOT AFFORD GAS. GO TO MIKE SHUSTERS BLOG AT MSNBC AND HE CONFIRMS THIS THEORY BY TALKING TO PEOPLE ON THE GROUND IN BILOXI.

(6) MEDIA IS FINALLY STARTING TO ASK ARE THERE ENOUGH GUARD????!!! AND EQUIPMENT HERE TO HELP THE FOLKS ON THE GULF. THEY ARE REPORTING THE MESS IN THE GULF—AND NOT SUGARCOATING IT—SLEEPING IN YOUIR CAR AND LIVING WITH REFUGEES WILL MAKE ANYONE A BETTER JOURNALIST. SPIN ZONE IS IN MELTDOWN. (TWO WEEKS AGO ON PENTAGON SITE POSTED A STORY THAT MOTHBALLED FLIGHT VEHICLES WERE BEING SENT TO IRAQ FROM ARIZONA—THAT SAYS TO ME THAT THERE IS A HUGE EQUIPMENT ISSUE THAT WE HAVE NOT BEEN TOLD . . . .)

(7) PLEASE FOLKS GIVE TO THE REDCROSS—MEDIA IS STILL SHOWING ROOFS WITH MESSEGES—"NEED HELP—DIABETIC AND HEART PATIENT—NO MEDS" HOW CAN YOU SEE SOMETHING LIKE AND THAT AND NOT BE WORRIED . . . .

(8) AIRFORCE ONE WAS NO LOW ENOUGH TO SEE SHIT FOLKS—CALL YOUR REPS AND SENATORS—RAISE HELL THIS IS A NATIONAL EMERGENCY . . . . THOSE FOLKS NEED US TO USE THE POWER OF THE BLOGS AND PHONES TO KEEP THE HEAT ON . . . .

SEPTEMBER 03, 2005, SATURDAY

TRAPPED, DEAD AND DYING DAY 6: A LETTER TO MR.BUSH AFTER HIS FIRST VISIT TO THE DISASTER ZONE

SATURDAY MORNING DAY 6 OF THE DISASTER

9AM SEPTMBER 2, 2005

DEAR MR.BUSH,

YOU LIED TO THE AMERICAN PEOPLE AND WE ALL WATCHED IT HAPPEN.NOW THE WHOLE WORLD IS WATCHING.

THERE ARE 1000'S OF DEAD IN LOUISIANA THAT DIED AFTER THE HURRICANE, MORE THAN 9-11. THEY DIED AND ARE STILL DYING WAITING FOR FOOD, WATER, SHELTER AND COMFORT.

THEY ARE MOMS, GRANDMOMS, DADS, GRANDADS, CHILDREN, BABIES, PREGNANT WOMEN. SOME WERE DISABLED AND ELDERLY, AND YES SOME POOR, MANY ARE BLACK.BUT THEY ALL WERE ABANDONED, LEFT BEHIND TO DIE. THEY COULD NOT "HEED" THE EVACUATION ORDER BECAUSE OF THEIR STATUS AS THE INVISIBLE WORKING POOR IN THIS COUNTRY. IT IS

ESTIMATED THAT IN NEW ORLEANS ALONE 100-150,000 DUE TO FINANCIAL CIRCUMSTANCES COULD NOT EVACUATE. HOW DARE YOU AND THE FEMA DIRECTOR BLAME THEM ON THE AIR FOR NOT LEAVING.

THE POOR AND SICK AND ELDERLY SHOULD NOT BE EVER ABANDONED BY THE LEADERSHIP OF THIS COUNTRY AND REPRIMANDED FOR NOT "OBEYING ORDERS", ESPECIALLY WHILE YOU STILL HAVE NOT SENT ENOUGH OR ANY TRANSPORT TO THE CITY, AND THE DEAD LAY IN THE STREETS AND THE DOME OF NEW ORLEANS.AND WHILE YOU AS LEADER HAVE NOT EVEN EXAMINED THE DAMAGE OR THE CONDITION OF THE PEOPLE.

THEY DIED WAITING FOR TROOPS TO COME.

THEY DIED WAITING FOR FOOD TO COME WITH OUR NATIONAL GUARD.

THEY DIED WAITING FOR WATER TO COME WITH OUR NATIONAL GUARD.

THEY DIED WAITING FOR AIR DROPS TO COME FROM OUR AIR SUPPORT.

THEY DIED WAITING FOR SHIPS TO COME FROM THE NAVY AND MARINES.

AND YOU ARE RESPONSIBLE.PERIOD.

I AM A MOM. I AM A NURSE. I ALSO HAVE HAD EXTENSIVE EMERGENCY AND DISASTER TRAINING AND HAVE WORKED UNDER DISASTER CONDITIONS AND SITUATIONS. THERE IS NOTHING IN MY TRAINING OR EXPERIENCE THAT SAYS THAT THESE VICTIMS HAVE BEEN DEALT WITH IN A RESPONSIBLE MANNER BY OUR LEADERSHIP. RESPONSIBLE LEADERS DO NOT ISSUE

Watergate Summer

SHOOT TO KILL ORDERS ON HUNGRY STARVED PEOPLE. RESPONSIBLE LEADERS SEND HELP IN 24HOURS. RESPONSIBLE LEADERS END THEIR VACTIONS AND RETURN TO THE WHITE HOUSE STAT. RESPONSIBLE LEADERS DON'T LIE TO THE CITIZENS TELLING THEM THAT THINGS ARE GOING "RELATIVELY WELL", AND REPRIMAND THE PEOPLE FOR NOT BEING ABLE TO SELF EVACUATE.

I AM STILL PLEADING AND BEGGING THAT YOU BRING IN MILITARY TRANSPORT AND EVACUATE ALL THE HOSPITAL PATIENTS AND STAFF AND THEIR FAMILIES AND PETS THAT ARE STILL TRAPPED, ALSO THE ILL FROM THE AIRPORT IN NEW ORLEANS NOW ASAP. PLEASE ATLEAST AIRDROP WATER AND FOOD TO THE HOSPITALS, ESPECIALLY TENENT AND CHARITY HOSPITALS. YOU SHOULD BRING IN THE NAVY AND FLEETS OF AMPHIBIAN AIR SUPPORT, AIR DROP FOOD AND WATER ON THE DIFFERENT PASSES AND TO THE CONVENTION CENTER AND THE DOME, WHERE 1000'S ARE STILL DYING. EVEN TSUNAMI VICTIMS HAD FOOD AND WATER DROPPED TO THEM BY DAY 5. AS OF YESTERDAY DAY 5, THERE WERE STILL CLOSE TO 10,000 STILL NEEDING TO BE MED-EVACED OUT OF THE HOSPITALS IN NEW ORLEANS ALONE.

I AM GLAD THAT FINALLY 2800 GUARD ARE THERE IN NEW ORLEANS ON THE GROUND, THERE SHOULD BE 40,000 IN LOUISIANA ALONE JUST AS THE GOVERNOR REQUESTED. IN THE TRI-STATE REGION ALONE PROBALLY 60,000 GUARD ARE NEEDED NOW. I AM CONFUSED DO YOU NOT HAVE ENOUGH TROOPS HERE AT HOME TO TAKE CARE OF OUR OWN PEOPLE. ARE MSOT OF THE GUARD AND EQUIPMENT OVER IN IRAQ? I AM CONFUSED WHY THE SOS'S BY THE MAYOR WERE IGNORED. WHY DID IT TAKE 5 DAYS FOR YOU TO COME SEE THE DAMAGE AND BRING REAL TROOPS IN? MINUTE BY MINUTE PEOPLE-FAMILIES, ELDERLY AND

SICK WERE ABANDONED TO STARVE AND ROT IN THE DOME, THE CONVENTION CENTER, AND THE STREETS OF NEW ORLEANS. THERE ARE STILL 2000—3000 PEOPLE ROTTING IN THE DOME ALONE—THOUSANDS MORE AT THE CONVENTION CENTER. YOU DON'T LEAVE PEOPLE WITH ROTTING BODIES IN THE DARK OF THE DOME OR OUT IN THE HOT FETID STREETS. THAT IS INHUMANE. AND THIS IS JUST THE REFUGEE STATUS IN NEW ORLEANS—THE MAIN EFFECTED URBAN REGION.

IN THE HOSPITALS THE NURSES AND DOCTORS AND STAFF HAVE BEEN CARING FOR THEIR PATIENTS IN 100 DEGREE TEMPERATURES, WITH NO POWER, NO WATER, AND NO FOOD. THE NURSES HAVE BEEN GIVING EACH OTHER IV'S TO TRY TO STAY ALIVE AND KEEP CAIRING FOR THE PATIENTS. IN ONE SETTING THE NURSES WERE TRYING TO FIGURE OUT IF DRINKING URINE WOULD SUSTAIN THEM BECAUSE THEY NEEDED TO KEEP THE IV SOLUTION FOR THE PATIENTS, AS THEY WERE RUNNING SO LOW. IN ANOTHER MESSEGE A NURSE WONDERERD IF SHE WAS GOING TO DIE WITH HER PATIENTS OF STARVATION AND THIRST, SHE PRAYED THEY DIED FIRST SO SHE COULD TEND THEM.

IN ANOTHER HOSPITAL THE STENCH WAS RISING UP FROM THE BASEMENTS WHERE THE MORGUES FLOODED, AND THEN NURSES AND STAFF HAD TO PUT THE DEAD IN THE STAIRWELLS BECAUSE THERE WAS NO WHERE ELSE TO PUT THEM.

AS A NURSE WHEN SOMEONE DIES IN THE HOSPITAL, THIS IS NOT STANDARD PROCEDURE. USUALLY THE PERSON IS TENDERLY BATHED AND RELIGOUS PRACTICES AND TRADITIONS ARE RESPECTED. ESPECIALLY IN THE SOUTH, PEOPLE ARE TREATED WITH GREAT RESPECT, THE DEPARTED IS GENTLY BATHED, DRESSED, AND SOMETIMES COINS ARE PLACED ON THE EYELIDS AND FAMILY IS ALLOWED TO SIT BY THE BEDSIDE AND

GRIEVE. PRAYERS ARE READ, HANDS HELD, AND SONGS SOFTLY SONG. IT IS A GENTLE RESPECTFUL PROCESS OF HONORING THE DEAD.AND THEN YES THEY ARE CAREFULLY WRAPPED AND TENDED AND DELIVERED TO THE MORGUE. AS A NURSE YOU HAVE PLEDGED TO EVEN IN DEATH PROVIDE COMFORT FOR YOUR PATIENTS, ALL OF THEM. THAT IS WHY THESE TALES OF THE ABANDONED HOSPITALS AND THEIR DEAD ARE SO PAINFUL AND INHUMANE TO WITNESS.

THEY SHOULD HAVE BEEN EVACUATED ON DAY 1. AND DAY 6 THEY ARE STILL IN THE DARK WITH THEIR DEAD PATIENTS AND THE ONES THEY COULD SAVE. AND NO ONE UNDERSTANDS WHY THE MILITARY WAS NOT BROUGHT IN WITH THEIR MASSIVE TRANSPORT EQUIPMENT AND CARRIERS, IS IT ALL IN IRAQ, KUWAIT AND GERMANY?

EVEN OPERATION BLESSING WITH ITS HUGE FEMA CONTRACTS THAT IS A PAT ROBERTSON ORGANIZATION THAT YOU AND YOUR DAD KEEP NAMING FOR PEOPLE TO DONATE ISN'T THERE. THEY HAVE HUGE MILITARY CONVERTED MED EVAC PLANES

THAT COULD HAVE BEEN BROUGHT IN DAYS AGO TO EVAC THESE HOSPITALS. I AM NOT SURE IF I AM COMFORTABLE WITH THE LEADERSHIP OF THAT ORGANIZATION BUT WHY HAVEN'T THEY EVEN BEEN ACTIVATED?

AND AT ANOTHER HOSPITAL STAFF BROUGHT THE PATIENTS TO THE ROOF FOR DAYS WAITING FOR TRANSPORT, THE TRANSPORT NEVER CAME AND THE PATIENTS DIED ON THE ROOF IN SWELTERING HEAT WITH NURSES AND DOCTORS CRYING.

NURSES AND DOCTORS TAKE VOWS AND PLEDGE TO DO ALL WITHIN THEIR POWER TO PROTECT AND SAVE

LIVES. THESE BRAVE SOULS HAVE COURAGE THAT YOU CAN NOT BEGIN TO FATHOM OR EVEN APPRECIATE. PROECTING LIVES AND SAVING LIVES IS A NOBLE CAUSE.

YOU TOO TOOK A PLEDGE TO PROTECT THE LIVES OF PEOPLE IN THE COUNTRY, NOT JUST SOME. ALL.

YOU HAVE DISHONORED THAT PLEDGE AND NOW 1000'S ARE DEAD AND MORE DYING BY THE HOUR.

IN AUGUST FOR WEEKS WE ALL WATCHED AS YOU IGNORED ARROGANTLY A GRIEVING MOTHER, MILITARY FAMILIES AND VETS SITTING IN THE DITCH BEHIND YOUR RANCH. YOU WANTED TO "GET ON WITH YOUR LIFE" AND YOUR 5 WEEK VACATION. AND YET, NOW STILL ON YOUR VACATION, YOU TURNED YOUR BACK ON MILLIONS LAST WEEKEND. IT WAS NOT JUST A MATTER OF NEGLECT—IT WAS CRIMINAL. ON SATURDAY YOU WENT TO ARIZONA AND PLAYED GOLF AND WENT TO A PARTY. YET THE WHITEHOUSE DID AUTHORIZE AND ISSUE A STATEMENT OF FEDERAL EMERGENCY ASSISTANCE FOR LOUISIANA. THIS WAS COORDINATED WITH FEMA AND DHS BEFORE KATRINA EVER HIT THE GULF SHORES. WHY WAS THAT AUTHORIZATION IGNORED FOR SO MANY DAYS? THAT ORDER IS TO PROTECT LIVES AT ALL EXTENT AND PROVIDE ALL AID TO EVERYONE, EVEN THOSE WHO COULD NOT EVACUATE. YET WE DID NOT SEE IT FULLY OR EVEN PARTIALLY IMPLEMENTED UNTIL YESTERDAY DAY 5 WHEN YOU FINALLY CAME TO THE DISASTER ZONE.

PEOPLE ARE STILL DYING MR BUSH AND THEY DID NOT DIE IN THE FLOOD, THEY ARE DYING WAITING FOR THE TROOPS YOU TOOK TO IRAQ TO COME AND SAVE THEIR LIVES. YOU NEED TO SEND ATLEAST 40-60,000 TROOPS AND EQUIPMENT TO THE DISASTER ZONE NOW TODAY

BEFORE ANYMORE DIE. GET THE TROOPS TO OUR GULF BEFORE ANY MORE DIE. AND TELL MR.CHERTOFF 1400 A DAY IS NOT ENOUGH. THERE WERE NEVER 4000 IN DOWNTOWN NEW ORLEANS. TWO HOURS AGO THERE WERE FINALLY 2800, AND THE MAYOR HOPES TO HAVE 7000 BY TONIGHT. AND THAT IS NOT ENOUGH. WHEN YOU AND MR. BROWNE AND MR.CHERTOFF SAID THERE WERE 4000 THERE, IT ACTUALLY WAS ONLY 400 TRYING TO HELP THE DOME AND THE CONVENTION CENTER AND THE HOSPITALS.

THE PEOPLE THAT HAVE BEEN SAVING LIVES AND DOING THEIR UTMOST TO HELP SO MANY WITH SO LITTLE AND WITH NO FEDERAL RESOURCES ARE TO BE HELD IN THE HIGHEST REGARD. WE KNOW THE FEDERAL GOVERNMENT FAILED THEIR EMERGENCY LIFE PROTECTING MANDATE OF AUGUST 26TH, 2005.

WE ALSO KNOW THAT YOU CONTINUED A VACATION, DINING, AND GOLFING WHILE PEOPLE WERE DYING. YOU DID NOT RETURN TO THE WHITE HOUSE UNTIL DAY 3 OF THIS DISASTER AND AT THAT TIME YOU "FLEW OVER" THE DISASTER IN AIRFORCE ONE AND NOTED IT. BUT WHY DIDN'T YOU CALL UP FULL MILITARY EVAC THEN ESPECIALLY AFTER YOU SAW IT?

WHY DIDN'T YOU SEND FULL SEARCH AND RESCUE TEAMS? WHY WEREN'T FULL AERIAL AND LAND ASSESSEMENTS ORDERED?

IN A CRITICAL DISASTER THOSE HAVE TO BE ORDERED SO SALVATION ARMY AND RED CROSS CAN COME INTO THE ZONE WITH THE MILITARY TO PROVIDE CARE.

AS AN AMERICAN I AM HORRIFIED AT HOW MY FELLOW HUMANS WERE TREATED IN THE SOUTH, ESPECIALLY IN LOUISIANA.

THERE IS NO EXCUSE, NO LEVVEEE SPIN STORIES THAT WILL CHANGE SEEING DEAD PEOPLE LYING IN THE STREETS DYING AND DEAD WAITING FOR RESCUE. NO LEADER SHOULD EVER TREAT THEIR CITIZENS IN THAT MANNER. THERE ARE ALMOST 100,000 EVACUATED TO NINE OTHER STATES,MANY ON THEIR OWN POWER, WE ARE GRATEFUL THEY MADE OUT AND SURVIVED THEIR RESCUES. THERE WILL BE A BODY COUNT THAT ONES THAT DIDN'T.

AT THIS POINT IN TIME DURING THIS CRITICAL JUNCTURE LIVES NEED OUR FOCUS. BUT WHEN STABILITY IS IMPROVED WITH THIS SITUATION, SOME VERY HARD DECISIONS WILL HAVE TO BE ASKED BY THE AMERICAN PEOPLE AND THE CONGRESS.INVESTIGATIONS WILL BR PURSUED AND IMPEACMENT PROCEEDINGS OF ALL LEADERSHIP INVLOVED WITH THIS HORRIFIC EVENT WILL HAVE TO BE REQUESTED BY THE AMERICAN PEOPLE. LIVES WERE LOST AND BEING LOST TO CRIMINAL NEGLIGENCE BY THIS ADMINISTRATION. YOU WILL BE GETTING THOUSANDS OF LETTERS STATING OUR CONCERNS WITH YOUR LEADERSHIP, OR LACK THERE OF.YOU HAVE FAILED YOUR MANDATE.

SIGNED: A MOM, A NURSE, A TAXPAYER.

PLEASE SEE: http://www.cnn.com/2005/05/09/02

PLEASE READ THE FOLLOWING WHITE HOUSE DOC: http://www.whitehouse.gov./news/releases, Aug.26th,2005 Statement Authorizing Federal Emergency Assistance for Louisiana., by the WhiteHouse and posted Sunday August 27th,2005.

In 2001, August 6th, while on another 5 week Vacation you recieved a Memo about Bin Laden, terror attacks on US soil with airplanes, which Americans did not learn of until summer 2004. Let us hope the above memo does not turn out to be another just Missing Document that the American People need to know Existed to Protect lives in Louisiana.

SEPTEMBER 04, 2005, SUNDAY

ABANDONED IN AMERICA: SITUATION CRITICAL

Today is Sunday September 4, 2005

Day 7 of this Disaster: DEATH BY KATRINA'S WRATH AND NOW FEMA'S APATHY

Please read the letter to Mr. Bush from Saturday, I am submitting it to many sources, here and abroad. I encourage that all of us, especially bloggers write far and wide so that the world can see that we are ANGRY with how this Catastrophe was mishandled and neglected. We as a People, can not tolerate any more lies or Apathy. It is time for the Charade of "Conservative Compassion" to end. The People of the South need to know that we are angry and want to help care for them. And that we NEVER want to see America goes through This Hell again. The Survivors of Katrina who are now refugees are courageous, and we owe them better, and more. The Federal Government and Leadership failed thousands. The Coast Guard and Fish and Wildlife who saved thousands are the real heroes. And now State Governors and agencies from all over the Country are coming to Aid the South.

PLEASE PLEASE WATCH CNN, AND GIVE THEM SUPPORT AND SEND THEM LETTERS TO SUPPORT THEIR LEVEL OF JOURNALISM AND REPORTING THE TRUTH. WATCH THE INTERVIEW ONLINE THE MAYOR'S INTERVIEW WITH SOLEDAD. CNN HAS BROUGHT IN THEIR WAR CORRESPONDENTS TO COVER THIS ONGOING CRISIS. WE

NEED TO SUPPORT THEIR HONESTY. INTERNATIONALLY WE NEED TO MAKE SURE THAT MEDIA REMAINS ONSITE DOWN IN THE GULF. I CAN NOT EMPHASIZE HOW IMPORTANT IT IS THAT WE SUPPORT THEM. THE HOMELAND SECURITY PLANS FOR SUCH A CATOSTROPHIC EMERGENCY DO NOT ADDRESS ALLOWING OUR MEDIA FREEDOM OF PRESS. THEY ARE TRYING TO BRING US THE SCOPE OF THIS TRAGEDY. AND AS IT BECOMES EVIDENT THAT LITERALLY THOUSANDS ARE DEAD, AND HUNDREDS OF THOUSANDS MISSING. THE BODY COUNT WILL BE HORRIFIC. THIS IS OF TSUNAMI PROPORTIONS.

CONSIDER THIS: FEMA HAS CHANGED THEIR 800 NUMBER THREE TIMES THIS WEEK—THIS IS NOT A WORKING SYSTEM.

FEMA IS PREVENTING THE DIFFERENT RESCUE AND RECOVERY PEOPLE FROM DOING THEIR JOB, THEY ARE EVEN PREVENTING RED CROSS AND SALVATION ARMY FROM PROVIDING CARE. (READ ARTICALES AT TRUTHOUT)

TO START DO GO TO CCN ONLINE AND READ ALL OF DR. GUPTA'S ACCOUNTS. READ ALL THE REPORTERS EYE WITNESS ACCOUNTS. KEEP IN MIND ANDERSON COOPER HAS WORKED HORRIFIC HUMAN DISASTERS INCLUDING SOMALIA AND ROWANDA—HE KNOWS HOW HORRIFIC THIS IS AND HE IS ASKING THE QUESTIONS THAT ALL OF US WISH SOMEONE WOULD ASK.

PLEASE ALSO READ TRUTHOUT

PLEASE ALSO READ BBC—THEY HAVE SOME AMAZING STORIES

WE AS AMERICANS NEED TO BE INVOLVED WITH THIS CRISIS, RIGHT HERE, RIGHT NOW.

THOUSANDS OF LIVES DEPEND ON THIS.

We must all try to focus on providing comfort and support to those effected. We all have monthes to work together to get them the much needed help and resources we know they need. We also know that the FEDS have failed on this mission miserably. We as citizens ALL need to do what we can to help our neighbors in the South. We are at a Critical Juncture in American History.

The Katrina Survivors have had harrowing experiences and yes sadly they are refugees now. Refugees is an interesting term.

Under International laws these people that had no way to escape and nowhere to go should have been provided and protected in a more responsible manner by our leadership and the Federal Government. The Officials lied and lied all week, and those lies did cause deaths throughout the Gulf Area. But first we need to get them medical care, shelter,clothes, food and water. Medical care will also have to include psychological care and support, many have horrific tales, adn the Convention Center and Dome people have a whole other set of horrors to contend with. These people will have PTSD.

And we will need to ask the President to bring troops, especially the Guard Home to take care of the South.But now we need to focus on saving as many as possible.

Many were Abandoned to Die this week, We need to take care of ALL the Survivors, and we may not like it but now indeed, hundred of thousands are Refugees. Under International Law, they are Refugee that should have been protected and then cared for in this Horrific National Catostrophe. And the States are already starting to organize and prioritize how to help all of these people get medical care, housing, education and food. It will be up to all of us to pitch in.

This Blog for atleast next month will be some very specific Focuses as this Crisis Unravel, it is not a Political Issue, this is a Human Issue. As a nurse of 20 yrs. with Disaster Training and Experience I will be working with the following listed below. My speciality is Environmental Forensics and it's effects on mass numbers—it is time to offer my services in any way possible to contribute helping our neighbors in the South.

(1) Red Cross (local): assisting with Displaced Persons

(2) Salvation Army: Logistics

(3) All of my spare time I will be gathering supplies to send to send to Veterans For Peace down in Louisiana.

Please go to Words Light Fires to learn more of the needed supplies.

On Thursday Night after spending days and nights on the phone and computer attempting to get help for people in the South, trying to get Water delivered, get Food Dropped, Get Air and Boat Rescue there, Get Hospitals Evac'd. As a Citizen, a Nurse, I used every resource I could find. FEMA has been decimated, DHHS the same, EPA the same, ALL of these are needed to work a Disaster. The Offices of Emergency Response and Preparedness—decimated. Please understand I am a nurse that has extensive Red Cross Disaster training,which like many of us I updated after 9-11, and then I even took related FEMA training.Before that I have all levels of experience: ER/EMT,PEDS&PICU, AIDS&CANCER etcetc.I have worked disasters. I can tell you that this Disaster has been mishandled since The Whitehouse and Mr.Bush signed the Emergency Authorization on Saturday August 26th, 2005.I would love to know if it was signed before or after the Golf and Cake in Arizona. And yes, I do not understand HOW the president waited days to fly over and did not get them the help they needed. And I don't understand HOW the Leader could wait until Day 5 of this Disaster to come to the scene.The World is Horrified—and we all should be.

We as a Country should not allow the Government's Failure to bring Shame to the rest of us.

All of these departments merged under Homeland Security and when that happened things did fall apart. All of this will need HUGE over haul. So I as a nurse am going to put my logistical skills and knowledge to better use. I have definently given up trying to call the Federal Government to do their job. And I now know that my FEMA training was a sad joke.

Thursday night I called FEMA one more time at 4am, I was put to a very nice lady, she and I talked. I again voiced my concerns of the week, I told her I was glad to reach a human, I was grateful. I told her I was worried sick about the people stranded with no food or water, and the hospitals, I said well who do I call about rescue, and Air drops. It seemed so simple.

She said "You can call the White House". I said "Isn't there anyone else? . . . ANYONE? WE ARE GOING TO LOSE 1000'S IN Louisiana?" And then we discussed options" Call WHOEVER you think will help, outside media, anyone, Louisana is now depending on all of you to help them, there is no one else." She said. And I said "Fine, I am contacting the International Community, and outside media" And then we both just sat in the Grim 4am dark and cried, and I know both of us were praying for people in the South. And yes, Friday I started that process in Earnest. This is not just about NOLA, there are 1000's effected in Mississippi and Alabama as well, thousands of displaced, wounded and sick in Rural areas, that seem as forgotten and forsaken as the people of New Orleans. The Poor of this Country are invisible to the White House.

But it is not just the Poor, it is also the Elderly, families, disabled, women and children, and infirmed. It is not just a Race issue. 1000's of people were and are Disenfranchised in this country, and hopefully there is still time to repair this Horrendous Disaster. But Folks we all have to be honest—1000's were Abandoned. ABANDONED IN AMERICA TO DIE.

I even have proof that FEMA turned down MEDI-VAC services that could have saved 1000's.

I called Beer Companies that wanted to send water—but they could not get FEMA to answer of let them.

Another example: Tenet Hospital is NOW evac'd in downtown New Orleans. Also the Tenet Corporation has rescued ALL of their Hospitals in the Gulf region. It sounds like they organized their own evacuation of patients and staff.

As a citizen I am asking you to look in your hearts and decide how you can help. I am sorry but giving to Red Cross may not be enough this time, it will take more than Money to fix this Disaster. And yes, later Questions and Investigations will have to ensue. And yes, Certain Responsible parties will have to face the Music and their Fates. We as Americans need to make certain that this Never happens again.

NEW BLOG: http://nolacare.blogspot.com/, will be up fully tonight.

This blog will still focus on issues related to Concern about this country and Katrina updates. I have created a new Blog related more to issues related to Refugees and Refugees Caretaker Issues, as well as the Pending Health Crisis that we face.

I started this because I was watching people trying to help and the reporters down in the NOLA Zone and I realized no one is telling them of the Hazardous Health Risks of what they are walking around in, is a Toxic Cesspool full of waste, corpses, and sewage. It will also have advice and support for people who are going to the area to render services and care. I explored what advice and care is being offered to those in the area. This is a Human Crisis that will have Huge Health Implications.

JANUARY 10, 2006, TUESDAY,

WHY NOLA HAS TO BE REBUILT

As an American NOLA has to be Rebuilt. And I am not just talking about the Business Sector. I am talking about it's Heart and Soul. I am talking about it's Culture. It's Way of Life . . . . that we all need to remember. (10-10-05)

>   It is a Way of Life,
>   It is deep hearted Blues,
>   It is Gin soaked jazz, and Grits, Hushpuppies, and fresh cornbread.
>   It is panfried shrimp with limes and hot sauce.
>   It is 3 day Gumbo that leaves you sweating and thirsty.
>   It is Sunday Church where the buildings rock and seismic sway.
>   It is the slideguitar pleading in the the still of a summer night.
>   It is another lonely Crooner sending shockwaves in an old riverfront garage.
>   It is women swaying in gauzy dresses
>   And men in timeless suits.
>   It is granmommies lullabying babs,singing
>   This Ol'Man with a hum and a roll.
>   It is a place where old folks are tended with gentle hands and respect.
>   It is where Family is a way of life.
>   In New Orleans a clock is merely an instrument,
>   But Time is a Place to Be.

{{{{{This piece is dedicated to a great NOLA chef who died last week-Austin Leslie of Pampy's Creole Kithcen, and Chez Helene fame. He died in

Atlanta, but he had survived Katrina. He had been on his roof for 2 days with his wife Victoria, they were brought to the Superdome and then the Convention Center, and then transferred to Atlanta. He was in the Hospital last week, but still wanting to get back to the Kitchen. He died last thursday. He was 71.}}}}}

UPDATE:

January 10th, The King in all his JimBeam-laden-swagger came back to NOLA this week- while they are in the midst of buldozing the Ninth ward . . . and declaring huge sections blighted

Imminent Domain (AKA Developers Wet Dreams).

Please keep these people in your thoughts and prayers, they are Lost.

OCTOBER 10, 2005, MONDAY

MISSING NUMBERS: LIVES LOST OR SCATTERED, SOMEONE BETTER COME TO THE TRUTH

For a variety of reasons that mostly don't matter in the scheme of things, I have not written for over three weeks. It does not mean that I stopped watching, breathing or paying attention to this World of Ours. It certainly does not mean my "Aides a.k.a Ass-Kissing—Lackies" are going to have nervously hand me a "BEST OF' Handmade DVD with Current Events on it.(Hopefully you all catch my drift about our Leader being handed such a DVD, and you of course know better than to think I have "Lackies", unless you count a feeble cat and deaf dog).

It means I had Some Things I had to take care of, and Some Other Things that Fate dealt me that led to a Temporary Blog Withdrawl that was rather painful and unexpected. During that time I was trying to read less, and watch less TV, but the truth is that I am a News///Media Junkie . . . . So I continued reading and watching, but I did have to take a break from writing so much. But now I am back. And there are Some Things on my mind. So sit back grab a cold one and lets mull a Few Things.

And I will be honest, it ain't pretty.

What is so odd is that over three weeks ago, we were still all reeling from watching the Devastation of Katrina and the failure of the Bush Regime to properly address basic Humanitarian Needs. And to be honest the Main Stream Media really kept the limelight on Bush's Blunders, and rightly so, and they helped ALL of us re-focus on the Human Condition which deserved our full, undivided Attention while Mr. Bush looked the other way for FIVE FULL days and continued to stumble the rest of the month with his Helluva Job Browie Blame Game. The Situation Needed our Anger, Our Angst, Our Phone calls, Our Emails . . . . But then in the past month some interesting Distractions have been coming dribbling across the news, screen and and print . . . I have a name for them:

CREATIVE DISTRACTIONS:

And now since then, we have been plundering through an assorted array of Creative Distractions. Offered to us like stale fingerfoods by the Host at a Tupperware Party Gone Adrift. (And yes, that does mean I am comparing MSM to a host of a sagging Tupperware Party). First we had to suffer yet more Hurricanes named to honor favorite past Playgal Pinups and Vegas Showgirls. There was Rita, Katrina's screaming baby sister that also seemed determined and relentless to unleash her wrath on the Gulf's Oily Armpit, dragging ATLEAST 24 Rigs all over with gleeful abandon. And then there was the Supreme Court Soap Opera, and in true Opera fashion the first act was a fulfledged snoozer. (I am sorry but let's be real, even Roberts' own damn fine, doting Donna Reed of a Wife was caught nodding off on C-span. So I am not the only person who with the Dramamine "Excitement" of Mr. Roberts almost suffered lockjaw from world record setting yawns in a 6 hour period.) And now it looks like the" Harry" Follies will start soon. (And let me be the first to say she will be confirmed with her Church Lady Ways and Attire, regardless of the scary Kathleen Harris Eye Liner). Just more Distractions from the Truth. And the Truth is that Katrina has been set aside like an Ugly Sickly Old Aunt that No One wants to sit next to at the Thanksgiving Dinner. But By Thanksgiving Dinner Someone, ALL of Us better be sitting next to ol' Aunty Katrina Again and asking Some Damn Hard Questions.

THE DUCKING FLU?

And Now we all are suposed to be scared knee high shitless of this Mythical Bird Flu that is A-Comin-to-Get—US. I am sorry I am not buying it—not now and not wext week. Because to be honest after Katrina I don't think they understand Public Health Emergencies—AT ALL. Period. (Unless we want to give obligatory "Credit" to the New—This—Month Mr.

Duck Tape FEMA that he might understand basic hygiene, more than the previous Horsehit Director). If they can not understand how to Air Drop Food and Water, how am I susposed to pretend that they are SOOOO competent that they Understand a Droplet Spread Disease? Or that they even begin to grasp the Goals of Hygiene can play in Disease Path? For example—leaving 1000's without water of any potable kind sitting in sewage for days on end may have indeed contributed to the deaths of 1000s'. And this isn't just the rant of a mom, or a nurse, it is merely common sense. And last year, there was some sort of Secret Problem with the Flu Vaccine—and so the Administration vaccinated themselves and their workers—2 million vaccines worth—and then announced that there was NOT Enough—and proceeded to blame it all on Chiron. Yet CDC, and the DHHS had also UNDER—Ordered the vaccine (atleast 14 million or so). So there was NEVER enough even planned to be distributed. But we all are suposed to Not Remember That . . . because now we are suposed to be Scared and Fearful of a New Flu . . . . I am tempted to call it the "Duckin' Flu'. Because it is giving this administration a New way to Duck Other Responsibilities . . . . like the Mess in Iraq or the Unresolved Issues of Katrina. And yes, It is indeed a Foul Situation, just not a Fowl Situation that the Leader would rather us focus on.

WHAT UNRESOLVED ISSUES?!!!

2663 ISSUES TO BE PRECISE . . . .

2663 MISSING CHILDREN . . . AND WHO KNOWS HOW MANY ADULTS? WHOLE FAMILIES GONE?! HOW MANY? AND SHOULDN'T WE ASK FOR THE SOLID NUMBERS, THERE ARE 1000'S STILL MISSING FOLKS . . . .

And my-oh-my there is quite a list of Unresolved Issues, but for now I have One that the MSM seems to have neatly sidestepped once Rita had finished doing her dance across the Gulf. The Friday before Rita hit, and actually the whole week before Rita, the Media spotlighted something rather Tragic—a consequence that Almost went under the radar—MISSING CHILDREN. And so CNN and then MSNBC spent almost an entire week dedicated to running pictures of Missing Children.

Photos were displayed on the side of the screen, and I believe at last count a fair number, <100, CNN actually assisted with actually reuniting the children with distraught families. We know that families were literally torn asunder by the Raging Surge and the crumbled levees, but that is ALOT of Missing Children . . . . And so tonight I am flicking over the screens and surfin' the net, and I see (Forgive me Father for I have sinned . . . .) yes, Geraldo Rivera (who I NEVER watch . . . .) over on FOX (also NEVER) and he is interviewing a Wellspoken, ever so Patient woman who is explaining to Geraldo that according to Project Alert, a group that works with other Missing Children Projects—that according to her group—there are indeed 2600 children STILL MISSING from Katrina as of today October 9th, 2005.

I spent all night looking at the photos on the Missing Children site—baby photos, and junior high graduation photos. The Photos tug at your heart, moments of pride and recognition pryed from a tattered scrapbook. Moments from Christmases and family gatherings and picnics, irreplaceable moments stolen and scattered. Faces scrubbed clean glowing with hope even with missing teeth and poorly chopped bangs. Names that ring across the page, Hope, Faith and even a little one named Heaven Butler. I look at her photo, her beautiful baby photo, I know her mother never meant for her name or her photo to be on the Missing Katrina Children's page. She named her that name believing her God had indeed given her a little piece of Heaven to hold in her arms.

And the more I thought about it, I thought Where is the Outrage—Where is the Horror. WHY aren't more people Screaming out in Pain, that is alot of children to be LOST? I mean all summer every time there was a missing white blond teenager—there was much Angst and Horror liberally buttering the News by the Day. And now 2663 Chlidren are STILL MISSING, LOST, from Katrina. There must be weeping mamas and granmommies for these beautiful children that are bewildered and bereft. Yet I thought about it, and if there were griefstricken families awaiting news and still searching, they would be raising Hell by now. Because that is what Moms do, they YELL for their children. And instead we have Silence. Deafening Slience.

WHY THE DEAFENING SILENCE ABOUT THE LOST

CHILDREN:

2663 CHILDREN LEFT BEHIND MR.BUSH . . . .

I think I might have indeed accidentally found part of the reason. I don't think we can Blame all of this on Mere Misplaced People Scattered Far and Wide. Part of me, the Pollyanna—Ever—hopeful side of me, was indeed drifting to that path. Yet part of me kept asking where are those Screaming Moms? And Dads? WHERE? There should be Lots of Noise by Now.

And then I stumbled onto a little PDF on a site called www.missingadults.org.

Distractions are created so we will look out the Window at something else, anything else.

Just not at the Ugly Disgusting Truth.

If your go to the www.missingkids.org site you will see the page laid out so that you can look at missing kids from both Hurricanes. And also not as noticeable, yet present on the site, a link to missingadults.org. And then you can link to http://www.theyaremissed.org/ncma/katrina/katrina_missing_adults.pdf. This document was just "updated" and placed in pdf format as of 10-7-05, and you can download as a pdf, it is 182 pages long.

It is 182 pages of missing Adults.

It is the Deafening Silence.

It is WHY there was NO Outcry for the Missing Children. It is Missing Families.

It is an oddly compiled, slightly organized, vaguely Numbered List of Missing adults from the Disaster Zone—it is JUST Katrina.

It is 182 pages with 50-60 Missing adults per page.

That means that there are 9100—10,920 Missing Adults from Katrina, that we are NOT suposed to ask about, or think about.

And it makes sense that 2,663 children are still MISSING or LOST if they were with their families that are Lost.

And that there is now a Deafening Silence.

There might Not be anyone to Yell.

So I am Yelling Now, in my little Blog. WHY is the Media NOT covering this???!!!! 1000's are still Missing, and they all did not just get dispersed asunder, they actually may be Dead. Even the Crappiest Papers Know how to Write Obituaries-properly.

It is time Someone Write the Obituary properly on this, and not distract us with other pleasentries of Tweety Flu and inflated Judicial Gossip. As a mom I want the Truth about the families on the pages, the children, the moms, and the dads and the grandparents.

At the Very Least I think we owe it to a little baby girl named Heaven Butler.

I Need to know if she went to Heaven with her mama.

OCTOBER 18, 2005, TUESDAY

FAIR GAMEGATE

So here we still sit waiting for the other shoe to drop. I am sure that over the next few days there will be more baby stroller threats, and hours and hours of Avian Flu coverage. And also the Saddam trial will most likely be aired LIVE, in a feigned attempt to justify the War in Iraq that is now hemmorhaging support by the hour. And Wilma is churning out in the Carribean, so there is even another distraction on the horizon that Bush would be wise to notice.

I have wondered of the media coverage of this whole event, the Fair Gamegate Investigation.

Many of us have been calling it Plamegate, and I have been thinking that maybe that is not fair to Valerie Plame.

(Remember Mr. Wilson was told be another reporter who too had recieved a Bait call from the White House the summer of 2003 that his wife was "Fair Game." . . . .)

I think about her, and how her life has been torn asunder, and thrown upside down, and all because she was trying to do her job. And I have thought alot about Joe Wilson, and I am rereading his Book, and I realize that their lives were basically destroyed because this Regime was hellbent on lying about the WMD, they were merely collateral damage. They are not the 1st messengers to be shot down. But Americans should never be treated in the manner that they were treated, and that is why I think maybe the situation should be called Fair-Gamegate, or even Bushgate, or Cheneygate. I think that Cheney and Bush lied about weapons and caused so many to die and destroyed a country. The irony is that they are the traitors, there was no patriotism in lining their pockets. And it was never about terrorism. It was about Greed, Oil, and money.

I think Judy and her article last weekend has brought out a lot of emotions.

I still am puzzled WHY the NYT has done such a crappy job on the whole story—and then I sigh, and realize their Investigations Unit has been sanitized, and is of diminished strength. I am wondering if they are under any gag orders regarding the Investigation, especially after the Notebook was FOUND in the DC offices. If you read the articles over the weekend it does not say that Judy found the notebook. It merely says she answered questions regarding the Notebook.

And the story by her fellow reporters was less than flattering, not even supportive, and surely not forgiving.

They wrote knowing she has tarnished their paper, and the damage might not be repairable, not at this point.

We should support the press, because right now we all Need the Truth, and Freedom of the Press, which surely has been placed in jeporardy. I wonder if we encourage the Press, the Media and our representitives is that going to make a difference.

A part of me does think that Fitz should have the Silence and Quiet to complete the Investigation, that maybe that will let him get the job done . . . .

I will say this the media has been very skimpy on covering the issue well enough—but the blogs have been very thorough- thank heavens . . . .

And about the Fair Game—I wonder how the White House feels the Game is going now . . . . now that they no longer hold all the cards. Maybe the lesson is that people's lives are never Fair Game.

OCTOBER 19, 2005, WEDNESDAY

KING GEORGE'S LIST OF DISHONOR

THE LIST:

UDATE 10-28-05

(enigma via CNN. 12:44pm 10-28-05 CNN read press release

INDICTMENT OF I. SCOOTER LIBBY of FIVE counts Press conference planned for 2pm with Special Prosecutor)

GO TO THE http://plamegatetimeline.blogspot.com/, for the full timeline of the players activities.

1. Rove?
2. Scooter?
3. Karen Hughes?
4. Mary Matalin?
5. Alberto?
6. Harry Miers?
7. Hadley?
8. Hannah?
9. Millerwise?
10. Ari?
11. Condi?
12. Bartlett?
13. Bolton?
14. Grossman?
15. Powell?
16. Tenet?

17. Rummy?
18. Negraponte?
19. Ashcroft?
20. Goss?
21. Andy C.
22. Barney?
23. Jeff Gannon/ Dale?
24. Doug Feith
25. Wolfowitz
26. Wurmser
27. Addington
28. Bush?
29. Cheney?

REPORTERS: This is a list of reporters that allegedly may have been part of investigation or Leaked to, this list is incomplete:

Novak, Miller, Cooper, Russert, Walter Pincus, Glen Kessler, Matthews who else?

*Barney? yes—Barney the Dog . . . . Dogs watch . . . . Doesn't mean he is a criminal—just a witness.

WHO KNEW WHAT WHEN??????

[I know other blogs have a more "complete" list, this is just my little list . . . of all those who remain suspect. I would say all that anyone that left the Realm, AKA scene of the crime, in great speed or under "unusual circumstances" may deserve a little closer scrutiny.]

REQUIRED READING VIEWING: (at this point we need a playbook—rent ALL THE PRESIDENTS MEN, better yet READ IT AGAIN)

Article: "Bush whacked Rove in CIA Leak" In NY Daily News, by Thomas M.DeFrank. Maybe the Daliy News is going to show the NYT what real journalists do. Read here, http://nydailynews.com/front/story/35107p-304312c.html,

Watergate Summer

(okay, I suck at links—so go over to Blue Collar—he has the whole article, and some interesting insights)

POINTS TO PONDER::::

[[1]] I have heard many say that this Administration is all about LOYALTY. A thought, That loyalty crap might be true in a Godfather Ethics way, but I also think this administration doesn't treat the "help" or the "grunts" well, I mean we have seen how the troops are treated, and I just bet there are quite a few assistants finding OLD emails, letters etc . . . . A Leak can go both ways . . . .

Especially when it is a Coverup to hide a Conspiracy . . . . Conspiracy to go to War based on Lies. The Slash and Burn Administration I am sure has an enemy list Behind the Castle's walls that is longer than the King's arm.

*   *   * Rawstory has the real take on this and does a much better job than I could ever attempt . . . *   *   *

[[2]] And one more little tidbit to ponder—what if a Fake Journalist had been planted in the Press Pool with White House Press Pass and Security Clearence to see if The Media were taking the Bait regarding the Wilson/Plame story???? WHO? WHAT?

I mean think about Gannon—you remember Jeff Gannon, also known at Press Conferences by DALE as called on by the King, as in Dale Guckhert . . . you remember right—Dale as in the gay.com fame . . . . and that the news was NOT the only thing he pimped. What if he was planted there not just to improve the King's image with planted questions, what if he was also there to see who was Eating the Bait about the Wilson/Plame story.??? . . . so yes, I have added him to the List—right under Barney. And for anyone who is interested Gannon is still in DC—last seen in September at the PRO-WAR rally carrying a banner with a buddy (sept 25th,2005).

[[3]] And as the Prosecutor starts zooming in on the Circle of Loyalty—' The Clusters with Roots" (Scooter's quote in the Aspens letter to Judy.) I expect we will have more Distractions: babystroller threats, tunnel threats, and other wonders. As to Real Distractions that should be monitored, Meantime 300 mile wide WILMA is screeching Pissed Off Showgirl Style through the Carribean. She actually might be a bigger Bitch than Rita or Katrina As of noon today, sustained winds are up to 175MPH. (Yes, now that we all are Hurricane Experts, that means she is indeed a CAT FIVE). Enigma the weather-wanna-be-girl is perdicting Landing Destination Sometime Late Saturday Night between Clearwater and Naples. And if I was on Sanibel Island I would be thinking about evacuation more than where-the-hell-did-I-put-the-duck-tape . . . .

*   *   *ENIGMA NEWS ALERT: GET YOUR POPCORN NOW: HARRY HEARINGS DATE SET FOR NOVEMBER 7.*   *   *

*   *   *ENIGMA NEWS ALERT II: (oh-to-be-a-fly-on-the-wall-moment) BONO AND BUSH had lunch at the Castle, Bono had the pasta dish, and the King dined on crow and some humble pie. And the Queen sat and batted her prozac glazed eyes.*   *   *

*   *   *ENIGMA NEWS ALERT 4PM: TOM DELAY—ARREST WARRANT ISSUED, go to Skippy, or Raw Story, Best of Blogs,or Agitprops for the full cockroach update . . . . Hey Bubba cleaned up yur cell for ya' real good—hope you look good in orange jumpsuits and those special little flip flops*   *   *

OCTOBER 26, 2005, WEDNESDAY

LOOKING FOR HEROS AND HOPE IN THE LAND OF CORRUPTION

Often you read this column and wonder about the nurse with the pissy, pithy insights and comments. (all two of my readers that is . . .) I also am a mom. A good piece of me sees the world though my son's eyes. I try to see what he sees, and sometimes I try to see what his eyes are searching on the horizon.

"Teach your children well". I have been walking around with this song in my head all week. You remember that song from the 1970's, by Crosby, Stills, Nash and Young. It is a song I lullabyed to my baby when President Clinton was in the White House. I would sit and rock him for hours . . .

When I was pregnant I walked in Peace Marches, at that point in time it was the build up to Iraq—the first one. I collected Peace buttons and sang peace songs left over from the sixties. My son now has usurped my music collection and all of my buttons. He also is now the same age I was when I had my Watergate Summer. Which over the past few months has become more and more haunting. Teach your children well, does that mean teach them your own history.

I grew up with Nixon and Vietnam. I didn't like Nixon, from early on. As early as eight when he was campaigning I called Nixon a name at the dinner table. To this day I see Palmolive, and I cringe and think of Mr.Nixon. I called him a name that I had learned while playing hopscotch on the playground, I wasn't even sure what it meant—but I knew it somehow suited him. And to be honest his name was Richard, so "Dick Head", could be just considered another version of his name. I also sadly grew up in a Very

Republican family where early on I was viewed with great horror and shock. My grandfather once exclaimed "if she doesn't turn around soon, she'll soon be turning into a damn liberal Hippie". Somehow that career path now held bohemian charms and allure, now that it had been condemned.

(Years later I would learn that there were Closet Democrats in the family, it would have been nice to know that while I was gagging on the green Palmolive).

Back to teaching Your Children, So I have tried to teach my son well. I have tried to teach him about What Matters. That we take care of each other in this world. That we look out for the elderly, the poor, our neighbors. That we try to do the right thing, even if it feels uncomfortable. That when someone is in trouble that we do what we can to help. That we don't bail on people. That Bullies are never to be tolerated. That whistleblowers are to be valued and protected. That Honesty and Integrity are more than mythical, they are valuable qualities to be embraced. And he watched Katrina with the same horror that I experienced.

As he is a boy, early on he started looking for heros in books and movies. And in the past five years he has been looking again. He has seen them all Bond, Spiderman, Zorro, X-Men, Batman etc. He even jokes about it," I think I am looking for Heros, because I am not going to see one on the news". I tell him to read To Kill a Mockingbird. He says "Maybe I am looking for an Atticus.

Geez I am looking for things that aren't here". We read All the Presidents Men and he says, "Whelp we don't have a Carl or a Bob, so how is this gonna end without them? "Hmm, I don't know . . . .

"You know none of the people that the news says are corrupt really go to jail. I mean look at Enron and all" (I try to remind him of Tyco and that Some have gone to jail.) And he points out it is not Real Jail. He is worried that we do not have a Justice System that works in this Country, and I am running low on proof.

"The Rackateer is not someone dressed in a black suit with a diamond stick pin. Sometimes it is someone outfitted in a grey flannel suit . . . .

When the rackateer bribes local officials and secures immunity from police action, the price exacted by corrupt law enforcement—incalculable in dollars-is paid again by the public. In short, organized crime affects everyone. It cannot be be the only concern of law enforcement officers. It must be the urgent and active concern of every citizen."

Robert F. Kennedy is quoted in Theft of the Nation by Donald R.Cressney.

He points out I was lucky I had heros, people that left their mark and made a difference, I had Robert Kennedy, and Martin Luther King, and even Rosa Parks. I tried to tell him that there have been different people that have tried to make a difference. We talk about this Plamgeate Investigation late into the night and we review the "Players", the inpacted, and the bad journalism that is indeed a player (NYT & Judy Miller). He reads alot so some of his mentors are writers, Howard Zinn, Al Franken, and John Stewart, and more. And he has been watching this Investigation closely, and he said "You know Joe Wilson is a whistleblower, and he and his wife are being mistreated because he spoke the Truth, Joe needs a Hero too. He needs Someone to tell the Truth. It is different than Watergate, Watergate had Carl and Bob, we don't have that this time. We don't even have Peter Jennings anymore.We have John Stewart. But there has to be some Justice, and a Hero to bring it."

So he's Watching and Waiting. And he also knows his future is being determined by Lies and he doesn't want to br drafted to fight for the Liers. And he knows it could happen. He also knows his mom won't let it happen.

And I sit and wonder will History repeat itself again leaving him jaded and cynical, and wiser.

Or will the process leave him bitter and confused.

Or will the Next few days deliver a Hero, an Atticus, to bring some Justice and Truth for all of us. Is Fitzgerald our Atticus?

Is this Plamegate our Watergate? Are we at the Tipping Point?

"We must accept finite disappointment,but we must never lose infinite hope." Martin Luther King

OCTOBER 29, 2005, SATURDAY

INDICTMENT DAY: EXPOSING THE MUSHROOM CLOUD OF LIES THAT HANGS OVER THE WHITE HOUSE (A LETTER TO "SAD" MR. BUSH)

(to my two loyal readers this is a blunt letter to MrBush, it might make him "Sad")

DEAR MR. BUSH,

I saw your Speedy—Gonzales—87-second Saddened Speech today out on the Lawn, after the Indictments that were announced 2 hours earlier. You came out all snippy, inconvenienced, gave your little speech, and then huffed to the Helicopter to go away to Camp David to lick your We-Got-Caught-Wounds. You said you were "saddened" by the Indictment. What the??? Sad? You should be Furious that Your Administration is Rife with Corruption. Or did you misspeak, and meant you were sad that Ol'Scooter got caught and your bud Rove is being Investigated still?

I guess the Only speeches that you show any balls are the ones where you get to be One of the Guys standing on a Pile of It-was-them-Evil-Terrorist-Let's—Fight'em-Rubble with a Megaphone and More Gusto and Bravado than a Beer commercial on a 99 degree day. But God Forbid if you face Evil in your own House, that is a different story. There are Rats in the WhiteHouse, large dirty unscrupulous rats. And these "evil-doing" rats need to be exterminated out of the White House.

I am a voter, a taxpayer, and I think still an American, whether you like it or not.

And I am a woman, a woman that does not support your right-wing-religous-crap.

And as a Woman living under your Regime I can tell you All about Sad.

About Being Sad. There are some Sad Statistics that you should face.

47 Million Uninsured. 37 Million Living in Poverty. 1 in 5 Children living in Poverty. Now that is Sad.

2000 dead and over 17,000 wounded because you and the WHIG team had dreams of Oil and Greed.

Because I gotta a theory that maybe Your Administration doesn't like Women.

See Alot of us think the Outing of Valerie was about the War and the Missing WMD's, and that you wanted to go after Mr. Wilson because he was a Whistleblower. I don't think it was that simple—because it was decided by you and the Boys up on the Hill that his wife was Fair Game—a Target. You didn't even care that she worked for the Government.

You all didn't care where she worked, but that she was a woman and That made her Fair Game-a way to send a Messege to old'Wilson. Sounds like a Klan Tactic—go after the Woman. "That'll teach'em".

We learned this week that Valerie Wilson, a mom with two small children did have threats and when she reported them to then FBI she was not offered any protection. She was told to call 911. I think about Valerie and Joe Wilson and the Hell they must have endured in the past two years.

I may not own a rapin'n'pillagin' gluttonous profits oil company. I may not be one of your crony chums in your base but I sure as hell matter. And as a woman I have watched how you treat Vet Moms, you remember the mom in the ditch-Cindy. And then there's Government Whistleblowers Like Bunny, you remember Bunny who blew the whistle on the Halli Goodie Contracts over at the Pentagon. And the whole world saw how you treated the NOLA moms, setting in the heat and misery of the Superdome and Convention Center with some white ass-in-Heckuva-Job-dockers claiming he couldn't see them.

We all watched Katrina, and wondered if you were rascist or drunk, or was it that they were Poor.

But as a mom I did think a fair number of the ones left behind were women and children, and elderly.

According to Hidden Government Records over 12,000 are Missing or Dead adults from Katrina, and 2600 missing/dead children.

I can't wait to see How Long You Can Cover Up Those Numbers.

But I had noticed that you covered up the Missing and Dead Children and Women with Great Ease.

You have had many photo-ops now down in the Hurricane Zone, but the Missing and Dead are not even mentioned.

In your eyes they are Invisible, they do not exist.

And Mr. Bush don't you dare think about Firing Mr. Fitzgerald in Saturday Night Cox Manuever, because he is trying to bring some Integrity and Justice and Truth back to this Country and the White House. And Millions of us are Watching him. And we will watch if there is a Trial, All of it. 86% of Americans support the Investigation of the Leak and the Coverup.

And Mr.Bush I know you are "Saddened" by what you think befell Scooter, but at some point you need to apologize to the Wilsons. Especially before you think about Pardoning ol'Scoot or Rovey. These Indictments were not "Tragic", they were and are Criminal. And maybe you need to think about writing an apology to some families in Iraq. And some vet families here. And also the family of MrDavid Kelley in England.

Criminals go to Jail and Criminals that hurt Women are not liked in the Big House. Think about it.

NOVEMBER 09, 2005 WEDNESDAY

THE KING AWARDS
THE MAYBERRY GULAG AWARDS

This afternoon was a special day at the White Castle, the King had the pleasure of awarding some more Freedon Tokens. He gave a irritated spasmodic little burp of a speech in the morning, and saved his Jim Beam gusto for the afternoon Prize Patrol.

The annual-when-I—feel-like-giviin'-it event when he awards WHO he thinks should recieve the once esteemed Medal Of Freedom.

Quick Mommy put on the popcorn and Koolaid it is time for the Medals of Freedom to be awarded. It never ceases to amaze me what the Dear Leader will do to desecrate these awards. In the 1940s President Truman gave Medals of Honor to the Brave who helped defend the Country with noble service in War. (President Kennedy was one of the few Presidents that recieved one before being president). In 1963 President Kennedy changed the Medal of Freedom to honor Civilians who had served the country with Executive Order 11085. It was awarded to honor people that have contributed to World Peace, cultural and signifigant public and private endeavors. "Any person who has made especially meritorious contribution to the security or national interest of the United States".

Now I could be wrong, but I think in the Dear Leader's brain the word meritorious means: "real good at sports or big TV star from the 1970's". And then of course he has also used the medal to reward "loyalty", (or his twisted version of that said concept).

So I was making a list of possible candiates for this year's Chosen:Gilligan from Gilligan's Island, Lance Armstrong, Clint Black for Patriotic Music at the Freedom Walk, Judy Miller and Scooter Libby for their fine coughgag Literary efforts. (Now the funny thing is that Mr.Bush has NEVER awarded ANY writers—isn't that shocking??? or has he??!!!). Jeff Gannon for his Press Skills. Bill O'Reilly for Journalism Endeavors. And gee, some Nascar guys, and some Rodeo guys. And Heckuva Job Brownie for his Katrina Work. Terry Shiavo for her Right to Life Work. And Pat Robertson for his wonderful diplomatic efforts with South America, and Mr.Chalabi. And some golf guy that I won't recognize.

Okay—so I am being sarcastic and rude. But his previous award icons include: Doris Day, Paul Bremer, George Tenet, And Tommy I got-no-exit-plan-no-peace plan Franks. It amazes me Women that sing and dance are considered patriotic, but not women that are writers or activists, or know how to SPEAK. Oh, wait that is right he doesn't give the award to journalists. (hey how about if he gave it to Dan Rather—now that would be a Popcorn moment.) So I re-examined the evidence, ooops, he did award ONE writer. In 2004 he awarded Robert Bartley, a writer for the WSJ in bygone days, and actually he awarded the man the honor after he was dead. He also did hand deliver a Medal of Freedom to the Pope in his dying Days. (His past awardees include Rita Moreno, Estee Lauder, and Arnold Palmer also).

Ans yes, I miss the days when it was awarded with all the prestige and honor that Kennedy intended to people that have made a huge difference in the world, and don't play golf, Nelson Mandela, Rosa Parks, and President Jimmy Carter and Rosalyn Carter were all awarded under President Clinton.

THE 2005 MEDALS OF FREEDOM?
(YOUR MAYBERRY MOMENT)

So today he gives out the Awards with all the obligatory pomp and circumstance befitting the little dictator. The Chosen are:

Aretha Franklin, Jack Nicklas, Muhammad Ali, Andy Griffith, Paul Harvey, Paul Rusesbuinga, Sonny Montegomery, Carol Burnett, and Frank Robinson, Alan Greenspan. Now I just have to say—the atheletes that he awarded did not JUST contribute to sports, they also broke color barriers, and also were Activists. And Muhammad Ali also has really helped educate people about Parkinsons Disease. Now about Andy Griffith, I am sure for folks with insomnia Matlock is sure a blessing, and we all know Mayberry.

(And yes, the WhiteHouse Website mentions that Ali was an athlete—period. And it also basically credits Andy Griffith with founding Mayberry like it is a REAL place in America.) So am I the only person who wonders if the Dear Leader is trapped in a Time Warp Video Store at night, that he hasn't seen anything newer than Matlock or Mayberry??!!!

And then I notice on the list is General Meyers, and this is what the WH press release says, ""His Tenure was marked by the Toppling of Brutal Dictatorships in Afganistan and Iraq and liberation of 50 million people." Now I don't mean to quibble, but HOW MANY did he KILL??? Come on I would like honest numbers of Shock and Awe? And the Taliban would be offended by the Dictator description . . . . I think Meyers whined about Paul Bremer and Franks and Tenet getting their dog collar trophies.

I also think that there are 1000's of troops and their families that should be insulted by these War-Toy-Boys being awarded for their lies and incompetence.

THE GREAT GULAG MOMENT: HONORING CRIME AND PUNISHMENT

Now I was worried that once again the Literary Greats had missed Dear Leader's Great Vision of Freedom, (I mean even Hitler had Propaganda Moguls), and then I saw a name I sort of recognized as a writer, but in a rather ill-described way. Matter of fact, the way he is described is less than Honest, and very circumspect. (Kind of like saying Larry Flint is a fine Romance writer . . .)

Near the bottom of the list, is the name Robert Conquest. (And yes, that really is his Macho cool name, that probably really fed Mr. Testrosterone Bush with absolute glee). Now I am not a betting woman—but I will bet $1,000,000 dollars that King George did NOT read anything written by this man, EVER. Now as of yesterday, the White House website stated that Mr. Conquest had written a great influential work in the 1960s called the "THE GREAT TERROR; STALIN'S PURGE OF THE 1930'S", and yes, that is the WHOLE name of the Book. I actually read the book many years ago in College. THE BOOK, is actually a history of Stalin written with even a hint of glory and admiration, and examines the genious of Stalin, his use of GULAGS to purge the country of PROBLEMS: ie: writers, and scholars, thinkers, and scientists, and yes, DISSIDENTS and ACTIVISTS, EVEN LAWYERS.

(Now the really Ironic side of me, would even hope that he is reading up on PURGES . . . hint-hint of his own little house)

It even goes into wonderful little details about INTERROGATION TECHNIQUES AND TORTURE. And yes, it was written in 1963 after Mr Conquest had been a communist for many years and then was a British diplomat, a "Soviet Laison" sent to Bulgaria. In the 1990s he was friendly with Christopher-interviewed-often-on-Fox-Hitchens. Now in 1997, His publisher asked him if he wanted to change the name of his book, because as accurate as it was, "THE TERROR", he thought maybe 35 years later a more suitable title should be chosen. MrConquest replied," HOW ABOUT I TOLD YOU SO, YOU FUCKING FOOLS".

So please mummy pass the Fascist cookies and would someone please explain to me what "FUCKING FOOL" put this "Writer" on the list to be awarded a Medal Of Freedom for OUR Country? Because call me a woman of reason and deduction, I would say all dirty sticky fingers should be pointing at the man behind the Curtain, The Lord Of Lies, the Biggest Dick in the White House. Don't you agree Mr.Conquest?

IMPORTANT UPDATE: CROOKS & LIARS HAS GREAT VIDEO OF MUHAMMED ALI GIVING THE CRAZY SIGN TO THE KING. HE SPOKE THE TRUTH, MAY WE ALL BE INSPIRED TO DO THE SAME . . . . EACH AND EVERY DAY IN OUR OWN WAY . . .

*   *   * also go to Blog With A View and learn more about Gulags—the right way . . . not the "Conquest" way . . . .

Links: http://www.whitehouse.gov/news/releases/2005/11/2005/1103-5html., http;//www.medaloffreedom/,

AUGUST 17, 2006, THURSDAY

THE LOST SOULS AND THE SOULESS THAT REMAIN IN POWER

* * *[It is now almost the One Year Anniverary of KATRINA and over the next two weeks I am going to post some Anniversay Posts regarding KATRINA, because while we have Criminals in the White House that let People Die, we need to Honor What was Lost Last August. This is Followup to the Story of Ethel Freeman—the lady that died sitting in front of the Convention Center, she died waiting for Aid, food, water, and shelter. Her son was forced by the Authorities to leave her, and it took monthes for him to find her. I originally posted this in November 16th,2005 and then again February 11,2006. This week her son filed Suits against the Federal Government. This is the Story of Ethel and her son, Junior.]* * *

* * *

IN HONOR OF MS. ETHEL FREEMAN WHO DIED ON SEPTEMBER 1ST DURING THE KATRINA DISASTER.

(This piece is to also honor the other Lost Souls of the Disaster that are gone, but not forgotten)

* * *This Piece was originally posted on November 16th,2005. I am Reposting it since I am honoring Women this week. and Since Brownie appreared before the Katrina Hearings, and maybe some people need to remember ALL that was lost.

And yes, this post is about the Woman who died sitting in her Wheelchair by the Convention Center and was seen by millions.

Ethel Freeman was finally laid to rest this week, Today. It is now seven weeks since Katrina struck the Gulf Coast. She was a strong woman with a frail body, she survived the Hurricane with the aid of her capable son, but she did not survive the Abandonment of the Aftermath. She was a fine woman and mother of Herbert Jr. "Junior" was known for taking beautiful care of his mother with love and attention to details. Matter of fact he had taken care of her for many years. She lost her Herbert Senior in 1976, so he has been the man of the house for many years. She was a grandmother and a great-grandmother. She had lived in New Orleans for many years, many of her neighbors knew her for 30-49 years. She was a humble quiet woman that was a part of the neighborhood in an gentle unassuming way. She worked for many years at the Tulane Medical Center, so she definently understood the importance of people recieving good medical care. In 2000 she broke her hip and within monthes her health slipped rapidly with heart problems that needed correction with a pacemaker, and also a feeding tube for her nutritional and hydration needs.

Katrina barreled into New Orleans and people battled it out at the Superdome, on roofs and in the Streets. They took care of their granbabies and their granmommies. We should hold these people with the greatest respect and admiration, and as I posted earlier in October there are STILL more than 12,000 MISSING OR DEAD ADULTS AND 2661 CHILDREN. (please see post dated 10-10-05, and it lists PDF that is issued by the government). The Government' Silence and Lies is not honoring of these dead families.

Junior rode out the storm, the worst storm in America's History with his mother. And then the flood waters rose, and after 30 hours he and his mother were rescued by boat and taken to the streets leading to the overpass. Junior pushed her in her black wheelchair to the overpass, through streets of flood slime and garbage and rising fetid waters to the Convention Center as they had been instructed by local officials. He pushed her there consoling her and telling her that there would be medical people to help take care of her and help rescue her and take her to safety. He pushed her with care as she was 91 years old and fragile. He worried about the effects of the stress and heat on her already weakened heart. And they arrived at the Convention Center to find 1000s of people languishing in the Heat with no food and no water, and no rescue imminent. They waited together there for FOUR days. He thought that she would be rescued first and instead he was ORDERED on a bus to places unknown. There was never any medical care at the Convention Center, never any food or water, or any one offering Comfort or Answers.

And he knew that Thursday morning that she was alone and frail, and that yelling for food, or water, or medical care was fruitless, there was no one and nothing. He could hear helicopters flying over, but he knew that they were not coming for her. He carefully placed a note in her pocket with all the needed information about how to best contact him. He wrapped a plaid shaw around her shoulders with tenderness and made sure that her soft pink terry slippers were still on her feet. He knelt with her and prayed.

And that same day Kyra Phillips on CCN around noontime got in a heated argument with Mr.Browne from FEMA, you all might remember it he refused to acknowledege that people were trapped at the Convention Center.He even said things are going "Relatively Well". He claimed he wasn't aware that 1000s were dying and starving at the Convention Center, he also said that "These people had Refused to Evacuate, they did not heed the Advance Warnings" implying they deserved their fate. He was interviewed with Ted Koppel in the same 24 hour period, and Mr.Koppel came right out and yelled 'Don't you all watch TV??" And now we all know thanks to his own self-righteous pompous emails that he did have access to TV and was mostly worried about his grooming, and his resturante meals, and his appearance of being "hardworking". He had to make decisions about how to roll up the Norstrom sleeves to send the right Image. And the same morning the Flyover President went on morning talk shows and said speaking for his own arrogant self that NO ONE Expected the Levees to fail. And all watched the Lies continue. (And the lies have persisted in the past two monthes with the Criminal Mr.Browne even getting paid for two extra monthes as a "consultant".) And millions of Americans emailed, made phone calls and tried to get help for the Abandoned Folks of the Katrina Hellzone.

And we yelled WHAT is Wrong with these "Leaders"? Are they Incompetent? Are they Ignorant? Are they Rascist? Is this Genocide? Is Our Country being run by the Klan?!!

Are these Men in fresh pressed shirts Souless? Clueless? How can they be so utterly detached and heartless? Do they have a Conscience? Don't they have grandparents and children? Wrapped in yet another ill conceived illusion they keep saying they are doing a Good Job, and are Hardworking . . . .

And meanwhile sitting in her black wheelchair with her weak heart and her empty feeding tube, and with 1000's of other distressed folks, all trying as best they could to look out for each other. Ethel got weaker and weaker, but she sat as tall as she could and hoped and prayed for rescue, just like Junior had said. She wondered where that bus took him. And she got tired in the heat. And she died.

And sometime that day some well intentioned soul pushed her over by the Employees entrance and hoped and prayed that someone would come back for her. And by later that day there was another soul placed with her wrapped in a white blanket. And photographers were horrified, and furious and they took the pictures of the fragile souls by the Entrance to Hell. And Anderson Cooper even showed her on LIVE TV, and you knew he did it because he was worried that she was alone, someone's grandmother, that was loved and deserved better. There was nothing exploitive in the footage. We all felt his agony and his pain. His outright grief-stricken Horror. The Outrage Knew no Bounds.

But our agony does not compare to that which Junior would experience in Alabama worried only to see pictures of her fate across TV screens and newpapers. And then his continued angst as it took SEVEN weeks to get her body back from the Government run Morgue in St.Gabriels. And finally today Junior was able to bury his beloved mother with love and care, as he had cared for her in life. And the Reverand said "It took Courage for Herbert to do what he has done and experienced".

But I have to say that we all know that Herbert Jr. is not going to picture her cared for, and loved and well tended this loving son will be haunted forever by the image of his mama sitting in the Katrina Hellzone, sweltering and abandoned by her own government. Was she abandoned by Arrogance? By Greed? Was She abandoned because she was Black? Because she was Poor? Was she abandoned because she was Elderly? Was she abandoned because she was frail and in poor health?

We hear so much from this so called Christian Right To Life Compassionate Conservative Regime that teaches and preaches Intelligent design, yet what we see is that it is coming down to the Survival of the Elitist, the Richest, and the Arrogant.

And Ironically Mr.Bush has placed many Lawyers in positions of Power, thinking that even if they are incompetent, that any situation can be Lawyered. Even if people have died, he has rationalized. He is Incorrect and it is about to be proven as Junior has hired some very fine lawyers to sue the FEMA and the Federal Government, because Ms.Ethel "was an Incredible Symbol of Neglect".(The Government failed Ms.Ethel and dishonored all the fine years of care that Junior provided).

Mr.Bush, I have a messege for you, when you have come home from your Imperial Road Trip you need to sit down and write Mr.Herbert Freeman Jr. an Apology. And before you ever set foot in New Orleans again to have another Dramatic Well Lit Disney Moment, maybe you should go to Miss Ethel's grave and lay some white roses to show honor and respect. And Bow your head in Shame.

* * *

The story above was compiled from over 40 newspaper articles. I had spent weeks attempting to research the Bodies by the Convention Center as well as the 1000s still Missing, like many other concerned bloggers. Please do read the Previous article on Oct10th regarding the Missing and Dead, this issue will haunt this country for many years to come. Whole families Gone.lost and dead, More than 12,000 adults and 2661 children.

Junior was evacuated to Alabama and he also met a lovely woman named Veronica that has been his support through much of this wretched ordeal. I like to think that Ms.Ethel in way had a hand in in helping her son find

Love, a caring soul in this Disaster. Junior is engaged to marry this other brave tempest tossed survivor.

* * *

My Great Grandmother was a Strong Southern Woman from Kentucky, she was widowed young and raised two headstrong willful boys in a small apartment. Her name also was Ethel. We called her Granny Ethel. She took in knitting, sewing and taught piano to make ends meet. She taught me that there are times to play the piano, knit socks for soldiers, and take care of neighbors, and also that Elders are to be respected. She taught me how to Set-a-table, cut Fresh Mint with scissors for the SunTea, and how to put lemon and basil and cilantro in Egg Salad and sprinkle with paprika. She also taught me how to call a Bluff. She also taught me that Evil Men can be and should be openly Cursed. During Watergate Summer, as I cleaned her tiny apartment, because by then she was blind, she was listening to the News, and she said, "Have they arrested that Evil Son-of-a-Bitch yet?" And I said No. She said in her toughest not so lady like drawl, "Well, they Better, he's getting those boys in Vietnam killed."

And I knew by that time that part of her savings had been used to send my one compassionate cousin (with the low lottery number) to Med School in Canada. Our family had conscientious objectors and soldiers, it was an interesting tense time.

{{And for those who have read of my Palmolive moment a few posts back for calling Tricky Dick a" Dickhead "one Thanksgiving when I was eight, she had heard about the event and the next time I went to see her she taught me how to make Angel Food Cake to compensate for the Palmolive moment.}}

My Granny Ethel tried to teach me how to knit, and how to play the piano, all without success. But she did teach me poetry. Below is her favorite.

* * *

Another Note to Mr. Bush:

Allie McNeil

The Next time you are in New York, maybe you need to go back to the Statue of Liberty and Ellis Island, if it is open to the Public yet. It has a poem called "The Collusus" that is honoring the Great Lady, but also is honoring the Plight of ALL Refugees. And at this point we have 1000's of Refugees that need to be remembered, sheltered, tended and loved.

". . . . Give me your tired,

Give me your poor, your huddled masses, yearning to breathe free, the wretched refuse of your teaming shore.

Send these the Homeless, the Tempest tossed to me,

I lift my lamp beside the Golden Door."

Emma Lazurus 1883

NOVEMBER 22, 2005, TUESDAY

QUESTIONS AT THE THANKSGIVING DINNER: WHEN WAR COMES HOME TO THE TABLE

In Honor of President John F. Kennedy:

"A Revolution is coming—A Revolution will be peaceful if we are wise enough;

Compassionate if we care enough; Successful if we are fortunate enough,

But a Revolution is coming, whether we will it or not. We can affect it's character, we cannot alter it's inevitability." JFK 1963

May we remember the troops eating MRE's in the Sand this Thanksgiving.

And other families going to lay flowers at the Cemetaries.

PART I: THE PASS THE GRAVY THANKSGIVING QUESTIONS

So we are approaching the Thanksgiving Dinner festivities. Many will travel to gather and feast, or lounge on the sofa and watch too much football. Families and friends will gather around the table and the stringbeans will be ignored and the gravy will be passed and questions will be asked. And I think we all know that the Focus will not be on the White House Spnining Point. In many ways I am certain that the White House would be more comfortable if we all focused on the Bird Flu, as they have been pimping it hourly now for days. And we all know it is to keep us from focusing on the Bigger Messes: Criminal Investigations and the Iraq Mess.

I watched an FDA hearing on C-Span last week and was stunned when a weasely looking man in a aged suit was explaining at a hearing that the Poultry population here in the US is not at risk of Bird Flu because the birds in this country are not ALLOWED to roam free under Bioterrorism Laws. It brought many interesting pictures to my mind. Do the birds have to carry little passports, do they have curfews and travel restrictions? So I stopped cleaning the Kitty pan and sat down to listen to this Animal Husbandry Expert. (Which by the way I think Scooter should have consulted him for his book—this Expert knew all about Caged animals, and besides his title alone would turn Scoot on). Anyways he was explaining that the birds are NOT allowed out to be Exposed to Flying Immigrant populations. All I could picture was the farms being "protected" by Red-Neck-Gun-Toting-Minute-Men on walkie talkies patroling the perimeters and scoping "We got us some Aliens, look like some Canadian Geese, got some funny sqawking, and don't look like they are from around here . . . better shoot'em".

You have to wonder how much this Expert gets paid, and how much was spent on the Bioterrorism Poultry Plan. And Doesn't anyone think that there is alot of money being tanked on Paranoia plans at this point. I mean how much is spent making sure that the white mice are traveling comfortabley as they go on the Dear Leader's Road Trips to test his food. (They are probally really sick of Arbys and Outback).

Back to the point, there will be uncomfortable questions and silences and some heated exchanges This Holiday. And maybe even some healthy dialogue and some healthy dissent. And hell maybe even some Critical Thinking. Maybe even some verbal battles down in Uncle Dick's Cave and Down at the Crawford Ranch. (Between the shots of Prozac and Wild Turkey).

PART II: THE HISTORY OF THE HEARTY THANKSGIVING DIALOGUE

So Thanksgiving for me is full of memories. (If I ramble like an old woman forgive me—I do have a point, it just takes awhile for me to get there sometime. And I was raised by Southern Women—they are not known for telling any stories with great speed. Now telling a Red Neck where to go—that can be done faster than a blink of an eye). I mentioned earlier the Thanksgiving that I was 8 and half and calling Nixon a Dickhead at Thanksgiving Dinner, with a table full fairly sober of Republicans (my relatives). The Dickhead comment meant I was sent to the powder room to have my mouth cleansed with Palmolive. I personally to this day—thought the punisment far outweighed the crime. I should have called him a Fuckhead—that would have earned the Soap. But Ce la vie.

So the following year rolls around, and my mother does the Domestic Goddess Routine, says she will bring baked goods for the Dinner. (Which means she went to the Bakery and bought lovely breads, and rolls, and re-boxed them). And then she made Home Made Pies—Rhubarb—from our garden. And she dressed us up and piled my twin sister and I into the back of the old Blue Dodge Station wagon with the pies and the rolls. And halfway to my grandparents she pulls off the road to have a talk with us. It is always a bad sign to be reprimanded before you have done anything wrong.

"Now I have worked really hard to make this a nice Thanksgiving and I will NOT have anyone Embarrass me Again this year is that clear? And that means that we will NOT be discussing the President this year—is that Crystal clear?"

The two carsick children in the back seat nodded dutifully. After all there was suposed to be Pumpkin Pie with whipped cream there, not just the hideous Sugarless Rhubarb pie. (And I can tell you Palmolive does taste wretched).

So we all sit down to eat. My Grandfather, Grinstead, Ted for short is at the head and he is serving and slicing. And the Aunties are chatting and laughing. And already one Social Fux Puax has happened as Granny

Ethel was complimented too loudly on her New Teeth and now she is so embarrassed that she won't open her mouth. (My Aunt Julia didn't mean to say it so loudly, but Granny couldn't hear her). My Aunt Julia has arrived from Kentucky and she is heavenly to sit by, she knows how to play the spoons, and tell 100's of Knock—Knock jokes. She also has stories from her childhood about her pet albino crocodile. And she likes kids, because she is a 40 year kindegarden teacher. She was like a pale version of Katherine Hepburn with twinkling green eyes and an easy laugh.

So I sit next to her. And she makes me laugh. I am actually pretty shy, don't like the huge adult dinners and fancy china and dinnerware. I am the one with bandaid knees, thick glasses, and anemic coloring that makes me people inquire of my mom if I am getting over the flu.

So the Glassware is tapped to start the dinner with some semblemce of civility. My Grandfather asks my sister to say the blessing. She does it pretty close to perfect, and my mom is beaming with pride.

And then the food is passed, and the Turkey is carved. And soon after all the food is distributed comes the time for polite conversation.

"Well, dearie, How do you like school this year? And what is your favorite subject? And what do you like best about it?

(I don't know why—but Southern Women always ask questions in threes.) Aunt Julia smiled warmly at me as she asked these, she was not trying to embarrass me, she really cared.

"She loves school this year and is doing really well" My Mom answered a bit too quickly to ease her own nerves.

"Oh, My, I would much rather hear from her, do you mind?" Aunt Julia was used to dealing with shy children and overbearing adults.

"Well, I really like school. I like Current Events, I have to watch the News every night and I get to buy a newspaper when I walk Home from school." (I felt very grownup to give this answer and it was the truth)

"What Interests you the Most?"

Off to the side I could hear air seep out of my mom like a tired balloon, an exasperated sigh. The moment had arrived where she was convinced I would embarrass her. A Curious nervous Silence had settled over the table and it was obvious Everyone remembered the Dickhead Moment and perhaps the captive audience was hopeful for an encore preformance.

"Well the thing I watch the most and I don't understand is the Vietnam War, I mean it doesn't make any sense, I don't understand WHY our soldiers who look like kinda young are over there getting hurt and killed in these gross swamps and in the jungle, and I am not sure who they are fighting or protecting? And if it is like baseball, I don't think anyone is really winning, I mean how can anyone win if they are showing the dying on the news every night?"

BAM. There is was the Big Fuck Up Moment of the night, the moment my poor mother had been dreading, and knew was coming. The palpable Silence hung in the air like fresh Skunk spray on a humid summer night. I looked over at my grandfather and his eyes were bulging and the vein was pulsing in his forehead. Hmmm, and I realized too late that the Pumpkin Pie was hanging in the Balance—Again.

Suddenly, the silence was broken by Aunt Julia, "I think it is fine that you are paying Attention and asking Such Good Questions that is what Americans need to do to help protect those fine young soldiers over in Viet Nam. Ted, Dear could you pass me the gravy . . . . It is a good thing that a nine year old is paying such attention? We can only hope that our President and Elected folks are being so thoughtful. . . . Don't you agree Ted Dear?"

She smiled at him, but her eyes were hard and determined, she was not to be trifled with.

He swallowed hard, and nodded in amazement and quietly handed her the gravy.

And just like that my Palmolive Dickhead Moment was Vindicated, atleast at the house where my Dad grew up.

[[[And now for the Ironic Epilogue to this tale. In the next couple of years Everything would rattle and change the Republican Framework of my childhood. The following Thanksgiving my Uncle Stu would not be attending because he was driving my Cousin Stu—the compassionate cousin with the really low lottery number, up to Canada so that he could go to Medical School for the next number of years. And My Aunt Julia was arrested at a Anti War rally in DC. And we were again in the back of the faded Blue Dodge Station Wagon, except this time we were going to Arlington to attend the funeral of my mom's nephew. The Thanksgiving Dinner at her sister's house had been interrupted by the KNOCK at the Door of two Uniformed Officers. The War had come home. The Thanksgivings were to change forever.]]]

PART III: QUESTIONS FOR THIS 2005 THANKSGIVING:

(Feel Free to pass the gravy and fire away . . . . feel free to add your own to the Comment section)

- [1] If the US supposedly went to Iraq to stop Sadam from using his Chemical Weapons on us or his own neighbors or civilians, why are we using Chemical Weapons on poor innocent civilians in Fallujah?
- [2] If the US suposedly was SO concerned about Saddam's Torture Chambers, why does the Cheney Cabal have Secret Torture Chambers set up in Secret locations in Secret Countries?
- [3] The US supposedly came into Iraq to end the Horrors of Abu Gahrab, why is it still being used? And why isn't it closed? And if the WMDs is not a problem, because they do not exist why were all these people being interrogated?
- [4] If The President is pardoning Turkeys can we expect certain people to be lined up outside the WH door to be pardoned?
- [5] What does Stay the Course Mean? Stay on the Golf Course? What course?

[6] What is wrong with bringing the Troops out of Iraq if the Iraqis want the Occupying the troops out?

[7] Aren't Evil Doers people who use Illegal Weapons—ie Chemcial weapons and drills, and imprison and torture people illegally? So WHO is the Enemy Uncle Dick?

DECEMBER 07, 2005, WEDNESDAY

MAMA DEE LEFT THEM BEWILDERED AND GODSMACKED AT THE KATRINA HEARINGS

Did anyone watch the Katrina Hearings? I know the MEDIA SHOW we are susposed to watch this week is the Bad-Dictator—Saddam Trial, it's being displayed on all the channels and properly spread across the Media like Fresh Buffalo Manure. And I know that the Bird Flu and the Broken Borders Crap are also being broadcast in Classic Diversional Fashion. Not me I scrambled to find the Katrina Hearings, and they were well worth the search. (Check C-Span—there will be late night re-runs) They were beyond Amazing. First off we need to give some Brass Ball Awards to the fine people who come forward to DC, and testified to what they saw, heard, and the Extent of Misery that was experienced by those in NOLAZONE during Katrina. These Fine People testified to the Arrogant at their Prescious Comfort Zone in the Marbled Halls of DC. They were eloquent and lyrical, even riveting in their descriptions and testimony.

And my-oh-my some of these "fine" reps had a Come-to-Jesus moments during these Hearings. The "R" word came up and the "P" word came up. Oh-Holy-Shit these men in suits did indeed turn many shades of paler pasty pale. (oh, and yes the words that came up over and over was Racism and also Poverty, echoing like shockwaves in this little Republican Shark Tank, because the Democrats are boycotting these hearings, geez, I sure as Tuesday hope that someone taped it or TIVO'D for them).

*NOTE TO READERS (ALL 4 OF YOU): Please do not be offended by reading this post. If I speak disparagingly of the Men in Suits on the Hill, please note that it is directed at their apathy and lack of concern for their fellow Americans. And yes, I am very worried that Color did indeed play a signifigant role in the Katrina Disaster. I am not the only one that has pondered WHAT IF the Disaster had Struck a Mostly White Upscale Golf Community in Florida—would things have been different? I think we know the answer . . . . hmmm, and Imagine that—the Katrina Hearings are not on cspan today . . . . I wonder why. And the White House is to be supoenaed next week for the Documents that have been witheld up until now. My anger is not directed in White Men in Suits, just The White Men in Suits on the Hill—who appear so stupidified and confused.

There were some Priceless Moments:

> (1) So Shay of Connecticutt asks, for some friggin' unknown reason, "Can we hear some examples of Good or Hopeful events that came of this Disaster"

(oh, yeah as we all watched TV during that week from HELL, that was the first thing that I thought of after CNNing for 6 days straight . . . .)

So one of the panel members, who is an attorney says "Well, I know that seeing the Looters feeding the Hungry was an Inspiring Sight."

There was a collective THUNK as the white men jaws hit the table.

And then the Lawyer explained about the Looters and why it happened, and the whities sat and scratched and squirmed, realizing that maybe asking for Heroic HAPPY Patriotic WHY I LOVE America tales was not a bright move.

> (2) Mama Dee is my new hero, this woman is the Lifeblood of NOLA, and she is the Queen of Integrity. She laid it out for these men, she rendered them speechless, Godsmacked and bewildered. She explained in her own way what the hell went wrong and is still wrong in NOLA and she did indeed bring up the R and the P words, alot. And after she was done there were grown men with hankies drying sweat and tears. She is so sharp she carefully and oh-so-subtley kept reminding these Repugs that yes-indeedy that

there was mountains of tapes, video and interviews and photos showing what happened that week, alot of it that was on TV and some that wasn't. For those who don't know her, she is an Amazing Fine Woman, interviewed over and over on many channels and by Anderson Cooper and others. She is Courage in Motion. She is a longtime Community Activist, and her house was The Hub of Rescues, survivors and Response. Food to Boats this is a One-Woman-FEMA. And the media and rescue people alike went to her house as a sanctuary and for meals. Her full name is Dyan French Cole, but everyone calls her Mama Dee. She was full of stories, some would make any mama's heart flutter. And others she told with sardonic wit and careful humor. She told about FEMA? RED CROSS and Military Air Dropping Barrel of Hard Rock Candy that was Expired. (Geez, they should have airdropped Dentists also). And she gently chided them "It wasn't just poor black folk, it was also poor white folk. So it is still Racism, not all of it was about color, it was also about socioeconomic status."

(3) Ms. Cynthia McKinney, rep. of Georgia showed up and listened and asked questions, the Democrats that didn't show looked arrogant. They should have listened to these tempest tossed souls with harrowing tales. As a Democrat I am embarrassed that such a stupid path was taken, it solved nothing and accomplished nothing, but was one more insult to the Witnesses to look at the Empty chairs before them.

(And have the Democarats Done ANYTHING to investigate this mess, or did they go to sleep on this too?)

(4) Horror Stories were shared about the Missing, and Still Missing. And the truth about the Dirty cops, and the missing young boys down there. And the Horrors of being poor and sick and black and not being ABLE TO EVACUATE. (What is it about these men, they can't understand that not everyone can go climb in their lexus and shimmy up the Coast and hang out in the Marriot for a few days, WHY OH WHY can't they wrap their heads around that???) And the Witnesses did also point out that WHOLE Families are STILL Missing. (Now yes, we know that Enigma has been ranting and raving on this very issue for monthes, but according to the

Hidden Numbers and my earlier posts, more than 12,000 adults and 2,661 children. And in my head that is like THREE Twin Towers falling all at once, and all of us just walking the other way).

(5) And the last point that was brought up and is still disturbing and gave me pause and shiver, and actually made the little panel Extremely Uncomfortable. The Witnesses reported that in the 9th ward Explosions were heard.(I have read this on Blogs as well . . . but I had never heard it said OUT Loud). They said that many people heard and then the water rose all that night. They also said that people were wondering if the Levees failed or if something blew them up or damaged them. It was also said that the pumps went off. (Why did the pumps go off—were they nuclear powered? And what about Nuclear Plant there—we have never heard if it was turned off or not—there were conflicting articles online that week, and yet NOW all the articels are GONE off the Internet—ALL of them have been removed.) Questions about the Explosions and about the Power Plant were actually not answered with any authority or accuracy.And I have tried to find out, but it does not appear that Entergy the Power Plant has had to appear at the Hearings, and they should. And I also wonder if the Army Corp has to appear and answer questions???)

(6) And I have another Question, Brownie and Chertoff certainly had to plant their behinds in the Hot Seat, when is Uncle Dick or the King's turn? I have a case of popcorn, I am ready. And I know we have not seen the Lord of Darkness or the King with live humans—unless it is to press militarized Flesh.

(7) Another Higlight was Lawyers describing that the Superdome, the Causeway, and the Convention Center became Concentration Camps for the people left there to swelter and starve, trapped by the government in these zones. And the men with guns that would not let them leave or move. (The Guard and the Black Water Boys I presume . . .)

(8) The Witnesses have been gathering much research and confronting the Government with their OWN research, including previous statements made by Brownie and Chertoff. Other Stellar moments invloved actual Math—the WHERE-IS-DAMN-MONEY-

CAUSE-IT-AIN'T HERE???And Why aren't the Guard still there? And WHY did it take SO LONG to get them there?

I could go on and on, in usual rant style, this I know many good points were brought up at these Hearings, and hopefully some good will come of them. But I am asking that the Witnesses be Heard, because we are damn lucky they survived to tell their stories.

* * *

(Please see last post on this was about Ethel Freeman,the woman in the Wheelchair at the Convention Center, who died waiting, "Lost Souls and the Souless in Power" and multiple posts on Katrina)

DECEMBER 22, 2005, THURSDAY

COUNTING THE COAL IN BIG BROTHER'S STOCKING

HOW DO WE COUNT THE LUMPS OF COAL?

. . . . with a smile. So let's get to it.

As some of you know the Enigma has been in a Really Bad Funk, some of it due to Snot Freezing Lake Erie Weather and some of it due to the King's Illegal Secret Spying Program. But thanks to some incredible blogging minds and due to some Big Fat Lumps of Coal in the White House Stockings I am feeling a little more positive . . . . It is true that I hit my head getting cookies out of the oven earlier, but I intend to enjoy this head throbbing giddy glee for a little bit longer . . . hell, even ten whole minutes.

LICKING IT AND GETTING STUCK

Okay, I know that sounds particularly dirty, or like something Scooter or Lynne Cheney would have in their Literary Wonders. Sorry to dissapoint. But here is what I mean. Earlier tonight I took my little Lilly dog for yet another popsicle walk in the Frozen Lake Erie Tundra and while we walked and skidded about I had a few little epiphanies. Poor Lilly is still having trouble with the ice—she looks like Bambi wide legging on the Black Ice as we cross the street. So we get to her little park and we have what I can only describe as a Ralphie Moment from a Christmas Story . . . . I was walking along and suddenly I looked down and noticed that Lilly was not moving and she had her head down. But then I noticed she had her mouth open. She had found an old French Fry Under about two inch Chunkette of ice, and her tongue was stuck to the ice. Now while I debated taking my cellphone and calling 911 (and how thrilled the Fire Department was going to be with the dumb redhead . . .) My Brilliant dog somehow got her tongue uncemented from the ice.

And while I was laughing at her, it occurred to me . . . . isn't this like Bush in a way (well, except we know that Lilly is Much Smarter). The More he licks at the I-Gotta-have—me-more-spying-power SaltLick, he is getting himself into all kinds of Trouble. He has licked so Hard at it and it is Hard Work, that he is Stuck now, Don't you think? And it isn't little trouble, it's Yur-Daddy-can't-Save-yur-ass-on-this-one Trouble. How big is the Ol' Trouble?

Well, well Let's Count the Lumps of Coal, shall we . . . .

THE LUMPS OF COAL IN BIG BROTHERS LEAKY SOCKS:

(1) THE ILLEGAL NSA SPYING (AND OTHER ILLEGAL SPYING) So it Leaks out this week that Americans may have been spied on Illegally, by our own government,and gee not by the FBI or some other Homeland Security Special Task Force, but by the NSA. And Bush comes out this week and gives a little "I-Am Here—to-assure-you "speech about how it was ONLY foriegn emails and phone calls with TERRAIST connections . . . hmmm, color me paranoid, but gee I bet not. So now 36 hours later, ooops, it turns out that well, it was NOT just Foriegn Soil emails, it was ALSO Domestic Emails (no shit). And now here is what is so interesting, READ Jay Rockefeller's Secret Hidden Handwritten letter to Mr Cheney about the New Program, and read what was causing him worry, it was about BATCHES, AND IP NUMBERS. Hmm, were they Data Mining? (I don't think Warrrants cover that?) Or were they just requesting LARGE Batches from Broadband Companies (Does the FCC Allow That, can we ask Powells son?—I mean Janet's Breast wasn't allowed to see daylight), and HOW DID they KNOW Which Batches to get IF THEY WEREN'T ALREADY SPYING???? And Jay's letter talks about Interception. Well, I don't think reading an email is

> the same as TAKING IT AND PUTTING IT IN A SECRET SAFE SOMEWHERE NOW IS IT???

Now if he already had the Expanded Powers of the Patriot Act, and was using the FISA court like a Carry out Resturante, and Homeland Security had Secret Special Task Forces doing some of the scut work, and the Pentagon was Spying on the Real Threats of Vegans and Cookie Baking Grannies—WHY would he need more Spypower? Maybe because he was already doing the spying on a larger scale, and needed a way to continue his activity . . . So what does it mean when a President spies on SO MANY (besides the fact that he is maybe Beyone Paranoid?) This is not about protecting me or you is it? It is about HIM being real scared of Something?

Something like what? Like People knowing he is Corrupt and Lying About a Phony Oil Driven War? Gee, that might be a way to Spy on them nasty Writers, and those Damn Enviromentalists,and those Damn Democrats, and those Damn Quakers,and those Damn Liberals, and those Damn Anti War Defeatists. This is NOT about Protecting Anyone, and NOT about Osama or Terra anymore.

> (2) So earlier today we learn one of the FISA Court Judges is resigning over concern over Warrants that were written, that the Secret Program might have been used to issue those warrants. And then in Thursdays' WAPO it is revealed that the FISA Court and Judges might not have known about the Secret Bush Program . . . . oooops. JUDGES DIDN'T KNOW??? . . . . that is a little different then they were not comfortable, hell, they didn't know??!!! So does that mean for THREE years they were writing warrants based on ILLEGAL SEARCH AND SEIZURE—(well, gee that is a Violation of the Constitution's 4th amendment, altough the 1st Amendment might be in there too).

*   *   * Here is an Off Topic Observation: Every Time the President gives a speech the Flag is right behind him, but it NEVER has the Olive branch—it is ALWAYS the Arrows . . . watch and see if I am right . . . . Hat-tip to my son for that one . . . it is haunting.*   *   *

And then to top it off, we also learn this week about the ACLU and 2330 pages of FOIA that show that all kinds of folks were being surveilled—Environmentalists, Poverty Advocates, and time will tell who else. (Greenpeace, and PETA of course). Does anyone think this is sounding like an ENEMY'S LIST? (and how come when ever they give these speeches about the Homeland Threats, and lists, they never mention Hate Crimes against Muslims? or the NeoNAZIS? or the KKK? and these are alive and well in Certain States)

And we also learn that there were multiple speechs given Supporting Renewal of the Patriot Act, and even ON FILM, where he says no rights were violated and that the Constitutional Rights were upheld. (Dates: 4-20-04, is the best footage so far. I will post the other dates at the end if someone is having cpsan urges)

> (3) So the Patriot Act didn't get kicked through after all, so today he came shitstomping across the Lawn and gave a little snippy-pissedoff-ginnedup—speech about how the Patriot Act expires January 1st and that we all are going to be in Danger if we don't pass it, the Terrorists are gonna Lurk and get us. So Osama is going to "Get" Us because George can't find another way to spy on HIS OWN enemies? Does he think we're stupid or paranoid like him? He will sure drag those 3000 exploited 911 corpses out every chance he gets. (godforbid Someone, Anyone brings up the Hidden 15,000 Fresh corpses of NOLA and Katrina, shhh)

[[So WHO helped him come up with the Secret Program Mis-Using NSA and FISA? Was it Gonzo? hmm, or maybe it was our favorite Church Lady—Harry? Or was it Soaring-like-an Eagle Asscroft? George Curveball Tenet? (shh,yes) Did Chertoff of Homeland Security Fame KNOW about this Program??? Take your pick folks . . . . Or maybe it was ALL of them.

HEARINGS FOR THE NEW SUPREME COURT CAN NOT BEGIN UNTIL THIS MATTER IS ADDRESSED, AS OUR CONSTITUION HAS BEEN VIOLATED, and THAT IS MORE CRITICAL. (and since Alito has relationship with Chertoff, he might be compromised)]]

NURSE NAG: So I am going to say this—please keep calling Senators, Media, ANYONE, write letters do what ever you can MAKE NOISE.... our country needs us to save it. I have said this before, and I will say it again, If Paul Revere was alive today he would be a blogger....

(4) Conyers deserves a Huge Gold Star and a Hug, read up on his work and DSM that came out yesterday, most Big Brass Alliance already know. And hey—he too has put forth the Impeachment Option, on the Table now with relation to the War and DSM.
(5) FINALLY FINALLY the Senators are finding their Brass Ones and Just in friggin time.... Now if they can just Not drop them Again....

Okay I am going to stop counting for now.... and get ready to count more tomorrow. Please Santa Bring us a little Coal every day for Ol' Big Brothers Stocking at 1600 Pennsylvannia Ave.

* * *

As Tongue in Cheek as this is... We are living in a Police State, and some of us have already experienced Surveillance. 1000's will end up having been on Enemy Lists. Suspect for What? Do we want to find out How Many this President is Capable of?

THIS IS IMPEACHABLE.... High Crimes and Misdemeanors are Real and Happening in your Country.... We Need to take back Our Country.

DECEMBER 23, 2005, FRIDAY

85% VOTE IMPEACH ON MSNBC POLL

MSNBC HAS "UNSCIENTIFIC POLL" ON SITE:

QUESTION: DO YOU BELIEVE THAT BUSH'S ACTIONS JUSTIFY IMPEACHMENT.

(HAVE BEEN TRACKING MOST OF EVE IT HAS BEEN FLUCTUATING BETWEEN 85 TO 88% VOTING YES)

As of 11:30pm 139,838 have voted, and 85% have voted YES; "BETWEEN SECRET SPYING, DECEPTIONS, LEADING TO WAR, THERE IS PLENTY TO JUSTIFY PUTTING HIM ON TRIAL? (yes or no, or others)

{WHOA that is one big lump of coal, considering most people were out eggnogging and last minute shopping)

http://watchingthenews.org/story/2005/12/23/163721/28, or Google MSNBC + Impeachment poll update: 8am 142,900 have voted, still 85% for Impeachment

Merry Christmas . . . .

DECEMBER 25, 2005, SUNDAY

THE LESSON ABOUT GRACE

Christmas Eve I ran into Jarad and he was Singing Amazing Grace, with a pretty good voice. And in the Grey wet stillness it was echoing off buildings and sounded sweet . . . .

In an earlier post I wrote about Robert, the Homeless Iraq Vet and how he hung out in the little park near where I live and where I walk my dog. I also mentioned Jarad, another Vet in that piece about Homelessness and PTSD and Vets. Jarad was in Iraq I, and has PTSD and self medicates a bit with alcohol, and that means he isn't always allowed to sleep at the shelter. And he has sort of a job, he calls himself a MetalMan. Here in Cleveland and in other cities around the country (Baltimore,Pittsburgh) Impoverished are finding a new way to make money.Used to be people collected cans and went to transfer stations to get money. Now it is Metal, any kind, copper gutters, ribarb and plaques off old abandoned buildings. We have this giant hole across the street where the City is I think trying to fix some kind of problem, it has metal sheeting and rods holding the hole together, and letting the Steam out and keeping the dirt and debris from falling Into the Hole. It is a Hole of about 20X10 feet.

Jarad had his old rattley grocery cart with him and had already harvested some placards and old rusted gutter pieces. I tried was trying to explain that he should not pull the metal that was holding up the barrier around the Hole. He was nice about me pestering him in his efforts, and I realized that he was just doing "his" job, and that my Engineering Rationales don't mean much when someone is Broke and Hungry. I knew that when I came back walking the dog, that the metal rods and more would be gone. My arguments were wasted breath.

And I came home and found an email from the Edwards, so nice and very kind. And it had a photo of them, and John looks young, but his eyes are so tired and old. And Elizabeth looks tired and ever hopeful. And there were the words that I had just heard Jarrad, the Metalman singing as he salvadged Metal.

"Through many dangers, toils, and snares, we have already come.

Twas Grace, that brought us Safe this far.

Grace will lead us Home."

And the E-Card wished Grace . . . .

And I was struck that I don't KNOW what Grace is anymore, not really. I wish I did. But it is lost to me.

IS Grace something I can still find . . . . And if it is a Place . . .

I need a better Map or a Guide . . . .

{{By Christmas 2005 My Husband had left to go back to the NW and my son and I were living alone in the City Loft. And I finally shared out little of our Life and our reality.}}

* * *

DECEMBER 25, 2005, SUNDAY

CHRISTMAS 2005: PUMPKIN SOUP, PANCAKES, POPCORN & PROMISES

Christmas was very quiet at Enigma's urban loft. The Xena warrior princess kitty (who thinks she is a dog) and Lilly the deaf barkless Basenjii (who thinks she is a cat) took turns lying in front of the fire. It rained by Lake Erie and there was a dingy grey haze that enveloped the city. And the temperature rose to 38 tropical degrees. (and after the below Brrrr Zero of last week—we were beyond happy for the tropical 30's). It was Pumpkin soup, popcorn, and pancakes. Our little tree is up in the corner with 20 years of reglued handmade sentimental ornaments. The ornaments are just part of a larger broken picture.

It was a very quiet Christmas. The last Christmas was spent in a old rotting Victorian Rooming House on the California Coast in a 20X10 Room with a very sick Enigma and a dying marmalade cat named Philo. It was rainy and windy and awful and just one more Christmas in a Strange place. This is our forth Christmas in a different place . . . . a strange not quite Home place. A refugee In My Own Country. And yeah due to being sick and not working much, the old Enigma Christmas budget was small . . . . too small. Many people had this kind of Christmas.

In 2001 I blew the Whistle on a big bad Evil Chemical Company to the Federal Government, I had done a County Wide Health Survey and the Results were staggering. I did it because I had sick neighbors and friends and It had to be done. I never thought twice What would happen next. I never thought my government was part of the collusion, the poison. This year the Big Evil Company sold Billions under price and they did stop all their dangerous polluting on the little contaminated town,even though they left their toxic mess behind. I never thought that IT would change Everything Forever. I was wrong.

The Big Company was pissed and the Government, this administration was not happy with the lil' nurses data and her complaints. The Company also had a long lasting relationship with the Bush Family, but I did not know that.The Nurse was harrassed and threatened, and she kept having to move her little family for safety. It didn't always work. I know most citizens don't Believe Their Government would spy on them or tap their phones, or look at their Library records or medical records.All agencies are being used, and misused to do this to 1000's of citizens. I am not paranoid, just pissed and really tired. Most people are naive like I was, but now I know what it feels like to be poked and prodded. I know also what the it feels like to be Abandoned by the Federal Government and be mistreated by Federal Authorities and have Trust demolished. I have complete empathy for the folks of Katrina . . . and the Aftermath they have experienced.

*   *   * If you want to know more about the Enigma tale, it is under Silent Fallout over on my links, (yes, I blogged my book) the intro, and other chapters over time will be up for interested readers.If any of you know a Good Agent I am interested. Please leave me messeges on watergate summer.*   *   *

But this year I am with my son, and our little dog and cat and we have a nice dry apartment. And that is Something to Treasure. I watch the folks, the Survivors of Katrina and the Tsunami, and the 1000's that have lost jobs and homes these past 4 years and I know that Change has to come. And I know that I have much to be grateful for, no matter how small they may seem to others . . .

And yes, our Christmas was pancakes and popcorn and promises to my son. Because Promises are all I had to give. But with Promises I give Hope and Faith for a better future . . .

Blessings and prayers to Blogatopia. Namaste.

DECEMBER 25, 2005, SUNDAY

ENIGMA'S PUMPKIN SOUP

So if you read the Enigma Christmas piece . . .

You read about the Soup—Pumpkin Soup.

so here is the Secret Receipe . . . shhh

2 cans of Pumpkin Puree
2 cups of water
1 cup of Amaretto Creamer butter (3 tablespoons)
1 tablespoon sour cream

Spices:

2 cloves garlic—sliced thin and lightly sauteed and then added to soup.

This is my new favorite soup—I plan to eat it until I am sick of it. It didn't Look very tasty, but myohmy.

Simmer on the stove, and when it is smokey and steamy, add 2 tablespoons of brown sugar.

Sprinkle with nutmeg, cinnamon, and sprigs of fresh basil and cilantro.

Allie McNeil

Now about the Creamer, you could also add regular Cream and even some real Amaretto. But I didn't have any Real amaretto . . . but be creative and explore it.

Served with buttered bread, or fresh bisquits or warm buttered cornbread it is Heavenly. Enjoy.

JANUARY 04, 2006, WEDNESDAY

BROKEN MIRACLES IN THE WEST VIRGINIA, 12 DEAD MINERS

BREAKING NEWS: OR BROKEN NEWS . . . . BROKEN MIRACLES DOWN IN THE HOLLOWS.

It is 3:08 in the morning, Finally a Press Conference was held by the Company, and the Bossman came out and Admitted that the 12 Trapped Miners were found Dead, and one Critical. Why the Sam Hell it took More than FOUR hours to identify 12 DEAD people, I can not even begin to Fathom.

(I have been watching TV for hours and I have been following the Miner Story. It is in my Blood. I come from kin in West Virginia and Kentucky, I have studied Mines a bit, but that is a story for another time. Please read this I am only writing what I am seeing, there are no online updates or accurate information to give with this post)

(Now at 2:46am Lynnette Roby with her son and daughter Kiki and Travis came out of the Church and ran over to CNN Anderson Cooper and told him that the News was Wrong. She told Anderson that the Mine Owner had come to the Church at 2:30 am and he said that only Errors Were Made and that there was only one survivor. She also said that he had come to the Church earlier and said that the Miners would be brought to their loved ones before they went to the Hospital, but that now the families were being told that the Miners were indeed dead. The families were horror stricken and you could hear yelling and screaming and fighting up in the Church. Right after this interview The Press Conference began by the Bossman of the Company).

At 10:30pm we were told that the Miners had been located and were told that the Miners were Found, and found Alive. That the Waiting Families were told this information waiting at the Church. And yet, all eve only one ambulance went by. CNN spoke with the local hospital, and the ER doctor they said had been dispatched to the site. (As an old ER nurse I am thinking that is not a good sign, sometimes in small towns the ER doctors are also the Medical Examiner). Yet the company said Nothing, and there was never a Press Conference, UNTIL 3am. Most of America has already gone to bed, thinking that the Miners were Alive, because NO Company Statement was issued. (As of 11:30pm I switched over to Dave Letterman, and I was still thinking well they say that the Miners are alive . . . so I was thinking well, we'll see how many to go to the Hospital and what condition they are in).

[No Families or Media were allowed to the mine site, and the Results of the Carbon Monoxide levels have never been made public, the ones obtained by a robot yesterday. So I am still thinking that Something is NOT Right. So this was nagging me . . . . and so at 3am I am thinking whelp I will check CNN one more time and see what is going on, and that is when I see the Press Conference . . . and the Redfaced Bossman is giving a conference, and admits that the Carbon Monoxide levels were well above 300ppm. That is too high, not compatible with life for long periods of time.Dead Canary High.}

The Bossman (his name was not on the screen) said that he went to the Command Centerto Celebrate the Miracle and he found out 20 minutes after the Initial reports and that some were Dead. NOW WHY the hell NO ONE said Anything? It would not be hard to give a report and say "We are concerned that some of the Found Miners may be Critical or Dead". These West Virginia Folks are smart—they know mining, hell if they knew how high the Methane levels were, those families would have been prepared for the worst.(I think it was very deceptive of the company not to release the levels earlier—it means they knew that the Company fostered False Hopes and caused the families pain they certainly did not need).

Even in the past three years since the last wretched Mine Disaster, it is known that many Protective Regulations have been rolled back and altered and it Deserves Scrutiny. (The Company was operating with a slew of Safety Violations, total of 208, enough to close the Mines). I also find it very odd that the last time that this happened in Pennsylvania, there were atleast hourly accurate updates. Once the families were confined up in the Church and the Media and the families were not allowed at the Mine site and Media not IN the Church, I think some Problems are going on. At the last Disaster, Equipment was shown, Mining Experts on site were Interviewed and Information was shared, partly because when information is shared this keeps Families Calm. I am wondering now that Mining and Energy is under the Government Reigns and Clouds of the Defense Dept. and Homeland Security did not BLOCK effective Communication to Media and Families. And it is also very obvious that the COMPANY was controlling the Outlet of ALL information. But if you were watching like I was you would have seen that the Media Coverage was Muzzled and Ineffective. And it was not for lack of trying, CNN, MSNBC and even Fox had all their best in place. The Company had HOURS to Correct The Mistake, instead they let the "Good News" sit for Hours. The Company let the Families "Jubilate and Celebrate" said the Bossman.

Randall MacCloy is the only survivor Minor, 27 years old and he is in Critical condition and was unconscious. He is now on a ventilator and being transferred to a Level One trauma level.

Sago is a small town, a Company Town, a mere Hollow in West Virginia, 418 people that all view each other as Family. Why did the company lie to these good hardworking people after 40 hours of Anguish . . . . Ask yourself this . . . .

We are living in a Culture Where LIES are Embraced and Perpetuated . . . . and there is fallout . . . and we are seeing it. Has the Mining Regulators and Safety Monitors experienced a Femanized Agency? And indeed the Mining Owner who knew 20 minutes after the Miners were found that they were indeed Dead, WHY didn't he say Something. I guess we do indeed have another Heckuva Job Brownie Award to give out?—to MrBossman (Mr Hatfield Blaming the Miscommunication . . . . Now I don't know ALL the details, but Intentionally letting these families wait at that Church to see their loved ones for Hours, that is Lying, plain and simple. And Lying by Omission of Facts Doesn't Clear ANY Blame.)

One Family member, Anna, one brave woman standing in the cold rain told Chad OBrien at 3:30 am "We was told that they were ALIVE and that they was going to bring them up here to the Church, then we heard Nothing for Three Hours. No one said Nothing. We Deserve the Truth, we are Americans, People should be Angry for and with us."

Families were and are so Angry and Hurt . . . . We should share their Angst and Rage. This Ain't Right.

UPDATE: as of today Friday January 6th, the International Coal Group has posted three small notices FINALLY on their website about the disaster, and set a Fund for the family, and posted the names of those effected, and the Dead.

I will be updating blog over weekend with mor information. Skeptical Oberserver has been following closely, and has good info. and also ALF-CIO has good information about this situation—google them + Sago Mine.

JANUARY 10, 2006, TUESDAY

THE ENEMY WITHIN

Articale II Section4

[All Civil Officers removable by Impeachment]

The President, Vice President, and ALL Civil Officers of the United States shall be removed from Office on Impeachment for, Conviction of Treason, Bribery, or Other High Crimes and Misdemeanors.

Dear Mr.Bush,

In the past month we have learned that American Citizens have been spied on by their Own Government. I realize that you want to call it "Eavesdropping". Eavesdropping is what strangers do in an elevator, what you have been doing is NOT eavesdropping.

You have been spying on Citizens, secretly, under false pretenses and utilizing multiple agencies to carry out your demands. We learned two weeks ago that Pentagon has been keeping files and investigating Peace Activists and Anti-War Protestors, and others of "Concern". That means that you and Mr.Rumsfeld are afraid of Quaker Grandmothers that Bake cookies and hold "meetings"? What makes them terrorists? We have watched you and Mr.Cheney fight our Elected representitives over Torture, as more and more stories come out about Rendtion: secret prisons and planes and Individuals tortured. And now we find out that you have been spying on American Citizens Illegally for Over three years, and misusing powers and laws and agencies to do so. We learned that even though you had the access and power of the FISA court and the Patriot Act you Needed Other ways to Spy on citizens. You have Violated the Constitution that you promised to Faithfully Uphold and the very laws that you vowed in January 2001 to Faithfully Execute.

Presidents that Lie to the Citizens and the Congress and do not uphold Our Laws are Impeached.

We have learned that 1000's of Citizens have been monitored, emails and also phone calls. We also know that you have authorized the FBI working in Conjunction with the Department of Homeland Security to monitor and Investigate people's records, including Library Records, as well as Medical records, and book purchases. If the Patriot Act even allowed your Administration do spy in this manner, WHY would you need More Ways to Spy by using the NSA in an illegal Manner. And we know that since the NSA was involved it will be almost impossible for Americans to learn WHO you thought were and are Terrorists in your mind.Tonight before you go to bed, you need to take a Long look in the mirror and ask, Who does threaten you Mr.Bush, WHO is the Enemy Within?

Are they Muslims? Are they People of Non-Christian Religion that you do not feel comfortable with? Buddhists? Are they People with Names that you can't pronounce? Are they people that speak in a different language? Or are they Anti War Grannies? Are they Gold Star Mothers that have lost children in your Oil War? Are they Scientists? Are they Researchers? Are They College students studying Political Science? Are they Lawyers that represented People that you do not respect? Are they Military Leaders that did not Agree with you on War Tactics? Are they Writers? Are they Ex-Ambassadors? Are they Whistle Blowers that went to the Press and tried to get the Truth out? Are they Vets who happen to be against your war? Are they Ex-Federal Employees who left in disgust with your regime changes? Are they Civil Rights Activists? Are there any Environmental Or Health Activists and Advocates on your lists? Are there any Nurses and Moms on the Lists of People You authorized to be spied on? Were The People on Your Lists that you felt Threatened this Country just "Fair Game"?

The Founding Fathers wrote Laws and Created Our Constitution to help Protect us as a People against Abuses of Power and Hubris. They wrote laws to Protect us, We the People, from Tyranny, from the Enemy Within.

(originally posted December 19th, 2005, some Quakers asked me to move to January . . . I will post the links in the Comments about Quakers being on spy lists now—Jan.14th, 2006)

JANUARY 16, 2006, MONDAY

NOW IS THE TIME

Dear Dr. King,

We have to listen to your words and your wisdom. Now is the Time.
We have to treasure the lesson and hold it close.
We have to pray for strength. Now is the Time.
We have to faithfully guide a movement as it grows.

There's a Change A Comin'.

We have to honor our sick, our elderly, our poor.
We have to be their Voice. Now is the Time.
We have to face problems that Power is hellbent to Ignore.
We have to take care of Each Other. Now is the Time.

There's a Change A Comin'.

We have to roar into oppressive winds thick with Lies.
We have to speak Truth against thick Walls. Now is the Time.
We have to know that Real leaders don't rule with Spies.
We know that True Power trusts the people. Now is the Time.

There's a Change a Comin'.

We have to face the Powers that create webs of deciet, We must.
We have to work as one, together. Now is the Time.
We have to do it for our children, otherwise who will they trust.
We have to show them another way to peace. Now is the Time.

Watergate Summer

There's a Change a Comin'.

We have to Know that the Change is on the Way.
We have to help it gain momentum. Now is the Time.
We can't turn out backs on it for an hour or a day.
We are the momentum, we are the Change. Now is the Time.

There's a Change a Comin'.

(enigma2006)

* * *

Words of Wisdom Below by Dr.King

Yes, We must stand, and we must Speak.
There comes a time when Silence is Betrayal.

Injustice Anywhere is a threat to Justice Everywhere.
(letter from jail April 1963).

Our Lives begin to end the day we become Silent about Things that Matter.

* * *

AL GORE'S SPEECH ON CSPAN TODAY—AT CONSITUTION HALL—ABOUT THE DAMAGED CONSITUTION AND THE KING.

No Blood For Hubris and Educational Whisper have the transcript and also Links.

CHINESE NEW YEAR
(AN AIDS TALE RETOLD)

[[This is actually a Tale about AIDS and Hope . . . . it was orginally posted for Chinese New Year 1-29-06. I was an AIDS Nurse for many years in Seattle Washington. I am reposting it to Honor The International AIDS Conference in Toronto this week.]]

So tonight it is Chinese New Year. Some folks start celebrating it at Sundown and some at Midnight. It is the Year of the Dog, the Fire Dog. The Dog in the Chinese Horoscope represents Loyalty, Everlasting Friendship and Infinite Courage and Mighty Fortitude, and Hidden Strength. It also is true in Chinese History, especially in the years of the Fire Dog, represent Much Change and Upheaval. I say this with great optimism for Change in the year to come. On the West Coast some resturants have big parties and banquets and Celebrations. There is much wonderful food, music and Fireworks. Some resturants have one night for the public and one night for the resturante families. It can be festive and jubilant, and truly welcoming, or a more traditional quiet holiday. And for some it is a time to resolve rifts and wayward relations, and for others it is a time of Reunion, and even Thankfulness.

I originally started celebrating this many years ago, and for me it is a quiet reflective time. Some celebrate it with gusto and great enthusiasm. Some celebrate it and welcome it with huge gatherings of food and family and friends. It was never like that for me, a time to gather, take stock, review and honor the past and those that are gone. It is quiet and full of solitude.I clean like crazy for a week, I re-organize, tidy even the closets that are best left dark and dusty. I scrub the front door and make Red banners with Caligraphy (Japanese or Chinese), that have warm thoughts of peace, prosperity, and inspiration (Couplets). And my son loves that no one but us really knows WHAT they say. (When he was little he used to call them the Secret Banners).

There are fresh flowers, lotus and irises, and sometimes Lillies. And since Rob was little I have fixed the traditional Long Egg Noodles symbolizing long life. And all kinds of tea. And Red Envelopes, with good wishes and trinkets, chocolates, and nuts. (and of course the Neatly pressed Money and polished coins) ALL to bring good luck. And the Dim Sun (Sweets) puchased from some little Chinese eatery as well as Fortune Cookies. I would wear Songbird Colors, and put lotus candles in the bath water. And even when many holidays were havoced in my life, this holiday I always loved and cherished, and it's simplest of rituals made me whole again.It was so heartwarming to believe that WE Create Our Luck. And at Midnight I would burn 9 sticks of incense with tenderness, remember those that have gone and honor Who and What they were. It was a simple holiday that held Hope. Always.

I worked as an AIDS nurse in Seattle in the late 1980's and one of my favorite patients Rick, became a friend. He was a talented artist, this friend that taught me about Buddhism and how to find my way with it. He was an artist and a poet that had worked and taught Art and English in Asia. I first took care of his partner Steve in 1988-1990, and as I taught him the finer graces of nursing to care for his partner, he taught me so much more. He taught me intricacies of Life even when dying. His partner was nauseous alot, so Rick would spend hours figuring out what SMELL made him feel better (S'MORE's fresh in the microwave and vanilla mint icecream on the bedside table were some of the best Comfort results). He taught me how to make "Russian Tea" (Which is Tang and Iced tea powder mixed and served steamy and hot, a heavenly concoction). He explained that a part of Buddhism is science and reading, and putting those into action and having faith that the Universe would help the Healing. I liked how he explained it and that it was not a matter of "Leaving it up to God". (Who personally I felt had failed miserably).

Rick would sit by Steve's bed and read to him from the I Ching, and chinese poetry, and from Confuscious, and Teachings of Buddha. He had rituals where he would serve tea and tangerines. He put ginger in the tea.He consulted a Feng Shui expert and they reviewed the horoscopes and rearranged furniture and brought in different colors to help Steve's comfort, and amazingly it all helped. And Rick would smile and gently leave books out for me about the Feng Shui, Chinese Horoscopes, and "The Barefoot Doctor". He was the first to explain to me that I was a Rat, according to the horoscope. (After the initial whiff of Insult, I learned quickly that Rats are Special, trustworthy, resourceful, take good care of their community, and have courage. So I decided to embrace this little part of me, and cherish what I could strive for.)

I took care of AIDS patients in Seattle 1988-1998, and this was quite a feat, for a good part of those years I lived on Capital Hill near many of my patients and my neighbors. And yes, as many of my neighbors became my patients there are also were lessons to learn about boundaries that became blurry and soft. I did homecare and also worked at a lovely little hospice that was called Rosehedge. (and still worked other shifts on the side, including ER and PEDS). (I had this grand idea that if I could just work alot of different areas—I would never burn out as a nurse).

Steve died first in 1990 and in less than two years I got a call that Rick was very sick. And by then we were stll friends, but I took a job at a nursing agency that I knew would take good care of Rick. Rick was shocked to realize that he had AIDS and that he had CMV retinitis.(He had been HIV postive for almost 8 years when he went into AIDS, he took amazing care of himself, even while caring for Steve.). He called me and said:

"I can't believe this, I am losing vision every day. It is so odd, it is like the colors are being washed from the sky. You think living in Seattle where it is so grey and rainey, that makes it worse?"

The saddest part was he was still grieving Steve when he got his own bad news, and it spiraled him into a huge depression. He gave up painting—totally. So I would go see him, and so would his friends, and we would all try to figure out what to do. I finally took the Phone number list off his frig and organized a Plan. I called Everyone, all his friends and neighbors, his "Care Chain". I set a a huge old Value Village Bowl on his front Hall table,called it the" Blessing bowl", and we all started leaving goodies in the bowl, to help him heal, to help him paint. Handmade playdough beads from my son,silvery gum wrappers, String, a birds nest, copper wire found in the Alley, cards and even tangerines and fig newtons and fortune cookies. And day by day he could not pass the bowl and not be tempted by what gifts were there. And slowly after many monthes, I arrived one day to find him painting with his head bent close and putting wire and beads on the canvas, and he said.

"I can't really see clearly, but I can feel the texture, and mostly I can FEEL Again" he lifted his head, and through the paint and glue and woven into his hair and face, I could see a wide infectious smile. And for the next few monthes I would always make him my last stop of the day. We would paint and weave, make paper with a dilapitated blender, and laugh and listen to music. And yes in many ways, I think that it was Grand Conspiracy that his friends and I pulled off. We were able to get Rick to paint again.

If you come to my apartment, I have many of Rick's greatest paintings.
I have packed them over and over on my precarious journey.
(and even ones we painted together, that I know in my heart are priceless)
I look at Them and they are not Just Art:

They are laughter at glue spilled on ugly old linoleum,
They are coconut shavings and melon seeds stuck on my clogs,
They are the the 1962 Hamilton Blender that vomited home-made paper on his kitchen ceiling,
They are homemade Minestrone Soup and Opera on Fridays,
They are the 16lb. bowling ball that "fell" out of the 3rd floor window.
They are courage against angst,
They are watching Willow 26 times,
They are Winter in Seattle, without the Grey.
They are Chili Cookoffs and "Friends& Sienfeld".
They are sandalwood Incense and tangerines,
They are Light in the Darkest of Darkest Shadows,
They are Chinese New Year . . . and Eternal Hope.anuary 29.2006

FEBRUARY 01, 2006, WEDNESDAY

THE WHAT IF GAME

I homeschool my son, which means that What he learns and How he learns is my job. It is a job that I hold precious. He likes to point out he has had to "endure" 5 years of Mr. Bush, and that he does not know what America is suposed to be like, he is only 14. He likes to point out that the Constitution and the Bill of Rights that I have now spent years teaching him don't matter to Mr. Bush. He also points out that Mr. Bush has not read History Books, American or World History. He also has been taught that part of how he learns is by disagreeing and asking questions. And he also knows that if he asks enough questions, he will end up being told to go look it up. Which means I have encouraged him to Argue, and fight for what is right. Which means that if he was in a regular school some poor teacher would be peppered with questions, and he would be in trouble alot. But his ability to think and question is intact.

He likes to come in my room, usually at bedtime, and ask some Killer Question.

KILLER QUESTIONS:

"Has any other Country ever bombed another another for Democracy?"

"And what Kind of Democracy is that—that requires Bombs first?"

"If Mr. Bush has had to spy on 1000's and listen and read emails and letters of so many, that means he does not really trust his own people? I guess we are lucky he has not arrested more . . . or maybe that is a matter of time?"

"How come the Elected representatives are all clapping, don't they realize that they look guilty too?"

"So Who does he have to Answer to? If not the People, the Congress, the Courts Who?"

"Isn't bombing a country for the sake of lies Wrong? Isn't that worse than Clinton lying about having an affair?"

The Questions have grown night after night, and his bedtime has grown later and later. And it is amazing how many nights I don't have the Answers. he said about a week ago, "I guess you don't have all the answers, but atleast you are still letting me ask Questions." I think he knows that he would never be allowed to ask These Questions in School . . .

THE WHAT IF GAME:

The Other Game that we played alot and has been Valuable is the "What If" Game. It goes like this.

I ask What if you had lived in Nazi Germany What would you have done?

What would you have done when the Government started closing Coffee shops and libraries and parks?

What would you have done when they started targeting peoples?

Would you have helped Hide Jews? (He used to joke that as many stray animals we used to sneak home and later have to announce to my poor ex—that the answer is fairly obvious)

If you lived in France or Poland Would you have helped with the Resistance Movements? (he was the one that pointed out that Bloggers are the ones spreading the late night Truth).

Would you have ever helped Spread the Truth? (with radio messages and underground newspapers?)

Allie McNeil

What if you knew that the Government of that time was lying and imprisoning people Falsely, what would you do?

Would you fight Back?

What If?

FEBRUARY 09, 2006, THURSDAY

FLORENCE, MY GRANDMOTHER

I know that I mentioned Flo in the post about my Great Aunt May, and I was going to write about her this month. Since I mentioned her, I think I should go ahead and write about her, and she holds a special place in my heart. And since this Administration is not honoring the Women of this country—I will go ahead and honor some. And later in the month I will explain Why I am honoring these women and holding them dear at this point.

Florence was born in July 18, 1914. She was named because her parents were in Italy right before the World War. She was concieved on this holiday trip, and yes in Florence. (and yes she was grateful that she had not been concieved in Pompeii or Milan). In the 1980's we discovered that she shared her birthday with Nelson Mandela—and she really liked that, said it was an honor. When she was little she was called Florrie. As she grew up she became Flo, and as my grandmother I called her Mimi. She was married to my grandfather Ted, he was a staunch Republican, and she was a Closet Democrat. (Which mostly means that her husband and mother-in-law Granny Ethel did NOT and would not ever know that was a Democrat and she had voted for shhh Kennedy).

Now here is the thing, I got on my mother's nerves, for a whole bunch of reasons. I am a little bit of a tomboy. I like jeans, not dresses. I read too much, and I am pretty shy. All of these things used to irritate my mom. So my grandmother used to take me to do errands and hang out at her house. (Now just to let you know—yes my family is fairly dysfunctional) But in the long run this arrangement worked because I got to know my entire family, especially my Aunties. I learned from them, their manners, and the Code. How to treat people, how to accept things and get on in life. So Gwennie may have been annoyed with the skinny peeked child, but the Aunties called me the Keeper of the Castle.

Now back to Florence, and the reason she was a Closet Democrat. She loved Ted, and she said that she had decided a long time ago what mattered and what would only cause pain. And she also knew that Ted, who was headstrong and ALWAYS right would waste alot of energy trying to talk her out of her political views. She also was still raising a teenager when I was growing up, so she was striving to be openminded in the 1960's. (My Dad's sister is 12 years younger than him). But mostly she wanted Peace at home. She also truly loved Ted, she loved him more than she loved fighting is what she used to say.

There love was documented in small beautiful ways. In the downstairs hall closet I used to go in there to raid coat pockets for Cinnamon Gum and Lifesavers. I used to love inhaling the smell of cherry pipe tobacco and my grandmother's White Shoulders perfume. The coats were hung with care, and the greatest secret was in the pockets of those coats and the golf bag. There were little love letters and note neatly tucked and folded. (And yes, of course I read them . . . . and someday I hope I find some notes in my pocket like that . . . .).

Flo was beautiful, she had smokey blue gray eyes and wavy auburn hair. (And yes, thank my stars I have her eyes, but that also means I end up looking into her eyes everyday). In the 1920's, and early 1930's she was a flapper girl, complete with beautiful beaded dresses, and dancing slippers. (And yes, my mother Also Sold THE DRESSES in a yard sale . . . my fury had NO Limits). She was born to a wealthy family, the only girl. She could have been spoiled, but she wasn't. She was one of the most giving people I have ever met. She was well schooled, spoke French, and painted and read, danced, and had beautiful gardens. Her yellow roses were incredible.

She was also a terrible cook, and had maids and cooks. (Which she used to joke saved her marriage). So going to her house meant that I got to spend time with Ida, Cal and Annie (the maids), and in many ways they were as special as the Aunties. They ruled the basement where they had sleeping quarters, a dressing room. In the laundry room they had a radio with Aretha blaring and the Kennedy Brothers hanging over the dryer. Sometimes I was sent down there to help, and other times I just liked to go sit on the dryer and listen to them and the radio.

Flo was a Real Lady. She had class in all the ways that mattered. She also was the Grand Dame in the neighborhood. If someone died, she organized all the neighbors. And that also was true if there a divorce, she was the first one to bring flowers, Silbers Cookies and support. She also looked after the Aunties who were all older in years, Aunt May downtown,

Granny Ethel in her little apt, and Elizabeth uptown. All of them were in varying degrees of vision loss—and all more stubborn than the next. By the time I was 16, I was helping her with the grocery, library, and doctor appointment runs for these stubborn ladies. And my mother periodically would need relief from the Twins. (Yes I am a twin). So we would go stay with Mimi. And my mother would go Rest somewhere for weeks at a time. (I never asked). And my dad worked out of town all the time.

Now Flo was interesting. I found out when Bobby Kennedy died and she was crying in the basement with Cal that she was going to VOTE FOR HIM . . . I was stunned. I watched these two women cry. Cal asked if she could have off to go pay her respects as the train passed and Flo said yes, by all means. I watched them that week in June, 1968, how they would hand Kleenex to each other, and pat each other gently on the shoulder and sniffle as they went about the house. Cal eventually lived down in the basement that summer because her apartment downtown got burned in the Riots. And that is why Flo was so insistant trying to get May to come uptown, but you know that didn't happen.

When I was in nursing school I went to visit my grandparents down in Florida,by 1980 they spent year part-time in South and part North.My grandmother had emphysema, so she did not do well with the cold. That summer, she showed me a lump under her arm, and I told her that she should be checked. She insisted it was nothing. I even called her doctor and asked him to check her for breast cancer. He was a SOB, and informed me that nursing students should not be diagnosing people, especially relatives.I almost ripped the payphone right out of the wall, and I was not the most polite creature.That fall she was run down, and I kept asking what the doctor said. he put her on vitamins and told her it was" probably hormonal, change of life "etc.(I told her that was absurd, that she was 68, she needed a BETTER doctor). Valentines day I called to wish her Happy Valentines day and ask if she got the Dark Chocolates I had sent. And I was going to tell her I was engaged. She told me that she had finally gone to Another Doctor.

Her initial Diagnosis was Breast Cancer, she was 68 years old. She had 4 lumps in one breast and it was also in 19 nodes. The doctor told her it was "Treatable". She told him she wanted to keep her hair, especially if she was going to lose both breasts.

("I don't mind being flat, but my hair is another story). I was the first one to talk to her after she got the diagnosis, she had not told Ted yet, he was playing golf. She had just met with the doctor. We talked and came up with a plan. She was so calm. She must have asked 20 times if I was upset.

She fought it bravely and worked hard to stay ladylike, that mattered to her. And due to Ice Cap treatments she did indeed keep her hair. I spent my vacations down with them. She would send me to cocktail parties with Ted, I was to spy on the ladies and pick out the ones that were okay, acceptable.

"If he is going to spend time with people after I am gone, I need to know that good folks will look out for him, and if there is one that is kind to him I can live with that". It took my breath away. I was stunned. (And yes, believe it or not she did pick out a new mate for him before she died, yet neither Ted or Helen knew that. But that is a story for another day).

I went to see her Thanksgiving 1986, she was 71 by then. I knew that she didn't have much time. She met my new husband. She had been too sick to come to the wedding. She was gracious and kind to him. And she was so sick by then. She ended up having lung cancer with the breast cancer. She would daintly cough blood into a napkin or a kleenex. (I never smoked again after that trip). I watched Flo and Ted slow dance to It's a Wonderful World in the Living Room, gracefully manuvering around her oxygen tubing, it took my breath away it was like they were 23 again.

I went home to Vermont and on Christmas eve I recieved a package from her. She and I had always shared shoes, I wear a size 10.5AAA (which for womens is huge).I thought oh good, shoes. Then I opened the package,and inside were her very favorite golf shoes white goatskin with lavender stitching.I had joked at Thanksgiving time that golf shoes would work to walk to and from the Hospital for work on the icey hills.As soon as I touched those shoes I knew that she was gone. I sat on my front steps and just cried as I held the shoes.

On that very day, Christmas eve 1986 My grandfather called and said that she had died at home, and that all of the Hospice plans that we had put in place had made it so much easier. She sent him to the store and he was gone 10 minutes, and when he came home she was gone. They were married for 50 years.He said that he didn't understand why she left when he was gone, and I explained that it was easier for her that way. She could not bear to say Goodbye to him.

* * *

These women are ever present with me, as I try to raise my son and be a good mother, especially these two.They tried hard to give me lessons about Dignity and Strength and Compassion. I am trying to honor them and their lessons. I know that they were right that we Must try to look out for each other and do the right thing. I know that they would have supported me as a Whistleblower.These women taught me how to take care of people, how to Listen, and so in many ways they did indeed make me a better nurse. I know that they would have understood why I am now divorced, even though I am the first in the family ever. (Although truth be told, Aunt May admitted that she would have made a lousy wife, she called her men the "library"). They would have understood my rage with this Administration for abandoning and mistreating so many and taking this country into a false war. And yes I know Aunt May would have called Mr. Bush names and had to put money in my swear jar.That is all from the Enigma tonight.

FEBRUARY 13, 2006, MONDAY

THE DUCK DICK MOMENT

I am not a Hunting expert by any shape of the imagination. I did work PEDS and PICU in rural New England, and I also have worked inner city ER'S, so that is my experience for Hunting and Gunshot wounds. But even with my limited experience I have some questions that keep banging around my head about the Hunting Incident.

(1) Wittington has not been seen since the incident—by Anyone? No interviews given? His wife? No photos? (You would think that by now the White House would have found a way for some folksy warm and cozy kiss ass photo to be "produced"?)

(2) He was out in the field with Cheney's Excellent Trauma (cough) trained team for atleast 50 minutes before they decided to transfer him by ambo—nor air medivac? A Crack team decided that a 78 year old man didn't need trauma care???—he was shot in face, neck, and head, and chest. (and wasn't talking "not responsive" we now have learned from Cheney). We later learned that he did indeed have pellets in his neck and larynx. (Did any vessels become nicked or damaged during the neck damage? His neck—throat thyroid, his AIRWAY .... ?)

(3) Has anyone else wondered if he had a heart attack? I mean he is 78 years old and was shot in the face and chest .... Did they have to do a little CPR out there in the field?

(4) Why was he driven to the FURTHER little rinky dink hospital and not taken BY AIR to the NEAREST TRAUMA CENTER? Is it because Witty has crappy insurance?

(5) How much liquor was consumed? Were blood alcohol levels done on Witty? Or on Cheny at any point in the first 12 hours?
Does Cheney's Heart meds conflict or interact with alcohol?

(6) Were any of the evidence saved from the scene—the clothes, the weapons?

(7) Has anyone looked at the Hunting Reports from the previous year, how many people were shot in the chest, and head while shooting quail during hunting incidents? (see link below) . . . answer . . . . ???

(8) Smoking Gun has report and some witnesses listed. The best part is where they say in ironic semantic fashion that Whittington "COLLABORATES" Dick's story. (Which considering he isn't talking due to laryngeal damage—that is just about miraculous)

(9) So the Pellets penetrated his clothes, and vest. The 30 yards theory is not holding up to that one.(Armstrong said this)

Pellets no only penetrated the clothes they penetrated his skin and oragans and tissue—heart, liver and larynx. (I am estimating 30-60 feet, but this means visibility would not have and should not have been impaired)

(10) Silence is deafening on this, no Interviews with Family? Lynne Stand By Her Man Cheney? THE WIFE? . . . .

(11) Cheney suposedly did not talk to Bush Until WHEN???? Sunday night? Monday? when?

The VP of our Country shot an OLD MAN in the Face, Head, Neck and Chest and here it is Thursday Feb 16th, and he is still in ICU and suposedly had a heart attack and suffered a pellet in his heart, liver and larynx. He also may have up to 200 pellets in his body, and if there are lead based that is quite a bit of lead.

Allie McNeil

And VP didn't give a press conference until WED to Fox . . . . the shooting was on SATURDAY????

Those are some of my nursey questions . . . . I don't know enough about hunting . . . . maybe this is a new Fair Game.

MARCH 06, 2006, MONDAY

THE CIGAR SALON

Everyday when I walk the dog there is a Cigar Shop I pass. I could cross over and go another way, but I take this route on purpose. Sometimes I take this route slow, so that I can do something taboo. Yes, it is true I love breathing deep those scents, it like standing in my Grandparents coat closet, the comfort of my grandfather's favorite cherry vanilla tobacco wrapping around me. And on another level it is my chance to do what I love, another taboo,shhh, Eavesdrop.

Why do I Eavesdrop? Because it is a Man's Salon, and they gather and laugh and talk. The people that go there Intrigue me, all kinds, men in overalls, men in sneakers,Chefs, Suited men in fine clothes, retired men,Cooks, and lawyers, men in Cleveland Browns jackets. All ages and socioeconomic status, and religions. They laugh and tell stories.

I would love to go in, I would love to just sit and listen to them as they puff and talk. I think in a past life I must have spent time at a Saloon listening to men talk and spit. (Let's be honest I don't think there's much demure Lady Activities in my past). Last Friday three men came out laughing and comparing Lists on Wrinkled folded pieces of paper. They were Arguing—goodhumoredly.I had to ask I was just too curious. It turns out that they have been keeping Lists of the Bush Failures, and trying to figure out which ones are High Crimes.

Allie McNeil

And the Lists were Long . . . . Much longer than I thought they would be. So here you go . . . . I am asking WHAT would be on your rumpled list and Would it be just a Failure, or High Crimes.It is just a list . . . . And we know it is long—but maybe just put your TOP TEN . . . . and hell tell me What kind of cigar would you try? . . . .

(okay, one small request NO Monica jokes . , . . please)

MARCH 07, 2006, TUESDAY

AIN'T NO LADIES HERE

Okay My son saw the other post and pointed out I sound kind of snooty, like I am "ladylike" and would never smoke cigars. (ahem, cough, hmmmm he might be kind of right). So I am putting one of his favorite stories here. And on another level I am just tired of documenting our travesty of a "government" right now, and I am tired of monitorinng Plamegate, Katrinagate, Locked&Loaded Dick, and Dukegate, Tommyboy's woes, and Casino Jack etc etc. So I am giving myself a break . . . .

When Son was four I was off from work and I was supposed to be cleaning the house. I decided that we could clean the Kitchen Floor with Shaving Cream. It was a hot summer day, and we were pretending it was Snow. We spread it across it the Kitchen Floor—TWO cans worth. It was Very Very messy, and we both ended up covered with it, head to toe. In the midst of this slippery sliding mess, the Doorbell rang. I fell twice trying to get to the door, but my son made it to the door. Smiling through the shaving cream. (he looked like the little tub kid out of the Mr.Magoo ad).

And this is what I heard as I was sprawled on the floor.

"Hi, I am spreading the word of God. Is the Lady of the House Here?"

(As I slid around the corner I could see what looked like a very nice lady in a dress with a purse and pamphlets, I kind of thought she might be a Mormon.)

And my son responded "Oh, Lady I am sorry, but there are no Ladies here, you can try next door. My Mommy is lying on the Kitchen floor".

Allie McNeil

I could just make out the stunned look on her face as son door slammed shut.

(oh, great now it sounds like mommy is intoxicated and passed out!!!)

And he slammed the door and ran back into the Kitchen, sliding and proud of himself.

Yup. No Ladies here.

MARCH 07, 2006, TUESDAY

SUPERMAN IS JOINED BY HIS ANGEL OF GRACE

We woke this morning to hear that Dana Reeve, 44, Christopher Reeve's Wife had died of lung cancer.She announced her battle after Peter Jennings died in August 2005. We watched her all these years as she cared for the love of her life after his riding accident. We watched her speak with such brave eloquence about the importance of caregivers recieving care and support as well as the need for Research. We listened to her speak after her Superman died, and knew that her heart was broken yet her courage shined as she spoke. She showed that being a caregiver and a wife and mother could be done with Grace. Last year she spoke on Oprah with her son by her side, showing that even in grief there is joy, as she looked at her teenage son Will with loving maternal pride. You taught us well Dana . . . . Rest In Peace Dear one.

> "Love bears all things, Believes all things, Hopes all things, Endures all things." I Corinthians 13:4-7

> "I honor the memories of those of us who are gone and I bless and honor the presence of those amoung us who stand tall like Evergreens."

Unknown

Allie McNeil

* * *

[Please leave thoughts and messeges below I will forward them to The Christopher and Dana Reeve Foundation. For each messege my son and I will donate $5.00 to the Foundation. Namaste.]

* * *

If you wish to leave Condolences for the Reeve Team or family, or donate please go to the following site:

http://www.christopherreeve.org/site,

[If you wish to know more information about the Foundation and Ongoing Work and Projects, please go to http:// www.paralysis.org/site, this site explains about the Christopher and Dana Reeve Paralysis Resource Center.]

If you wish to snail mail a contribution in Dana's name:

The Christopher Reeve Foundation (CRF)
636 Morris Turnpike, suite 3a
Short Hills, NJ 07078

MARCH 09, 2006, THURSDAY

WOMEN'S VOICES

Today we are to Celebrate the Strength and Courage of Women.

May the Voices of the Women below Inspire us to reach for More . . . . or atleast think twice about it . . . .

> "I stand at the alter of the murdered men and while I live I fight their cause."
>
> Florence Nightingale

> "When you get into a tight place, and everything goes against you, till it seems as though you cannot hang on for another minute, Never Give Up then, for that is just the place and time the tide will turn."
>
> Harriet Beecher Stowe

> "Never doubt that a small group of thoughtful, committed people can change the World. Indeed it is the only thing that ever has."
>
> Margaret Mead

> "Don't give or sell your soul away. Hunger for the taste of Justice. Hunger for the taste of Freedom. All that you've got is your soul."
>
> Tracy Chapman

"I always wanted to be Somebody, but I should have been more specific."

Lilly Tomlin

"Everybody talks about people, but nobody does anything about them ".

Fran Lebowitz

"The basic teaching of Buddhism is the teaching of transciency, or change. That Everything changes is the basic truth for each exsistance"

Shunryu Susuki

"Be patient toward all that is unsolved in your heart and try to love the questions themselves.Do not seek the answers, which cannot be given you because you would not be able to live them. And the point is to live Everything.Live the questions now. Perhaps you will then gradually, without noticing it, live along some distant day into the answers."

Ranier Maria Rilke, Letter to a Young Poet

[[[and just to make you smile: guess Who said the following: "It's not true I had nothing on. I had the radio on".]]]

*   *   *

For those who arrived late to dinner . . . yes, it was Marilyn Monroe . . . . of course. (But the guesses were wonderful . . .)

Now for Number II: Let's see who gets the Brass Ring this time . . .

THE QUOTE FOR FRIDAY MARCH 10TH;

"Life is about not knowing,
Having to change,
Taking the moment, and making the most of it,
Without knowing what is going to happen next."

MARCH 09, 2006, THURSDAY

UGLY TRUTH GREETS THE KING ON THE TARMAC

This week March 20th, 2006 Mr. Bush came to my town on the Third Anniversary of the War. He arrived at the Airport, no GOP Dignataries arrived to greet him or shake his hand. And Ohio is full of such GOP Strong Men, Mr Noe, Mr. Voinovich, Mr. DeWine. It was a striking moment watching him come down the stairs of the plane and search the empty tarmack with his eyes. It was a telling moment of the State That Supposedly Gave him this Presidency of 2004, now the Touchdown of a Failed Presidency.

The Protestors showed up by the 100 in the town center, and only a handful of his supporters showed up across the street dressed in Red, White and Blue and carrying small feeble signs. They huddled like lost soccer moms, and only held their signs waiste high, before they left quietly.

He gave a speech at the City Club to a echoey chamber of the Elite, another belly up to the Podium Moment. He rambled, he cajoled, he snickered and made strange inappropriate jokes. He seemed out of touch, like the Drunk Uncle at the Thanksgiving Dinner that no one wants to sit next to, much less get into a sparring match. The applause was tenative and polite like what you would hear at a Golf Tournament when an Old Timer makes a safe shot, but needs a Mulligan.

His speech was susposed to reassure and impress, but the problem is that the carnage from Iraq and the Katrina Zone outweigh his words and render him impotent. His poll numbers continue to sag like an old woman's dress drying in the breeze on a stormbent clothesline. His Blunders are now measured daily in dead bodies, and the whole world is watching.

He can't Drive the Podium, so the bigger question is should he be driving the Country?

THE RISING

[reprinted from March 13th, 2006]

I live in an old office building that is now loft apartments. Behind my building is a large auditoreum that is named after the couple that built it and their names are in lights on the building. So we call it "The Bert & Iris". The best thing about this building is that it has sand and gravel roof. Yet to the Gulls in the area it is a Beach . . . . an urban oasis, the Bert&Iris Beach. They flock there by the hundred.

About a week ago early in the morning I watched them, and they did something entirely different. They all went silent and were motionless for a moment. And then with some unknown hidden signal they all rose up at the same moment, hundreds of them. ALL of them. The synchronicity of that very moment took my breath away.

The Rising.

MARCH 23, 2006, THURSDAY

ANGELS AMOUNG US

Dear Mr.Bush,

You came to Cleveland this week to give a speech at the City Club to the Elite and Wellheeled. No GOP Dignataries arrived at the airport, or even introduced you at your Luncheon. You proceeded to drive the podium once again intoxicated with yourself. But you took a Intricate Route to your event so you would not have to see the Shredded Streets or the People of the Broken Hearted Inner City. You didn't take the time to see the Real People of Cleveland. The Real People were not standing with your handful of supporters. The Homeless and Disenfranchised of this City should not be blurred as you speed by in your motorcade. They have names and faces and stories. And your "Leadership" is killing them. In my mind they are not Invisible, they are Angels amoung us, teaching us what we need to Embrace and Remember, and hold dear as part of We the People.

* * *

IRIS:

I live in the heart of Downtown Cleveland. My Son wanted Urban, he wanted Gritty, he wanted to live in the Old Section of the City. We have lived here almost a year it as comfortable as old shoes now. Yet there are parts of it that still tug at my heart. Last summer I decided that I wanted to make a documentary about the Homeless Here. Supposedly there are 10,000 that live in downtown Cleveland, and maybe as many as 3000 of that Downtown Number are Homeless. Last summer I met a fair number of Homeless because I walk my dog 5 times a day. (Earlier I wrote a post about Robert a homeless VET). But over time I have realized not all of them want to be filmed, if I can get them to talk and make eye contact, it is a gift. Over time I take the time to learn their stories. Last summer I gave out Water and Sandwichs, and I know this summer I will do the same.

I met Iris last summer. I met her because she was taping her glasses together. She is Jamacian and in her 50's. She has training as a nursing assistant. She is a mother and a grandmother. She has been on the streets since last June. She left an abusive drinking husband, "Very bad Man". She talks about him quietly, and with such dignity. She had to leave, she said he would kill her if she stayed. I have hardly seen her during the winter. But I saw her about a week ago, as the crocuses appeared. She sits on a bench in front of the University in the evenings. We spoke and she admitted that she is going to take the bus and go find her sister in Florida . . . (Since I have been here I have ended up giving money to people to leave, take a Bus Somewhere, Anywhere.)

I asked her is she had a place to go at nights. "I go where I can be safe. One of these nights I may join the Angels".

She states it so factually, there is not emotion, no tears.

So Mr.Bush I have to ask, why should this fine woman be on the Streets? Why should she suffer? Do you care that she is one of the Grate People that might freeze to death? When you left downtown Cleveland did you see people staking out the Grates downtown with their blankets and bags?

METAL MEN:

Mr.Bush,Did you see the Metal Men with their grocery carts driving about the city, peeling copper plating and spouts off buildings? Did you see their clothes, rags held together with rope and duct tape? Did you see their raw hands and bloody knuckles. Do you understand the desperation that makes them search dumpsters for Metal?

JAMES & DENISE:

The Night you came I saw James and Denise in Front of the closest Pizza parlor. I have given them money, when I have it.

I feel guilty getting my small pizza on Fridays in front of them. I always feel guilty getting such a luxorious item in front of them. So I give them some dollars and I always get them muffins and drinks if I see them on my way in to pick up the Pizza.

They have been together for a long time. Denise has MS, and James is a VET with PTSD. I give them some money, but I can't give them a Home, or Shelter, and I can't get them off the Street. And it tugs at my heart that my street is FULL of Empty Buildings and yet people are sleeping on benches and under bushes and on the Grates.

So Mr.Bush, do you have a conscience? Because you gave your delusional speech, but I know that you don't Know We The People. And I know that they are the Invisible and I worry that they are as Iris said Merely Angels Amoung us.

MAY 06, 2006, SATURDAY

WATCHING RUMMY EAT CROW

This week Rummy was made to eat 2.5 minutes of heaping steaming crow at a speaking event. He pretended to be gracious and humble and made his usual snide jokes and pretended that the Women that raised complaints about his Lies were merely pesty flies at a picnic. Yet out of that melee came a Calm Clear Wellspoken Voice throwing Honest Questions to the Sweaty Secretary, questions based on the Rumster's own Pompous Quotes (lies).And Ray McGovern, of 27 years of Civil Service, most in the Employ of Intelligence, mostly the CIA, asked these questions as a Patriotic Hardworking American. And Rummy pretended to be offended, and then graciously spoke to Security in a patronizing manner, "Don't take him away yet". Ray was undaunted, and asked The Questions that needed to be asked, based on Rummy's own Verbal Spillage. [CNN yesterday actually put together a Full Montage of the Mislaid Quotes (lies) of that poor Bastard Poor Rummy]. For this was not some longhaired Kent State Hippy of the Vietnam Era, this was an educated eloquent man with Brass Balls and a sense of Honor. If Ray McGovern ever comes to my hometown he is more than Welcome to Dinner. Who needs Jack Baur?? We don't, we have Ray. McGovern . . . He is now officially on my Must Meet and Shake his Hand and say Thank You List . . . .

MAY 14, 2006, SUNDAY

HAPPY MOTHERS DAY

Happy Mother's Day to Blogatopia. May you be spending the day with those you love and enjoying the day. I am a Mom, I always wanted to be a Mom, there is no more important job. It is the Best Job I have ever had. Moms are the glue in any family. They patch the jeans, clean up sticky messes, fix broken toys,take care of upset tummies at 3am,wipe runny noses, tenderly apply bandaids on those little people wounds,make Pancakes on Sundays and cookies on rainy days,hold hands on long walks, watch SpongeBob and read Harry Potter at all hours. Moms try their Best to teach the Bigger Lessons and the Importance of Small Moments.May you all have wonderful Small moments.

Happy Mothers Day to all of you wonderful Moms and Dads.

* * *

Children Learn What They Live

If Children live with criticism,
They learn to condemn.

If Children live with hostility,
They learn to fight.

If Children live with ridicule,
They learn to be shy.

Allie McNeil

If Children live with shame,
They learn to feel guilty.

If Children with tolerance,
They learn to be patient.

If Children live encouragement,
They learn confidence.

If Children live with praise,
They learn to appreciate.

If Children live with fairness,
They learn justice.

If Children live with security,
They learn to have faith.

If children live with approval,
They learn to like themselves.

If Children live with Acceptance and Friendship,
They learn to find love in the world.

author: Dorothy Law Nolte

JUNE 11, 2006, SUNDAY

FATHERS DAY 2006

Being a Dad . . . .

It is as simple as a warm hug on a cold night.
It is learning to ride a bike on a crooked sidewalk.
It is hot dogs dripping with mustard on a crisp fall day.
It is Friday movies and popcorn.
It is Star Bellied Sneetches and the Cat in the Hat.
It is finding the Perfect Pumpkin for Halloween at Craven's Farm.
It is Hotwheels in the Hallway and long races on Rainey days.
It is cookies and fresh crayons waiting to be shared.
It matters . . . .
Everyday.

JULY 20, 2006, THURSDAY

TABLE MANNERS, PIGS AND SLAVERY

So in the past few weeks we have had to watch our King in all his fratboy glory embarrass our country in a way that goes beyond description. On the way to the G8 the King decided to stop by Germany and make an ass of himself by once again driving the podium drunk and blathering on and on about PIGS in front of the Leader of Germany. (Please somebody turn off his Mic I thought to myself). At the G8 Conference we watched the Feeble King have a lovely discussion with Tony-the-Poodle-Blair, what a mastigating Wonder of Diplomacy. Complete with Chewing the Fat I guess, and even a few foul words and a bit of spit. Lovely, but let's Leave the Mic on this time I thought. And to complete the Spectacle, the Mike was indeed on. OOOOPS has new meaning, but apparently the King isn't even ashamed of his blunder. And then there is his Reach and Out and Touch the Chancellor Moment—Lord Have Mercy, he gave her a quickie like she was a lonely Cow Hand down on the Ranch. So Bad Manners aside for Cowboy King, was that Enough Embarrassment for the week?

No, of course not.

I was folding laundry and decided to watch the NAACP speech—thinking that it would be the shortest speech of his life. And after his "Spare Parts" Speech yesterday as he Vetoed the Stem Cell Research Bill, under (cough,cough) the cloak of Moral Courage, I was thinking that it could only be a minute blundering boggling moment.

I of course was Wrong.

Watergate Summer

For some reason King Cowboy (after five very long years) decided that since he has been missing his People of Color (like when he Missed Them during Katrina), and now that it is indeed an GOP-Sinking-Faster-Then-Hoffa-Lead-Shoes Election Year he should give his 2.0% Base some Longlost attention. (I just want to point out that I was always pretty certain that 2.0% Of the People of Color that vote for Bush must include Condi and her Stilletos?)He tried his usual tactic of bring a little giggly-jokey-Aren't-I-Cute-Light Moments, yet the crowd responded with a Frosty Silence. Then he went on to Give Them The Speech, he was trying to deliver passion, but it came out as Wrathful Raging Blithering Ranting with undertones of a sophmoric imitation of old Hitler Film Noire Glory.

He yelled at the Poor Audience, and his Volume increased as The Now Painful Speech lumbered on and on like a Crippled Man that has lost his Cane. He Brought up so many Wonderful Issues.

(1) He reminded THEM that President Lincoln was the Last BEST President THEY ever had.(are you gulping with nausea and embarrassment yet?)
(2) He Brought up the 'STAIN OF SLAVERY". (huh . . . The Only Stain I see is standing at the Podium embarrassing the Entire Country . . . and Why would he bring up Slavery???—is he hoping it makes a comeback? Is he hoping to convince Someone, or Anyone that Voting Rights are safe because Slavery ended? Just when you thought he really isn' THAT Braindamaged . . . . he sets a new cerebral path of Shame.
(3) He told them "Ownership" of Anything is good for them (I know, I know, How STUPID is he?).

His Volume continued to rise and make my skin crawl. Remember when you were a Kid and Uncle Lester would arrive Drunk to the Thanksgiving Dinner and he would tell Off Color Man-from-Nantucket Jokes and get Louder and Louder as NO ONE laughed, and you would have to serve More and More PIE to him, to attempt to Silence him? I found myself praying for someone to Serve Him Pie.

And yet he rambled On and On, hemmorhaging like a Bloody Femoral Gusher . . . stumbling through the Valley of No Child Left Behind, then Vacumn of the Wonders of Home Ownership, and then into the I-Have-No-Shame-So-Kiss-My-White-I-Stole-YOUR-Vote-Twice-AssLand   of Voting Rights.

And yes I hoped and Prayed SOMEONE, yes, ANYONE would yell out "LIAR". But the Audience was so quiet and polite, and the Hired Poorly Paid Bussed In Golf Clappers continued to clap at odd Moments that threw off the Inept Podium Driver.

Finally I-Need-An-Excedrin-NOW speech came to a screeching Halt, and Julian Bond arrived on the Stage and came to the Podium and let the President know that the Speech was coming to an end, the King nodded at him in that NOT Now Laura Way and kept driving through his speech haphazardly to the lackluster Conclusion.

You can only throw so many socks and towels at the TV and Yell "You Fucking Lying Piece of Shit" so many times before your animals hide under the sofa.

So Folks here is my ten dollar Question, IS THIS WHAT IT HAS COME DOWN TO? A DRUNK INEPT IMPOTENT S.O.B DRIVING THE PODIUM DRUNK AND FONDLING FORIEGN CHANCELLORS ANDSPITTINGFOODANDIGNORANCEINTOAMIRCOPHONE AT A STATE DINNER AND BLATHERING ABOUT SLAVERY AND VOTING RIGHTS AT A NAACP CONFERENCE?

Okay if you too suffered through this Wonder of Speech give me Your Thoughts and I will give you my Compassion . . . or atleast a stiff Drink . . . . of Mylanta.

(and yes, I have thrown $5.25 into the Foul Language jar and I didn't even call Condi what I usually call her . . .)

JULY 21, 2006, FRIDAY

BAKING IN THE SUN . . .

Okay . . . This is going to be one of my stranger posts, but I have to blog on this, have to. I was walking home from a downtown grocery store and it was mostly a pretty normal hot humid sticky walk UNTIL . . . . I almost stepped on IT.

There it was lying on the dusty sidewalk limp and fragile and abandoned and lonely.

A small crowd had formed, staring at the little lifeless form. No one wanted to touch It or pick It up, or move It. I mean Someone might come looking for it, or even be missing it. Kind of like a Lost Pet, maybe an Ad will appear in the paper.

People stood staring, there was a hushed silence and much head shaking as people smoked cigarettes waiting for the bus.

Then a girl of about 16 did something really funny, she pulled a flower out of a giant planted pot, and laid it on top of IT, and then everyone just had to laugh.

Okay, so by now you are wondering what IT IS?

It was a Toupee. Dark Black and very greasy, with the scalp part plainly visible. Yet laying there on the hot sunbaked sidewalk it really did look like a small wounded animal, almost like Road Kill.

As we all stood looking at it, finally an older woman went over with a CVS plastic bag and picked it with up with military precision, treating it like a Black Plague Rat and she dumped it in the nearest trash container and gave a HRUMPH and "hmmm, Nasty" as parting words for the Burial.

AUGUST 05, 2006, SATURDAY

DANCING WITH REALITY

So last weekend I did something silly.

I KNOW I should be oh-so-embarrassed.

I went to Craigslist and looked up MEN for this area.

It turned out to be an unexpected moment to giggle and outright laugh.

My son has joked that I should "get OUT THERE", which sounds almost exciting, even somewhat interesting—like a Travel Channel Show I might TIVO . . . . "OUT THERE& How to get there & WHO to meet There".

But then over on Craig Crawford's site I read how Sheila—Sensible Sheila met a man on Craiglist.(I think she hired a plumber first, and that went well so voila. I bet I have this story messed up—but you get the general romantic novel drift here) I was more than intrigued and even slightly inspired.

So I hooked up to the List in my area.(for some reason it felt forbidden, in a kind of good way . . . and I am not sure why.)

So there it was a List of Men in my area.

Some wanted Women—proportionate, some wanted SOME areas to be BIGGER than others, no one wanted Motherly women raising teenagers or children (that's nice) and 40 apparently is NOT the new 30 (yup another crappy myth shot to hell—good).

NOT ONE posting was looking for a Woman of Substance . . . or that had Strong Values, or a Good Heart, or a Sound Mind. Nope, ladies it all comes down to tits and legs . . . and some ass.

And some arrogant little men even posted that they Wanted Women with a Job, and Good Income. (I guess it was all about wanting "independent" women-joke-gag-spit)

There were men seeking Polka Dancers ("Must have strong legs, like accordian practice and MUST Enjoy Polka Dancing THREE nights a week). Another one that intrigued me "Moving to Ohio in August, would like to meet good woman to help resettle. Signed, married in New Jersey).

Yup, that was my WTF moment????

Are Men really This Shallow, or only in Ohio?

I am not really looking I guess . . . after all.

But What a Reality Check . . . .

Is it wrong to think that men still like women of Substance?

Whatever happened to curling up Sunday Mornings with newspapers and coffee and newpspapers or blogs? (Planning The Date on the Phone)

Whatever happened to Long Walks in the Rain? (Date#1)

Whatever happened to meeting at a gallery and not talking for 2 hours, and letting the tension build? (Date #2)

Whatever happened to Dinner in small Italian Resturante? (date #3)

Whatever happened to Dancing Real Slow in the Moonlight?(date #4)

yeah, I know it is 2006, I am living in the wrong damn age. Sigh.

AUGUST 06, 2006, SUNDAY

ABOUT MOTHERING

This is not one of my prouder posts, but IT needs to be Blogged, it is not really a ladylike moment for the Enigma. So here it goes.

Okay . . . so I am not a Perfect Mother. I actually think there is No Such Thing.I think we as Moms, as Women do out best to care for the Children of this World.And it requires Patience, and Insight, and mostly alot of Heart.

So I say this and now I have to tell you about my Saturday Eve Trip to Wendy's.My son and I have Rituals, they are very Important.The Saturday Night Chili and Frosty are key to the Whole Week.

So I am in line in the Drive Through, and there is a Battered Purple Intrepid in front of me,inside I can see a Mom driving and three kids of different ages bouncing around and dancing and singing with the radio. I can hear Usher wafting my way.One little girl turns and gives me a big gaptoothed smile for a fleeting moment. Now admittedly they are not being cooperative, they are excited,hungry, and grooving to Usher.

I hear the Mother say LOUDLY with an edge," If you all don't quiet down, Somebody gonna get It".

The three stop wiggling as much . . . and heads start ducking below window level.I am thinking that this is indeed a Woman of Her Word. Poor Kids.

The radio grows softer, as she pulls up to the Service Window to retrieve The Food.

She is now yelling again, "I done you told to shut up!!! What part didn't you get!!?"

And I hear a soft whimpering question mumbled from the back seat.

And then out of Nowhere I see her big beefy arm swing back—pretty much without warning and get flung towards the backseat. I had already noted that all three kids had sklunked down in their seats. But she caught Someone, she hit Flesh. SMACK.

I was disgusted, and horrified. And the nurse part of me noted how No One fought back or even said OUCH. This is a Mom that Hits. Shit.

So I was sitting there FUMING. Thinking. This Mom gets AWAY with This . . . ALOT.

The Next thing I know I did indeed get out of my car and walk down to the Now Silent Car sitting by the Service Window. As I approached I heard The Mother" I want My damn Fries, What is taking so long??"

I waited until the Service Girl talked to her. Then I approached. And I Confess I did not use my nice let's talk voice.

"Look as a MOM I saw WHAT You just did, and it is NOT Okay at all. You shouldn't hit your kids EVER. And Kids if your mom hits you, Like That—you go to an Adult and get help. This IS WRONG.Got IT?"

She turned out to look quite a bit bigger and beefier up close stuffed in the Intrepid, yet she was still sitting in the car. She Started to stutter and spurt through an answer that came out something like" WHAT THE????"

And I stopped her. I said "Look you can't argue with what WE ALL SAW you do. And I am asking you to go get some help, and be better to your kids. But know this I got your license plate and I would be more than happy to call the Right People to STOP You from Hitting. Got It? Good."

And while she was still sputtering and cussing I walked back to my car.

The guy behind me in line, in a big ol battered Ford Pickup I guess saw the whole thing, he gave me a BIG Thumbs up as I got in the car. By the time I got to my car, she had pulled out. I am not even sure she got her godamned Fries.

So I pull up to the Service Window, still can't believe I did Something That Impulsive. But still knowing that I had to do it.

The Window Girl says "Wow . . . you either really brave or real dumb, but I am kinda glad that you did That." And the three other workers behind her were nodding in the same stunned way.

"And yeah, well as a mom there are THINGS YOU DO NOT DO . . . AND HITTING KIDS IS ONE OF THEM".

So here's the Thing I guess, I think sometime Violence requires someone like Me to get out of my godamned car and comfort zone and do the Right Thing . . . Let's just hope it's not part of my Saturday Night Mom Ritual.

AUGUST 12, 2006, SATURDAY

TRAVEL REFLECTIONS

So I have thought alot about the NEW Travel Restrictions that will make us all Safer. As a Mom—I think they are more than absurd. ANY parent trying to travel with children will testify that snacks and liquids are a matter of Life and Death. And anyone flying with little people that do not have snacks and drinks to help their little eardrums cope with cabin pressure changes will testify as well. And we all know that the Airlines basically treat people like Baggage or is it Freight at this point? There are no drinks or peanuts/ snacks on most flights, people have been bringing their own snacks for years . . . since 911. And here is the thing, about those 911 Hearings—one thing was forgotten, about the Boxcutters. WHO brought them on board, well according to early articles, they were snuck on via the FOOD Service Servers, which for all of the Airlines was a Food Server named Argenbright (okay so the spelling may be wrong). But it was a Texas based company . . . that George used to invest in. My Point is that there are Pieces of this Damn Puzzle that have never been properly examined and still haven't. So now it has come down to Lactation Inspection and Ridiculous Restrictions. And as a woman—well, yeah, hell make the poor women throw away hundreds of dollars of toiletries, that seems somehow like something this administration would enjoy. IF this does indeed EFFECT ALL AMERICANS—fine—take away Condi's Comforts too . . . and Lithium Laura . . . (Scary . . .)Hell Take Away The Kings Drinks . . . Let's be Patriotic . . . but safe . . . . Together. But let's not inspect what is in the Freight Section of the Plane. That would be too costly.

And my other point is that as I was traveling around the blogs on Friday I noticed alot of people said that they have not flown since 911 and I don't think that it has anything to do with BEING SCARED . . . I think it has to do with COST and HASSLE . . .

Oh, and yeah, WHY haven't I flown . . . cause I am on a Godamned List . . . cause I am an Environmental Health Advocate (aka a mom and a nurse . . . and a Normal American). So I only know Bus and Train Travel . . . . But please share with me, how many of you are traveling less and why . . . I bet it isn't cause you're scared of Terra.

AUGUST 22, 2006, TUESDAY

HUMANITY IN THE DIRT PIT . . . .

I have a little story . . .

I took Lilly for a walk this morning.

I was half asleep, and a bit blurry eyed.

It was early, I try to take her out before the Construction Activity and Traffic gets bad.

I live on a main Artery where there is Huge Construction now with Huge Earth Movers, and Back Hoes, and other gigantic yellow dirt monsters.

I always wave and talk to the construction guys, they are nice guys, family guys.

I see them alot, sharing sandwiches, cigarettes and laughing.

And they are even nice to my little dog throwing little left over lunch snacks.

So this morning I took her out, and I was foggy brained asleep.

I am sure these construction workers have seen me stumbling around with her these past 5 monthes, and always wondered if I would fall in a hole with her.

Today I came back inside, drank tea and watched Cspan, still trying to get rid of this friggin' cold. And it dawned on me hours later, that I had lost my cellphone. Now I assumed it was lost in my apartment.

But I could not find it anywhere . . .

I was a little worried, cause I just fired SBC this week, and it really is my only link to the world.

And if my son needs me . . .

And all those applications I have sent out.

Yikes.

But no phone.

(Not like I could call someone for help?!)

So at 1:30 pm, after lunch I take Lilly out and while I am walking something almost magical happens.

This older white haired construction fella in his flourescent vest says

"Hey Lady, You lost Something?"

He asks with a shy smile.

And then he holds up my phone, and nods to the Pit next to him.

I could not believe it. I obviously expressed my thanks and was so happy, gave him a big dusty hug.

"Yeah, and I bet you thought Chivalry was long dead?"

"No, But I have had my doubts about Humanity."

AUGUST 24, 2006, THURSDAY

OUT OF CONTROL: AIDS IN BLACK AMERICA

I try hard not to promote TV, unless it is Something that really needs to be seen. There are two shows that I am promoting this week, Spike Lee's Documentary on HBO on Katrina. It will indeed break your Heart. Maybe some of the Elected Reps will watch it while on "Recess". I can only hope.

The Other Show I am asking people to watch this week is called "Out of Control: AIDS in Black America", it is on tonight at 10pm ABC. This was the last documentary Peter Jennings worked on before he died, and there is a segment in which you can see him at his finest. Terry Moran worked on this Special for over a year, it is about a Hidden Crisis in this Country. AIDS is Huge in Black America in this Country. It is being ignored and denied on so many levels, yet it is rampant. And it is about Sex . . . and Lies.

Lies about how we Talk about It . . . How we Teach about It . . . . We need to find a way to teach our Young and Talk to Our Young . . . And Protect them. We need to find a way as Men and Women to talk about Sex.

We can not be Treating AIDS and SEX the way it was treated under Reagan, because it is already causing staggering rise in Numbers in HIV and AIDS in all ages, and male and female . . . . We can talk about AIDS in Africa—but we ignore Here At Home? WHY? How can that Happen? And why are we letting it?

And we have hourly Viagra Ads and Cialis WHERE are the CONDOM ads, we should be seeing them on as much as more than the Wonder Drugs. STD and HIV Numbers are up in the 13-23 age group, and that can only be blamed on Abstinence Programs and a lack of Education and a lack of Protection. Leading cause of Death in black women 23-44, AIDS. Black Women HIV infection rate is 14-20 times that of white women. We need to examine Why this is happening. It is not just about Relationships, it is about socieconomic situations, about healthcare, and about Hidden Stigma . . . . When do we talk? When?68% newly diagnosed HIV—Black women. Women should matter more than becoming a blaring statistic. If it were a White Women Epidemic would it be getting noticed?

And yes, it is also about the Religious Right and how they have Infected our Government, and it does have effect on Medical Decisions and Care. The Stem Cell Debate and the Right to Die Debate is all effected by these People that have limited Medical Knowledge forcing their beliefs into Policy. It is Wrong, and it is indeed Killing People.

So I am asking you to watch this Special tonight, and ask some hard questions. I also am asking that you watch with your kids, and ask the Questions together, and that you Talk . . . . to each other . . . . about Sex and about Love . . . about Relationships.

SEPTEMBER 02, 2006, SATURDAY

DATE FOOD: SPECIAL DIP & MY GRANDFATHER . . . .

The last couple of years my Grandmother was alive she was battling Breast Cancer. She and my grandfather were living in Florida. I was living North going to Nursing School and I would go see them on Holidays and try to help when I could. The final year I went down and my grandfather had developed a new Friday Night Ritual, he would go to Cocktail Parties. It turned out that my grandmother was worried about him, and worried that he would be lonely, she knew she was running out of time. So she developed the Cocktail Plan. She taught him how to make Finger Foods and Dips and sent him to the Parties. She even made sure that Certain Friends invited him to Certain Parties in the Golf Community. I came for one holiday and she said "I don't want to think of him being alone, this way I atleast can make sure suitable women look out for him. So I am teaching him how to cook for dates. Oh, Well, I might even have to help pick him out a wife." She said this very seriously and very lovingly. I would wince. He would do all of this in good cheer, but I saw the pain in his eyes, behind the smile.She would remind him to polish his white shoes and smile at him, and he would use Fantastick and a Handi-Wipe sing offkey "Hey, Good Looking". He would smile back at her.

[Earlier this year I wrote about Flo in February in two seperate pieces on the blog—"Florence My Grandmother" and also "April 1968". She was an Amazing Woman, if you want to read more about her. They were married 45 years.)

She did indeed die Christmas Eve many years ago, and yes, one of the Friends that had been close to both of them did indeed marry my grandfather, just as she has hoped and prayed.

For many years with my son I recently realized I was still doing the Friday Night Finger Foods, Pigs in a Blanket, Fondue, and cheese and crackers . . . .

Overtime my grandfather Ted became a Dip Inventor. This was his very favorite, and I don't think he would mind if I shared the Secret Recipe.

SECRET FAKE CRAB DIP

2 16 oz packages of Phili Cream Cheese
One small jar of Artichoke Hearts packed in Water
Kethup
Worstershire Sauce
Lemon
Cilantro

Soften the Cream Cheese, and then place in mixing bowl.
The Add Wostershire Sauce, about 3 tsp.
The Ketchup—about 2 tablespoons, enough to make it a pale salmon color.
Then drain and chop the artichokes finely.
Then mold into a mound shape put lemon wedges around the sides, and sprig of Cilantro in center.
Place in Frig to chill for atleast 1-2 hours.
The put Wheat Thins on plate while it rechills.

He would show up to parties in his green pants and white shoes and proudly bring his "Special Crab Dip".

(And yes he would call it that . . . and it was quite a hit.)

SEPTEMBER 02, 2006, SATURDAY

BUNNY LOVE: TALES FROM ENIGMA ANIMAL HOSPITAL

Larry and Rita Argue Over Celery (Starring Larry and Rita) video

This is a new Series off YouTube, and I am in love with these two, and even better their Home Movies have wonderful piano accompaniment. Enjoy.

* * *

I have a thing about Rabbits . . . true Bunny Love.

My first rabbit I brought home when my son was just a baby. I actually went to the Pet Shop to get a Budgie, but ended up with 2 Budgies, that could not be seperated. And then in the cage beneath them was this lonely depressed long hair lop bunny. Maybe it was the big glossy brown eyes or the long low hanging ears, but he looked so sad. It was funny, I brought home the budgies, and then I went back to get more Birdy supplies a few days later, and the Bunny was clearly looking sad. The Sales girl joked that maybe he missed the Birds that had been his upstairs neighbors. I decided if he missed his neighbors that much—they needed to be together. So I brought home George.

Now George was no ordinary bunny, he had quite a history by the time he reached us. He was a Pedigree Show Bunny, and also had been a Magician Bunny—when he was younger. But his career took a signifigant turn when it turned out that rooms of Excitable Children at Birthday parties led to a Little Excitable Bunny—who had an Incontinence Problem. Then he became a Show Bunny, getting Ribbons and also granted some Exciting Stud Duties. By the time I brought him home he was 4 and quite a character.

He loved chasing us around the House especially if we were wearing Fluffy Slippers. Unfortunately this led to him falling in Love with my son's stuffed animals. But what happened to Barney was unspeakable. Now truth be told when my son was 2 and half we begrudgingly let him watch Barney—and sad to say for all of one month—he loved Barney. And then the phase was over. And the Stuffed Barney was left alone on the shelf. Well, George made sure that Barney was never alone again. And in some respects George was more fulfilled and never again were slippers or legs humped.

George lived to the ripe old age of 11. Along the way we acquired Thumper and Benny. Benny was a 20 pound New Zealand Rabbit that was found in a Ravine and was brought to us Christmas eve wrapped in a Blanket. A Desperate Neighbor said they did not know what to do with this bunny, but that if she kept him her Boxers would dine on the poor thing. Over the years many animals arrived this way, for some reason many neighbors assumed because we were medical—nurses that we would have Vet skills. The list was amazing, mice, hamsters, a hedgehog, a chicken with a head wound, and even a three legged Painted Turtle, a Pregnant Skink, and a Walking Stick. (that is just naming a few). And so the Enigma Animal Hospital was run by son and myself. And my poor Ex had to put up with all sorts of creatures and helped feed and construct many interesting habitats. And for many years my son wanted to be a Vet . . . . He loved them all and tended them all. The First patient had been a Guinea Pig named Gimpy with a broken leg. And yeah, it is amazing what Landlords don't know about.

Benny the Christmas Bunny was 20 pounds of docile love and so mellow. The first few days we had him he literally lived in my son's room, lounging with the stuffed animals, a giant white Easter Bunny. (And yeah I have to be honest my son was already having Santa doubts at 4 and a half—and having this magical Huge Bunny arrive was very reaffirming, "Gee, Maybe Santa knew he should come live with us." My son said this and I agreed readlily.) Benny lived in my son's room until he was 12 and a half, and my son read him books every night for many years. I would walk by his room and hear Benny nibbling on his bedtime snack, and Rob reading. I still have some of the Books that Benny chewed on as well (I guess he thought that they were part of the Snack). He had two Roomies through the years, both guinea pigs, Albert and Emily. But first and foremost Benny was my son's roomate, and for many years my son always had a huge cage built by my ex just for Benny, at the end of his bed.

Then last but not least there was Thumper, he just passed away the Summer of 2005. He was 15 when he died. He was much like the bunnies in the video, he would play chase. He also played frisbee, we used to give him Container lids and he would throw them around and then chase them and run away with them. For years our cat Xena slept on Thumpers cage. He liked watching golf and soccer, and game shows and talk shows. He had been a Lab Bunny in his youth before he came our way. We figured this out when we found a Tattoo Number in his ear. His cage had to face the TV, and so he could eat and watch. If it didn't he wouldn't eat, period. We kind of guessed that his lab cage had been near a TV.

All of our bunnies used a peepan to take care of business, once they were trained, I could leave a pan out or leave the cage door open and they would do their business. This meant that for many years we gave our Rabbits Hop Time. You do have to remember that they need to chew, so you do have to make sure you make certain that ALL electrical cords and phone wires are not within reach. All of our bunnies liked snacks, cinnamon toast, cheerios and apples. And yeah, when we lived in houses where we had a garden, I did indeed let them dine in the Garden. Also if rabbits are fixed, especially the boys they aren't as aggessive and the humping can be greatly curbed, it would have been nice to figure this when we had George. They were some of the best Roomies we have had, they were Family.

SEPTEMBER 26, 2006, TUESDAY

DEAR MR. BUSH, YOU ARE A WAR CRIMINAL.

Dear Mr Bush,

I know that you and your henchmen don't read. I also know that you don't care that we all read and write letters and pay attention to What is being Done in Our Name. We are Still Americans. We value WHAT The Founding Fathers Set Forth in in the Constitution and the Bill of Rights. There was Nothing set forth by the Founding Fathers that precedented that we, as Americans llegally Imprison Others.There was Nothing that allowed Our Government to Imprison, and Torture Others Indefinently. There was Nothing about Renditioning People, Hiding, imprisoning, and Torturing them in Secret Prisons. There was nothing about Building Secret Harmful Prisons on Communist Islands. There was Nothing that allowed Our Government to Declare False Wars and to Occupy Countries Under False Pretenses.

I do not Live in Bushland, I do not abide your Lies or False Laws, or manipulation of Real Laws. I Believe in Peace. I believe In Justice. I believe in Truth.I believe that You will need to be Imprisoned and Impeached for the Coward of a War Criminal that You are.I am a Patriotic American, you are Not.

OCTOBER 05, 2006, THURSDAY

FAST FINGERS FOLEY AND GIMME ANOTHA PIE DENNY . . .

Okay, I am a mom, and I have a teenage son and to be honest I am fricking horrified by the this latest GOP Stinking Coverup. And I am not fooled for a minute by this steaming heap of a scandal, this situation concerns HUBRIS, and how MANY knew that Foley had a PROBLEM BEING TOO "INTERESTED" IN CHILDREN, AND BEING TOO "FRIENDLY". In True Let's Protect the Pediphile Fashion, these men in suits have been protecting a predator in their midst, leaving Innocent, Idealistic Children at Risk in the Page Program in DC. And the situation has deteriorated rapidly, by the hour with the lies and the DENIAL piling up by the Fast Fingers Foley's Bus of Shame.

Someone should get these poor boys out of the way. I watched that video of Foley Meetin'&Greetin' the Pages, and my he is practically licking his damn lips with glee and anticipation. This is an issue about a Real Life Predator, it is not about being gay, or having an alcohol problem, or a traumatic childhood. Look at his ONE Sentence Resignation—not a single apology offered to his constituents. He snuck off to Rehab, I don't think that speaks to a Drinking Problem—I do think that speaks to guilt. A man that is not safe with Children and Knows it, and has been caught.

And why the Hell didn't ANYONE do ANYTHING IN 2003??? There are children involved, and they are far from home, and Vulnerable . . . . Was Uncle Denny waiting for them to grow up? (Foley wasn't)

Watergate Summer

So here are Some of the Enigma's Questions for the Enigma Cafe . . .

1. WHY the Coverup? Because MORE have IM's and Emails and "Friendly Activities" to "worry about".
2. Is it at all related to the Abramoff/ PAC Monies (being funneled by Preston/Gates/Ellis)—that were busy being shuttled around Red State to Red State—and the Money was used to HUSH. (especially, just imagine if GANNON—you know Ol' Jeff or was it Dale Guckhart has Oh—God-forid-and—I—am—dying-anticipation PHOTOS????)
3. Did Fast Fingers Foley work SO HARD on the "exploited children" legislation so he could PROTECT HIMSELF??? OR ENJOY THE INTERNET—AND THEN LATER CLAIM (ahem—cough—gaggag) it was "RESEARCH"???
4. WHY did the FBI not investigate when it was brought to them in July 2006—WHO TOLD THEM TO STOP???
5. Does ANYONE remember the summer of 2001 and the CANDYMAN SCANDAL??? (AND ALL THE COMPUTERS—THOUSANDS OF THEM THAT WERE SEIZED IN FLORIDA AND TEXAS, AND YET NO ONE WAS EVER REALLY ARRESTED—ALBERTO HUSHED THE WHOLE DAMN THING UP . . . . HMMMMM) . . . . I wonder . . . .

Okay that is enough for this hour . . . . by Friday you KNOW there will be so much more . . . .

OCTOBER 10, 2006, TUESDAY

SPEAKING TRUTH TO POWER

[reprinted from March 2006]

Are we looking for Heros? Are we looking for Voices that speak the Truth? Are we looking for Someone to Speak up Against the Criminal Administration? I watched the Harpers Magazine Impeachment Panel on March 2,2006 (it is being aired on C-Span this week). The Panel was made up of some very well respected folks speaking very honestly about Impeachment and Options. They also pointed out that Speaking up to this Administration is Intimidating for All, even our elected Representitives. They also pointed out that The People need Someone to educate them regarding High Crimes and Abuse of Power. John Dean explained that the Watergate Impeachment Process actually took time, but it also was aided by the People, the Public Demanding the Truth.

* * *

In Spring 2004 I found a book about Robert F. Kennedy that spoke about this issue. This Book spoke to me at a time when I was disillusioned and sad about leaving my home due to circumstances beyond my control. I had driven over 1500 miles hoping to find a safe home for my son and pets after too much harrassment due to my Whistleblower situation had escalated. I had lost faith in My Government. This one book gave me Hope. The book is called The Spiritual Biography of Robert F.Kennedy, written by Konstantin Sidorenko. I sat in an old dilapitated Victorian Rooming House on the California Coast. It was very stormy that spring and the power would go out, and I would sit in the Dark and read this book while the Sea raged, seals bellowed and gulls squawked. This Book made me realize that the Truth needs to be Sought, but it needs a Leader.

A Leader that has Courage and Heart, and is willing to take on a Journey fighting a larger darker Evil. I sat in the Dark and realized that we are in the Dark waiting for that Leader to come to the Helm of the People and Speak Truth to Power.

The Book spoke about taking a Stand on Controversial Issues in a Time of Social And Conscience Unrest, because it would bring Change. Bobby Kennedy took a stand on an Unpopular War and also took a stand against a Sitting President. He reached out to The People, but he didn't just Reach to the people, he Listened to them and their pain. There were many that needed to be heard, college students, coal miners and impoverished in Appalachia, Watts, migrant workers, women,minorities, and more. He remembered the Real People, and he came to Them, he hit the Streets. He was fearless, but not reckless. He was compassionate but fierce in seeking Justice and Change. He remembered We the People had built this Country, Our Country.

It is now March 2006, we now Know Some of the High Crimes and Abuse of Powers, and we know that our Country has suffered, and Our Constitution is Suffering. And now Millions of Americans are as disillusioned as I was in Spring 2004. I am not alone in the Dark anymore. We are waiting For a Voice to arrive on the Scene. Someone who remembers We The People and how Important Our Constitution really is to Our Country.

We Need Someone to Speak Truth to Power.

Now is the Time.

OCTOBER 12, 2006, THURSDAY

LATE NIGHT AT THE ENIGMA CAFE

It is now October 2006, and we are still Waiting. Waiting for Change. I am reposting this because I wanted to share it again.Post was originally posted May 20th, 2006]

* * *

May 20th 2006.

So here we sit at the Enigma Cafe, stirring our coffee, and waiting for someone to show up with fresh bagels.It has been a long spring, all of us waiting for the other shoe to drop.(Actually I meant The Turd Rove to go down in the Plamegate Leak Scandal or the Abramoff mess) . . . if you know what I mean . . .) It has been raining and wet here, and even my son has been hanging out and restless, which means we have been telling stories and drinking too much tea and coffee.Storytelling here is not just about biding time, it is about nurturing the soul and stoking the hopes. When you are done listening to this little tale may you sit down and tell a story from your past, one that matters and makes a teenager ponder with a resounding ohhhhhhh. So cozy up a little closer, let me top off you cup. Here is a story . . . .

PART ONE: MIRACLES IN THE DEEP END

My son is 15, the age when you begin to ponder What you want to be. He was asking How I became a nurse, which is not an easy answer because I never actually wanted to Be a Nurse . . . . and involves being 11 years old and a miracle at a swimming pool . . . . in the deepend.

Watergate Summer

When I was 11 I was very sick for many monthes with a blood disorder and by summer I was finally better, but I looked like a Concentration Camp survivor. I had spent many monthes lying in bed watching the Wild Wild West and Perry Mason and wishing and hoping I would be better by summer. Summer arrived and I was finally better, but it left me weak and looking like Olive Oil. My mother decided that we needed to take a trip to visit my Dad in the Midwest, he lived in a modern apartment complex that had little to offer lonely skinny kids. (actually there were very few kids even at the complex).

My mom was glad to be on "vacation", which meant that she would sit by the pool and try to sell Shakllee products (which was some sort of godawful version of Amway crapola) and read her romance novels and tell us to "go play". (Which is insulting to any 11 year old). So I spent the summer reading things to make her worry—Crime and Punishment and Exodus, for starters. (and yes Smart Ass that I am I told her that I liked the violence and the sex—just to watch her eyes roll in her head and that vessel in her forehead pulse). I knew that I would spend my time hiding every part of my ostrich being with sweatshirts and towels by the concrete pool at the concrete complex. The whole complex still smelled of wet concrete and sand, there were no birds or trees even, so the pool was really the only place to go to escape the oppressive heat of the apartment.

(My Dad owned an aluminum sideing business in the Midwest, and the first 6 weeks of summer were spent surveying his plants, absorbing Kentucky and Ohio etc. and listening to my mother complain. The second half of the summer was spent in Florida. I spent a good bit of summers hiding from the sun and my mother and reading as many books as possible).

One overcast grey morning we went down to the pool and my mom went to the "Adult End", and sat with two other women and drank iced tea and read Good Housekeepings. I retreated to the other end of this strange pool where I knew no one and tried to read for awhile as I hid under my towels. I tuned my mother out. The "guard" was at the other end of the 60 foot long Peanut shaped pool, sitting on a chaise lounge talking too loudly to a girl friend and listening to the radio. The Beatles drifted on the Coppertone breeze as they giggled about boys like the chatty highschool cheerleaders they were. I painted my toenails with a black marker and cracked my bubblegum and realized that I was going to have to brave stares sooner or later and go in the pool.

I sat on the edge of the deepend and dangled my feet in the murky greenish water, because it wasn't sunny it gave the water a opague listless coloring. While sitting there I noticed a shadow down beneath the ladder. I leaned a little closer to the water and tried to see better, but I still couldn't make out the shadow. Suddenly I had an awful feeling in the pit of my stomach, the kind of gnawing dread that makes your heart pound. I realized Something was Very Wrong. I threw off my sweatshirt and jumped in the pool and as I came up for air I tried to navigate my way to the Shadow, and then I realized the Shadow was not a shadow at all . . . . I dove down to the Shadow.

As I got closer I could make out the figure of a little girl.

I had never seen a dead person, but I was pretty sure that she might be dead.

She was down in the deepend, right below the ladder to get out, her limbs splayed limply and at odd angles. She wasn't the right color, she was greenish in color and her hair was straggled about her head like a seaweed noodle halo. Her eyes were closed as though she was merely sleeping. She had been playing with a snorklemask and it was stuck over her mouth and nose, I remember looking at her and realizing what had happened, such a sad simple mistake.

The Dread had now changed to a different emotion, one of Cold Fear, because I didn't know what to do.

I decided that she looked about 8, I could pull her to the Ladder, and then yell for help, it would be so simple. It wasn't.

I went to touch her arm and it was ice cold, and it felt so heavy, like picking up a huge Yule Log. Dead Weight had a new meaning. I was stunned. I tried again, and could not pull her up. I began to realize that it was just her and I alone down in the DeepEnd, and I wasn't sure if she was dead or alive. The Silence was deafening and roared in my head. My chest was beginning to hurt but I knew that I could still hold my breath for a little longer. I then looked down at her and went over to the ladder and grabbed her by the hair. I grabbed on with all my might and pulled and dragged and hung on to the ladder. And as I got to the top of the ladder I screamed to the guard. It didn't come out very loud becuase I was out of breath. In a very hoarse garbled voice it came out "She's Dead". I was not trying to be dramatic—but I was really scared she was. The Guard came running and soon with her and her friend helping the girl was lifted out of the water. And they had to pry my hand out of her hair. They had a hard time getting the mask off, it was suctioned sealed to her face. She was still a wretched green and cold. I watched the guard give her breathes and turn her over and try to get the water out and the air in. I was stunned becuase as she did all of this I realized that the girl might not be dead after all. I realized that Hope was in Action at that moment, not just wishful thinking.

The guard stopped to take a breath and she looked up and yelled, "Call the Police and Fire, I will need more help. And get blankets." I didn't ask why, I ran to our apartment right by the pool and called the police on the phone and gave the address, and grabbed the new Sears Americana Blue polyester comforter and blanket off the guest bed in my Dad's apartment and ran back to the pool. By the time I got back, less than 2 minutes later the little girl looked a little better. And I as I stood watching she threw up all over the wonderful new blanket I had just brought down. I knew in the moment of seeing the vomit that maybe she was going to be okay, I was relieved and happy. (I didn't even hear my mother grumping about the blanket). And after she threw up the green color started to fade from her face and she took her first breath and gasped. And she cried. And all of us standing there were crying. And the Ambulance came and took the little girl away to the Hospital, and the guard's friend went with her, because she was all alone—there was no one to go with her. I was wondering where her mama was? And it made me wonder if that was why no one knew that she was Missing, or below the surface too long.

My mother stood yelling at me about the "wasted Blankets" I never heard her because in those few minutes Everything was Different. I went back to the Deep End and sat looking at the "Shadow" area. Thinking I never ever wanted to NOT Know What to do. The guard came over and just sat and neither one of felt like talking, not yet. We both sat and dangled our feet. "It's Too Late" by Carole King came on the radio and we both quietly sang along.

She looked over at me and lit a cigarette, her hand shaking slightly. "You know I thought she was dead too."

I sat silent and wordless and stunned.

She explained, "Yeah, I know a guard isn't susposed to say that, but for those couple of minutes I didn't Know What was going to happen. You did a good thing, you know that?"

And I finally said" But I didn't know what to do."

And she looked at me hard, "Yeah, but now you will always want to Know What to do, so that will make you try even harder to save someone. Because now know you can. That's how it works. Come see me later, I have an extra Red Cross Lifesaving book out in my car."

After she finished her cigarette she stood up and looked at me, and said "Saving someone is about the trying, you never know how it will turn out, it is more than Hope . . . . some say it is about Faith."

And that is how I became a Lifeguard . . . . the Nurse story is for another day.

We all have stories of How we became Who we are . . . . and how we got there.

NOVEMBER 01, 2006, WEDNESDAY

GIFTS FROM IRAQ:ROAD KILL AND THE WALKING WOUNDED

NEED MORE REASONS TO VOTE?

[THIS POST WAS ORIGINALLY POSTED NOVEMBER 2005, AND IRAQ IS WORSE THAN EVER, MORE THAN 600,000 DEAD IRAQIS, AND 2800 US TROOPS, AND 103 IN OCTOBER ALONE. 98,000 are now being treated for PTSD—up over 20,000. More than 41,000 have been treated for wounds, how many have been sent back into this botched battlezone is unclear. There are between 128,000 US troops-140,000 in Iraq, and suposedly there are over 450,000 Iraqi soldiers yet the Country is disintegrating into Chaos at best and Civil War at worst. And we don't have enough National Guard to protect Our Own Country and or the crumbling situation in Afganistan.]

WE NEED A BETTER DEMOCRACY, AND REGIME CHANGE in the United States.

* * *

We have seen alot of the King giving speeches and posing coquetteishly for the Camera these past few weeks, always with the Militarized Backdrop in full effect. (I don't think I have ever seen him pose with any wounded yet—atleast not recently).

And as more die and are wounded, and more Real Veterans demand a Timetable, and to bring the troops home, there are some issues that have been left unacknowledged. I am talking about the Gifts of War—this War, the Walking Wounded and the Road Kill that are invisible to the King.

This post covers several issues: Homeless Vets, PTSD, and Medical Care for our Reservists. It is about the Abandonment of these issues and people, and the hidden heartache that stretches across Our Country. Again it is indeed a longer post and told as a true story, about the real people that are effected. So it is dedicated to Jarrad and Robert and Iris, my neighbors, just three of my Homeless neighbors, and dedicated to what they have silently Endured. And Robert's story is shared below. I think he would want people to know that sometimes things are not as they appear, and that No One should be Invisible in America. I saw King George's Delusional Speech Today, yet another pissed petulent tirade, and I listened to him pontificate His Victory Plans and Schemes. I don't think he knows about the VETS, and I know he doesn't know Robert and the 74,000 PTSD Sufferers, and the Ticket to Hell he has given them. This is Robert's Story, his Reality.

(links will be posted with Part II of this tale, and this is Part I in a series))

BENCH PEOPLE AND GRATE PEOPLE

I live in Cleveland, but I have a suspicion that this scene is not so unfamiliar and might indeed be happening in towns and cities across the country. We live Urban, I moved here 6 monthes ago, and my son wanted Urban, edgy, "Real". He wanted a converted Urban Loft. He is 14,he is 6feet4in, he is Black Hightops, cargo pants and Rolling Stones and Green Day infusing on his iPod, idealistic teenage angst pulsing through the apartment. He lives and breathes John Stewart, Michael Moore and Al Fanken. We had been living out West, and he wanted a Change. He got It. I have wanted him to see All Sides of America, our America. Not just the Feel-Good-Post-Card Version.

Suposedly 10,000 people actually live in our downtown region, in the heart of the downtown. I have my doubts, it seems like less than that. Suposedly 3000 of downtown residents are homeless. (And the Homeless medical clinic has a patient load of 600-800, so the numbers actually might be accurate. I will keep researching it). I would see them as I walk the dog and go in search of better coffee than I can make. But statistically

I view the Homeless as my neighbors, because they are. I carry extra gum and change. And in the summer I delivered iced water, cold drinks and cheese sandwiches, and bandaids and cool wipes. And if I had extra change I would give them enough for a $2.99 Egg meal at the Johnnies Diner on my Street. And I know the Gyro Guy gives out meals—he appears to be a gruff hairy Serbian fellow that never smiles, but he has a heart. And the Homeless I see on a regular basis I have learned their names, and heard their Stories. It was the least I could do. They all have stories, illness, lost homes, and mostly Lost Jobs. And sometimes they let me take their pictures. (One day I will post the photos). First their Stories.

On errands to the library or the small little market I pass blocks and blocks of vacant buidings. Buildings built between 1900-1930, most have beautiful architecture, dignified lines and graceful curves, Art Deco with a Slavic Flair. You can look at them and imagine that they were once bustling with offices and business. Now the windows are hollow like an old lover's empty eyes, it is a permeable grief palpable at each bustop. In the heat of the summer the Homeless found benches to rest on. During the day behind the churches benches are staked out like prime beach front property, but it seems to be a hospitable process. And at night the Homeless gather in packs (for safety) and hide from the police. And I can't understand why those lonely empty buildings could not somehow be used to provide shelter for some of my neighbors?

Now it is Winter, and we have had some bitter nights and cold that makes your bones ache. In the Winter at dusk as the temperatures drop the Homeless look for Steamy Grates to lay on. They carefully arrange mats and blankets and use their bags as pillows. They wrap their feet in plastic and baggies to keep warm, and some wear socks on their hands as mittens. And during the election the Mayoral Candiate made sure they were removed, "relocated", so as to not clutter up the walkways near her Campaign Center. They are picked up in Vans and taken to the other side of town, away from familiar services and safety. And yes, there are not enough shelters and it is a System that is beyond repair, because it gets so little spotlight. The Campaigning focused on issues for the pearled and well healed, not the patched and blighted.

And from listening to many of the Stories as I walked my dog 4 times a day. I have learned the Circumstances that had contributed to their Homelessness. Many of the Public think they must be drug addicts or drunk, and that is mostly urban myth. Some have wrestled with substance abuse, and some are in need of medical care and mental health care. And a large number are Vets, of varying ages and service, and a shocking number are from the Gulf Wars—BOTH of them. Within the first few monthes here I had met three back from Iraq with different stories and damage. It was compelling and it was disturbing.

ROBERT: BACK FROM IRAQ

Robert was one of the first vets I met, and it was a challenge because if it was up to him we would never have met. Except for he was intrigued by my dog. I have a sweet little rescued honey colored hearing impaired Barkless Basenji. Her first few monthes here she was rattled by Big Buses and loud city noises. But the little park across the Street became her park, "Lilly's Park" and not shared with too many other dogs. She has a way of trotting up to people and sniffing quietly like a little fox. It can be endearing, but it can also be annoying.

Robert used to sleep over on a Bench over by the Law School at the University, part of "Lilly's Park" . . . The first time I met him it was because Lilly went up and quietly and gently sniffed his head. He jumped awake and I apologized. He didn't smile, he would not make eye contact with me. Yet he did look at Lilly and patted her just once very cautiously on the head. His eyes were sad, haunted like an old man. His face was well lined and his hands gnarled like bark of an old tree. He turned away quickly and went back to sleep. And I walked away quietly. I would see him but quietly give him his space, it seemed like he needed quiet. And over time Lilly kept wanting to see him. So over time she would go to visit him and I would not talk, I would just let him pet her.

One day a Truck was backing into the parking garage, while she was visiting him on his bench. And KABANG!!!, the truck backfired. Some students near by lunching laughed. But Robert slammed to the ground and covered his head. I asked

"Iraq?" He nodded with etched pain" in his eyes, like he had stepped on glass. And slowly he went to get up. I offered him my hand. 'Robert "he said. The eyes were looking down again. I knew he was embarrassed.

"Those godammned trucks" I said and let him pet Lilly. I knew that he had PTSD and that he needed help, but that trust was fragile and if I offered unsolicited help or talked too much he would move on to another bench. I decided that in the long run Lilly was what he really needed more than chatter from a nosy nurse. I knew that it was a silence worth nurturing, to help him heal.

Over time I learned Robert's Story, piece by piece. He was in his late twenties, he signed up for the Reserves after 9-11.

He spoke with a Southern drawl, he was from the South—"Roots in Alabama and Louisiana, got family there".

Parts of his story didn't make sense, pieces were fuzzy, and I think it was for him as well. He had signed up and been sent to Iraq, in the beginning. He explained that when he signed he never thought that he would go Anywhere, he thought that he would helping at home, protecting his family and friends. (I wonder how many share this tale). He said first folks were sent off to Afganistan and he was relieved not to go there. And then monthes later he found out he was going to Iraq. And he went. He was a driver, and I am not sure What exactly happened, some sort of shootout and an accident, that he could not discuss with his eyes clouding over. He hit his head and left him with some damage. Yet that didn't get him sent home. He was there until end of May 2003. I was unclear what brought him home and he would not discuss. He did tell me he had the Nerve Disorder. I said the PTSD. And he said it was awful dreams while waking, and unprovoked flashbacks. He is one of the Walking Wounded, and as he said, "Hell, I'm just glad not to be one of the Road Kill".

He would twitch while talking. I don't even think he knew he was twitching. He knew he wasn't "right". "Can't hold a job, can't think straight". I asked him if he was getting help—for the PTSD. And he looked at me and laughed bitterly. "You'all don't know nothin". And I told him he was dead right—I did not know enough. He said that Medical care is given for only two years and that's it. (I really thought that didn't sound Right). And the only "care" I could offer was egg sandwichs and Lilly's unfaltering attention. He said the care that was "Offered" was a joke, "Re-Exposure Therapy" and schizophrenia meds, all of which he claimed left him even more injured, more damaged.

In September I saw him, Katrina had happened. He said that he wanted to get Home. He didn't care anymore if they knew he was sick. "Can't hide it forever, maybe after all of this it won't matter I ain't right".

He wanted to get home and help his uncles the Shrimpers. I gave him Greyhound bus money. And I prayed for his sake that he could go there and help his family, find some Meaning again. I also prayed that no more devastating Hurricanes would hit down there. (And yes, i worried about him when Rita hit the Gulf). I never saw him again. I walk by his bench and Lilly still looks for him.

I hope he is in a Better Place. I hope he made it Home.

PTSD FACTS:

Post Traumatic Stress Disorder is what was known in WWI as Battle fatigue. Currently it is our Military's Biggest Dirty Little Secret. I am sure Rummy would rather change his underwear in front of the Press Corp than discuss how Big a problem this really is. I understand that each War has it's own Hells and Wonders. The Korean War gave us MASH units and Vietnam brought Agent Orange. And the First Gulf War gave us the Gulf War Syndrome and the Horrors of Depleted Uranium, and the wonders of Denial. Yet all wars and Miltary action can cause PTSD. (Even Police and Fire, other High Intensity Work can leave nervous system damage.) My Great Uncle Stu had suffered it after WWII, but it was a nameless disorder that was not properly treated and he was suposed to come home go to school and work. (Story for another day).

AT THIS TIME THE VETERANS AFFAIRS ADMITS TO TREATING 74,000 with PTSD on disability, and most of these are military that are Home now and not in service any longer. Many can not work, and qualifying for Disability benifits has been nightmare of a wrestling match.

They come home and their work and relationships ALL suffer, and many end. This is the most that are suffering at one time. Is this number accurate? Most likely not. Many have been refused care, or put on waiting lists, or should come back down the road for more followup. So the 74,000 might indeed be the tip of a Huge IceBerg of Broken Souls. Robert's Story is just one of thousands, and after researching PTSD on the VA websites, I learned Everything he told me was True, the "Re-Exposure Therapy", and the Meds, and how as a reservist he only gets two years of care.

This is Part I of my Vet Series, the next part will have links on more hard data, and also will have the other half of the story, and if the Medical Care is bundering and inadequate, but the Housing part of the Story is just as mindbending. And sadly, ironically, the next part of the Story does indeed Award another Heckuva-Job—Brownie—Award to yet another of the King's Crony Buddies. We will call him the Rennaisance Man—and he istruly deserving.(I will post links and also ALL updated Stats—that have been rising steadily since Summer—and have had to be updated TWICE since July).

As the weather continues to whip at us with cold wind and snow, I am asking that the next time you see a Homeless Fellow or Lady please stop and reflect that there is a story there. And like Robert they may indeed be a Vet, a Homeless Vet discarded by this Administration, Used, Spent and Wasted: Just More Walking Wounded and Not Yet Road Kill.

* * *

> "I may be compelled to face danger, but never fear it.
> While our soldiers stand and fight,
> I can stand and feed and nurse them."

Clara Barton

[Clara Barton,founder of the Red Cross, worked with Dorthea Dix to advocate on behalf of Civl War Vets, that they be provided safe care and shelter during ALL phases of Battle and War]

Allie McNeil

* * *

<<< Stats: Atleast 200,000 Homeless Vets look for a place to sleep every night, and the stats show that there are atleast 500,000 Vets Experiencing Homelessness per year under this Current At War Administration. I read the 27 Victory page book online, and the Chapter on Sick Homeless Vets seems to be MIA. Part II of this story will have ALL the stats and Links related to Homeless Vets. Part I was just to tell one VET's story, and make certain he wasn't just a number. So stay posted.>>>>

DECEMBER 13, 2006, WEDNESDAY

REPORT ON CIVILIAN CASUALITIES IN IRAQ: LANCET STUDY

CONGRESSIONAL BRIEFING ON THE LANCET STUDY OF 650,000 EXCESS DEATHES.

This report is available on CSPAN, there was a panel discussion/congressionalhearings on the Lancet report. (LINK on Title is IRAQ BODY COUNT—CIVILIAN)

* * * Please see other post: "Numbers don't lie, People do", and see link to titland that links to the Lancet Study itself. * * *

(On Sunday nite I watched the Lancet Hearings on Iraq, cried, and threw up. I also took notes . . . . I lack the heart to rewrite the notes at this point—but I do want to make sure they are available. This week I will tidy them up for all two of my readers.)

The CSPAN Hearing is based on Hopkins Resarch on Deathes in Iraq March 2003 until Aug 2006-the number is 655,000 dead based on the research of Les Roberts and Gilbert Burnham, and Senator Kucinich and Ron Paul held a hearing—Basement of Senate building—no one really there- just about six press people—public not there—does not look like it was well publicized.Juan Cole from University of Michigan was there—to address questions and concerns aboutMiddle East History. It was originally on Monday Dec11, 2006 on CSPAN 2.**(The Next day Kucinich announced his run for pres. I do think it is related to his concerns over Iraq.)

(1) SENATOR KUCINICH LED THIS PANEL and Hearing, Juan Cole was on Paneland the two investigators from Hopkins that worked on the Lancet study.Les Roberts and Gilbert Burnham. and there were 4-6 press, and no other audience, it was held in the basement of the Senate Building.

It was set up to review the Lancet study and three years of research.

(2) These surveillance/measureing methods have all been used in War Zones:Bosnia, Afganistan,Kosovo and the Congo, Orignially Dr.Berkal tried to collect the day and work with Jay Garner.

(3) Dr.Gilbert Burnham co-author explained how the studies were done, in a conflict situation it is very difficult to do cluster studies, but that is what is done, although it is more difficult to do with GPS the way W.H.O. reccomends. They are not just trying to measure death—they and mortality in given populations, they are also trying to measure health needs, birth rates,pregnancy, disease, malnutrition, but samplings of any of these is very difficult in areas where thiere is such violence.

(4) Methodlolgy might indeed be flawed, due to flawed sampling or other effectors of inaccuracy—but they are thinking that now the flaw is not getting all the bodies proplery counted, not that they over counted or numbers were too high.The estimates for flaw—taking into error account—would lower range at the most conservative to 390,000, but with new numbers or estimates or measuring tools it may be closer to 950,000.

* * * 3000 for Oct 2006 alone.

Deathes are indeed rising. Not all bodies are counted.If bodies are not identified and no death certificates are given—they are not always counted. Death rates march 2003—Aug 2006—est 655,000.

(5) 601,000 DUE TO VIOLENCE,

DEATH DUE TO ILLNESS, NUTRITION, COLLAPSE OF PUBLIC HEALTH AND HEALTH CARE, SHORTAGE OF MEDICINE,

AND SECURITY AT HOSPITALS, FLIGHT OF WORKERS, LACK OF CLEAN WATER,FRESH FOOD. 45,000 ESTIMATE.

(6) DR.JUAN COLE, HISTORIAN U OF MICHIGAN EXPLAINED HOW THESE STATS CAN SHOW/ DEMONSTRATE THAT THESE NUMBERS AND CRITERIA CAN INDEED INDICATE A CIVIL WAR OR EVEN GREATER CIVIL CONFLICT. THESE ARE SIGNIFIGANT. GUREILLA AND MILITIA MOVEMENTS, COULD BE DUE TO HIGH UNEMPLOYMENT-%60—VERY HIGH. VERY HIGH RATE OF DEATH AMOUNG YOUNG MEN. WOMEN ARE FLEEING—TO SYRIA AND JORDAN (PROSTITUTION) KUCHINICH ASKED HOW MANY ORPHANS (AL—CHECK HUMAN RIGHTS AND UNICEF, cause these numbers are not known)
(7) THESE NUMBERS OF DISPLACED PEOPLE ARE SHIFTING EACH MONTH-100-200,000 MONTH—DR.B stated. This also means that migration numbers will make it difficult to track people.
(8) JUAN COLE ASKED ABOUT WORKFORCE-

HE TALKED ABOUT DESTRUCTION OF ECONOMY. USUSALLY WOMEN WOULD—BUT THIS IS NOT GOING TO HAPPEN DUE TO CULTURAL GENDER SEGREGATION, AND ALSO SECURITY. BUT IT COULD EFFECT RECOVERY AND REDEVELOPEMENT. INSTABILITY AND SECURITY IS EFFECTING NEIGHBORHOODS AND NOT JUST WORK ZONES.SOCIAL FABRIC IS TORN. VICIOUS CYCLE OF VIOLENCE. MORALE IS DESTROYED, NOW MEDICAL STUDENTS ARE TRYING TO CARRY ON MEDICAL CARE. SOME OF THE HOSPITALS HAVE ONLY HANDFULS OF DOCTORS, MANY HAVE FLED—AND ARE NOW DRIVING TAXI'S IN EGYPT AND JORDAN.

(9) STUDY HAS BEEN DONE NOW TWICE 2004 AND 2006. STUDY IS NOT COMPLETE AND ACCURATE BECAUSE OF LACK OF SECURITY.THEY WOULD LIKE TO STUDY HOUSEHOLD EFFECTS AND MIGRATORY

PATTERNS. AND THEY WOULD LIKE TO STUDY THE LONGTERM EFFECTS.
(10) LES ROBERTS MENTIONED THE "CONTRITION"— THAT GREAT HARM TO ANOTHER POPULATION AND PEOPLE COULD BE STUDIED, PENTAGON HAS NEVER EVER GIVEN ANY ESTIMATES OR SUMMARIES OF TRUE COLLATERAL AND CIVILIAN DAMAGE. HE SPEAKS WITH FEELING AND TRUE CARING OF WHAT HAS HAPPENED TO THESE PEOPLE AND HOW THEY HAVE BEEN HARMED.
(11) BODIES ARE FOUND EXECUTED, AND THEY HAVE BEEN TORTURED, WITH DRILLS, AND CHEMICALS AND WORSE, AND THEN THEY ARE EXECUTED. THIS IS VIOLENCE THAT CAN NOT BE IGNORED. THIS IS WHAT A CIVIL WAR LOOKS LIKE. DENIAL IS JUST GOING TO LEAD TO MORE DEATH. (COMMENT WE DO NOT HAVE TIME FOR DEBATES ON SEMANTICS-PEOPLE ARE BEING SLAUGHERED IN THEIR OWN HOMELAND—TRYING TO PROTECT THEIR OWN NEIGHBORHOODS).
(12) THIS IS NOT AL QUEDA IT IS CIVIL WAR. said Juan Cole WE HAVE COMMITTED CLEOCIDE (LOOK UP THIS WORD). JUAN COLE ASKED WHAT WILL VICTORY LOOK LIKE? THEY DON'T WANT TO HAVE OUR TROOPS IN THEIR NEIGHBORHOODS.
(13) "TRUTH AND RECONCILATION IS IMPORTANT" SENATOR K. RON PAUL ALSO WORKED ON SPONSERING THIS EVENT, HE IS ALSO A DOCTOR. HE WROTE A LETTER ABOUT THE PAIN AND SUFFERINGAND THE CONSEQUENCES THAT HAVE BEEN INCURRED TO THIS POPULATION.100,000 VETS AND SOLDIERS HAVE BEEN DAMAGED IN THIS WAR HE WROTE IN HIS STATEMENT.

WATCH THE WHOLE THING, AND ESPECIALLY THE CLOSING STATEMENTS IT WILL MOVE YOU. OBITUARIES ARE NOT JUST ABOUT NUMBERS, THEY ARE ABOUT PEOPLE.

Watergate Summer

* * *

Enigma's closing thoughts . . . .

How many grave yards will that fill?

There are not enough morgues . . . .

655,000 is alot of people.

Stadiums vs cemetaries . . . .

6 people in the damn room and NO other elected officials other than Kucinich . . .

DECEMBER 20, 2006, WEDNESDAY

THE CHRISTMAS SHOES

In an earlier post I wrote about my Grandmother, Florence. I still miss her, and she has been gone for 20 years.

She died when she was 71, I was a young bride, a nurse living in Vermont when she died. I was a child of 1960's and she was a big piece of my Growing Up Years. I learned Everything from her.(You can read my post from last year if you clink the title).

I placed this post between her two favorite Christmas songs.

She was Many Things.
Unconditional Love.
Love Notes in Pockets.
Juicy fruit and Peppermint lifesavers.
"White Shoulders perfume"
Silk not Cotten. Cashmere sweaters.
Linen Suits and Italian Shoes.
Yelow roses with dew.
Beautiful smokey grey eyes.
Wavey Auburn hair that had copper highlights in the sun.
Slowdancing with my Grandad . . . Nat King Cole and Johnny Mathis.
Moonlight Sinata and Pachabel and Handel.
Beautiful White goatskin golf shoes, with lavender trim.

She loved golf, getting up early and walking the greens. She never got good at golf, she was not the most competitive person, she enjoyed being outside with friends. She had emphysema and they moved to Florida for her health, where they also played golf to help her lungs. She would end up battling Breast and Lung Cancer.

In the 1980's I did my best to help her battle her Cancers and then helped her find Hospice Care. In November 21 years ago I went to see her and take my new Husband (my sweet Ex) and we joked about the Ice in Vermont and having to walk up and down icey streets to the Hospital to work. She joked that her golf shoes would work well, that the spikes would do fine on the ice. I didn't think anything of it, until later, much later when Christmas 1987 came and I recived a package. I was happy to see it looked like a shoebox. It was Christmas eve. Flo and I had always shared shoes, I wear 10AAA, not a normal shoe size, but the same size as my elegant sophistcated grandmother, and when she got tired of different shoes she would send them my way. That cold icey December day on the Front steps of my apartment building and realized that she had sent me shoes, feeling warm and loved in that moment, just like I had numerous times. Then I opend the box and saw the beautiful white leather shoes, and also felt my heart sink because I knew that She was Gone. It was my Very Best present, I knew that as I sat there crying on the icey steps in the Vermont Snow.

Sadly she died Christmas Eve. A part of me is so sad that she died that close to Christmas, her Favorite Holiday. She loved Christmas, she collected cards and gifts year round. (Which meant as kids we spent alot of time rooting through her house Searching for the Stash Spots). She had sent out her packages as usual, so she did not think she would not be here. She was battling lung and breast cancer, and she was in Hospice Care at the time. But I know she thought she still had a little time.

She sent Ted my grandad out to the store and she passed. He was so heartbroken. I really believe that it was too hard for her to say goodbye to him, to let him go. And yet a part of me has never let her go either.

Once you have had such a grandmother you can not help but believe in Angels. On Earth and in Heaven.

HONORING LENNON . . . and Peace.

Tonight is the 26th Anniversary of one of our greatest geniuses being slain.

(This post is being reposted from last December 2005. Please see the Song that is posted tonight as well. I am sitting doing exactly what I was doing a year ago, watching CSPAN as the House has late night Vote, and I am blogging, praying for a better Future. I am eating cookie dough and drinking eggnog, and of course seeking inspiration over on YouTube, and of course I found some Lennon there . . . . Good night Bloggers.)

For me there are certain times of the year when I am filled with Loss, this is one of them. (The Deathes of MLK, RFK and JFK are the other hallowed dark days). I can not help but remember these Brave Souls and ponder what might have been. I remember the night that Lennon was shot like it was yesterday. I came home from working late as a waitress, my outfit stained with lobster and butter. (I held a number of jobs through nursing school—but lifeguarding and waitressing would pay most bills).

It was bitter cold, and I was rushing up the stairs to my walkup on the third floor. I was singing White Christmas too loud and off key. I was carrying a bag of Christmas supplies for a little Midnight get together I had planned to have with neighbors, Creme De Menthe, Baileys' Irish Creme, And Egg Nog, and cookie dough. I came up the stairs and I could hear muffled crying. I turned the landing to my apartment and found my neighbor Micheal sitting on the stairs crying, his head down buried in his fisherman knit sweater.

I stopped dead, I stopped too fast and dropped my bag. Only the Baileys broke. I had known Micheal for many years, and I had never seen him cry, even when his stepdad died.

What? I asked. He just said 'Lennon". WTF???? I thought I heard wrong. He explained it had just happened.

We both sat for quite a bit staring at the puddle helplessly seeping out of the bag.

We went inside and watched TV, and it didn't change a thing.

It didn't take away the reality and it didn't provide any comfort.

We stayed up the rest of the night, and sat on my fire escape with as many would fit. People showed up who I didn't know neighbors and strangers, it didn't matter. The Grief bound us in the moonlit night.

We lit candles and sang Beatles songs until 4am. And played Double Fantasy relentlessly on my record player. The Cops that came to tell us to be quiet ended up sitting on the Fire Escape and doing shots of Creme De Menthe. (They weren't bad singers). There was no Kleenex, only a role of Charmin passed around.

For the rest of my days on a Cold night when I smell candles burning and Creme de Menthe I think of Lennon and hear IMAGINE being sung off key.

Maybe tonight we need to remember Lennon for a little while and oh, I can't help but think of the Music he would have written about This Mess of A War and this Administration and religousity wrapped crap, from the Patriot Act to Gitmo. He would have kept us humming and singing, Thinking too much and Protesting more. And it's 25 years and we are back we started. Tonight again there will be candles lit at the Enigma Cafe.

Imagine All The People . . . .

*   *   *

Since I can't sing . . . . some Quotes from Lennon.

[1] The More I see, the Less I Know.

[2] Reality leaves alot to the Imagination.
[3] Possession isn't nine-tenths of the law, it's nine-tenths of the Problem.
[4] My role in society, or any artists or poets role is to try and express what we all feel. Not to tell people how to feel. Not as a Preacher, not as a leader, but as reflection of us all.
[5] Our Society is run by insane people for insane objectives. I think we're all being run by maniacs for manical ends and I think I am liable to be put away as insane for expressing that. That's whats insane about it.
[6] Love is a Promise, Love is a souvenir once given, never forgtten. Never let it dissappear.

* Date Corrected: since I originally ran post on Dec 6th, Some other lovely tributes: The Defeatists, Snarky the Badtux Penguin, and This Ol' Brit's . . . .

Please also see the YouTube song above . . . . I keep thinking that John would have loved Youtube—don't you think? Please see the great YouTube below.

Original Quotes are still on this post . . . as poignant as ever. Peace.

FEBRUARY 01, 2006, WEDNESDAY

LETTER TO THE COWBOY CRIMINAL KING: WHAT YOU DON'T DO TO MOMS

A Letter to the King:

I realize you have to give a Glory Speech to Celebrate all of your crimes this year. And I realize that you gloat as often as you breathe, but NOW you have gone too far you have Crapped on the Constitution and Arrested the Patriotic Mom of a Dead Soldier that was INVITED to the Capital because YOU didn't LIKE her t-shirt. Wow you really signed and sealed Your Bully status tonight.

Cindy Sheehan was in DC today for a series of Conferences and was also invited to come listen to YOUR speech by a California Rep. She came quietly to listen and she was wearing the Clothes she had been wearing ALL day. On her T-shirt was the NUMBER OF THE DEAD in the Iraq Oily War. And she was removed from the Balcony and ARRESTED AND EVEN ROUGHED UP and held for hours while you gave your Speech.

Please go to Brad's Blog and Yep, Another Godammned Blog, and see the complete story and the Links. I am too Ripping Mad to even spit straight. And Please Watch Cindy in the AM on Good Morning America and also read CODEPINK. And while we all are at it—we need to call and Write the Dipheads at CNN and tell them learn how to REPORT the Story—maybe bring Arron Brown back—because SHE WAS WEARING A TSHIRT, NOT UNFURLING ANY FRIGGIN BANNER, AND THEY NEED TO ISSUE AN APOLOGY NOW.

Allie McNeil

So let me get this straight Mr. Bush you gave a speech about the "Importance of Political Freedoms" and you had a mom arrested for wearing a Tshirt in the House of the People. You even spoke about the Poor People of Iran living under a Dangerous Regime. I fear that you were warning them that you are planning to go there next and bring them some sort of contorted Democracy like the One Here or the One in Iraq.

And Back to the Point. Mr Bush I hope you and your friggin GOONS read this. YOU DO NOT ROUGH UP MOMS IN THE CAPITAL OR ANYWHERE ELSE ON AMERICAN SOIL, AND YOU DO NOT ROUGH UP MOMS OF DEAD SOLDIERS. IT AIN'T RIGHT, IT AIN'T DECENT, IT AIN'T EVEN AMERICAN, SO YOU THINK MOMS WERE YOUR PROBLEM BEFORE?—WELL YOU HAVE A WHOLE NEW BALLGAME ON YOUR HANDS.

PHONE NUMBER FOR THE FUCKING WHITE HOUSE: 202-456-1111 (1) (1) PLEASE DO FEEL FREE TO JAM THE DAMNED SWITCHBOARD AND COMPLAIN.

JANUARY 01, 2007, MONDAY

2006 YEAR OF TOIL & TROUBLE

So every year I stay up on New Years Eve and put together a HUGE Jigsaw puzzle . . . and reflect on the last year. In this case much of the last year was indeed a Jigsaw Puzzle, waiting for the Pieces of this Corrupt Morass to basically fall into place. I read the CNN Top Story list and was almost laughing at how much they Forgot? So this is my list . . . I pray it is a little more accurate reflecting WHAT needs remembering . . . .

Here is a Random List of WHAT I will remember, as a Bloggeress . . . . And Remember this is in NO particular order.

(BUT if you think I forgot Something, please do let me know)

*   *   * Please also see the Ava Lowery video below, shamelessly stolen from Crooks & Liars it sums up the year nicely*   *   *

WHAT SHOULD BE REMEMBERED:

1. Democrat Tsunami November (FIRST time in 6 years MY vote was counted)
2. Iraq and 650,000 DEAD Iraqis (and how Afghanistan is a frigging mess and not getting covered)
3. BUSHCO continuing to lie and hump their Fake, Delusional War on "Terra"
4. How Iraq was not called a Civil War until December (after the effin Election)
5. GOP Repug Corruption and Resignations
6. MORE Unfolds about the Rendition and Gitmo mess

7. Lebanon bombed beyond recognition (and how the press never did the story again)
8. Al Gore and Inconvenient Truth (and Global Warning)
9. Sago Mine Disaster (and Media Mess)
10. Keith Olbermann's Special Comments
11. Micheal J.Fox (His Courage during the Elections)
12. Katrina Hearings (last winter—and then media and Senate and Congress dropped ALL of it)
13. How Millions Effected by Katrina—(the Survivors are STILL missing and not being properly taken care of)
14. How the Katrina TRUE DEAD NUMBERS are not being told
15. Stupid Ass New Airline Restrictions (hair gel and lipstick????)
16. NSA Spying Crap Conitnues to Unfold
17. Lost Faith in Media: CNN (except Anderson), NYT, even WAPO

Reading Vanity Fair and Harpers, and the Rolling Stone for GREAT Investigative Pieces

18. YouTube
19. And How Bloggers and the Internet Covered WHAT the Media Wouldn't
20. Corrupt Geeus Mongers (Haggard & co)
21. METH: and how the Media is STILL ignoring it
22. The James Family in Oregon (Survival and Tragedy)
23. The Lost Climbers on Mt.Hood.
24. Tornados at Christmas in Florida

LOSS:

Coretta Scott King
Rosa Parks
Steve Irwin
James Brown
Dana Reeves (and Chris before her)

JUST DEAD (I ain't crying) CATEGORY:

President Ford
Kenny Lay

Illegally Dead:

Saddam (Sorry but I don't think the 30 day Appeal Process Criteria was met—I am not even sure WHO hung him)

JULY 13, 2007, FRIDAY

FRIDAY GIFT.: . . . 7.13.07

(The Story of My Grandmother's Amazing Crabcakes . . . .)

I have decided to make some changes to my blog . . . . gasp . . . No, Nothing drastic. Every Friday I am going to try to post a reciepe and some music, just a little gift to you all for your weekend. By the end of the week, I need a break from the Criminal Corporatocracy of everyday life, and I can only say the EFF word so many times when vessels start pulsing and I begin rummaging for TUMS.

When I am frustrated I like to break dishes for my mosaic project or cook or bake . . . . or clean.

Enigma Crab Cakes:

WHAT YOU NEED:

Crab (16 oz. prepicked Lump and canned—Fresh)
One Mini Heinken
One tin of Old Bay Seasoning *Critical*
One Egg
Hungarian Paprika
Garlic Powder (NOT salt)
Parmesan Cheese (the powdery kind)
One jar of Mayo
Dijon Mustard
Box of Ritz Crackers
Buttered Glass baking pan

(1) In a bowl mix the Crab and even it's canned juices, with cup of mayo, 2 teaspoons mustard, and one tablespoon of Beer.

(2) In a seperate Bowl, Bowl A, crush up about 30 Ritz Crakers, nice and fine, then add a dusting of Old Bay, and some garlic powder, and some paprika . . .

(3) Now crush up some more crackers, about 20 and add them to the Wet mixture and then sprinkle with parmesan cheese(the powder kind), just sprinkle lightly.

(4) Preheat oven to 375 degrees.

(5) Now take the crab and measure with your hands, and make balls gently molded with your hands.

(6) Once you have molded, then roll in Cracker Bowl until the ball is fully covered with crackers, then place in the baking pan.

(7) If mixture is too wet, don't be shy about adding crushed crackers to the Wet Bowl.

(8) Make the balls, and place in circle and in pan, so there is space between to cook.Sprinkle more Old Bay lightly across the top.

(9) One can makes approximately 8 Crab Cakes.

(10) Bake for approximately 30-40 minutes.

Serve with salad, tomato aspic, potato salad, and garlic bread . . . . and fruit . . .

* Background: This is a 4th Generation Baltimore Reciepe, handed down through the women of my family. Grandmother Flo taught me . . . she would stand in the kitchen and crack open a Heiniken and my grandfather would come and stand and nibble on the crackers and the crab and drink a beer, and she would put on Johnny Mathis and Nat King Cole and then they would slow dance while they baked . . . . and I would sit and soak in the smell of the Baking Crab and Heiniken . . . . Old Bay wafting on a warm summer night still melts my heart . . . .

AUGUST 07, 2007, TUESDAY

SUMMER DREAMS . . . .

{photo by Mack Sennett in 1917: He was the person who filmed silent comedies and early talkies, and he made Charlie Chaplin famous. He knew how to film spontaneous moments and comedic moments. He was a photographer, film-maker, actor and artist. This photo shows how he can Catch the Moment . . . . I was struck by how he caught these two girls reaching out to each other in the Moment.}

* * *

I have been having dreams about my Grandmother Flo*. Summertime always reminds me of her. In the summer I used to stay with her and she used to make wonderful Sunday dinners, Baltimore Crabcakes (her version), deviled eggs, potato salad, tomato aspic, and for dessert Ice Cream Pie. I used to sit on the counter and eat the melted Coffee Ice Cream. She would take me to Church Rummage sales and she let me buy any books I wanted, thanks to her I read Ian Fleming before I saw any Bond movies. She would take me to the library on Saturday mornings and let me lay on the marble floor chewing Juicy Fruit and reading in the Reference Section. I still am amazed that she didn't rush me or even question what I was doing. Later she took me to see Love Story, Dr. Zhiavago, and even my first Bond Movie. She always shared whatever she had, whether it be mini-sprinkled treasured Purells, cold coffee, or stale peppermint lifesavers in her purse.

When she went down the hall the faint smell of Yardley Lavendar soap and Camay soap, White Shoulders dusting powder and Estee Lauder Lemon Spray Mist perfume followed her. I would see my grandfather sniff the air when she walked by. At 10 I thought that was romantic, as much as watching them slow dance on the porch during a Thunderstorm. They had been listening to Johnny Mathis, but the music stopped due to the storm, but they kept dancing. She had her head on his shoulder, the soft auburn waves. He smelled of cherry tobacco and Old Spice aftershave, and he was lightly humming. She was wearing a cotton dress that lightly swished and she had bare feet . . . . And there was an owl hooting in the old elm behind the house, and the scattered hum of crickets and frogs and it smelled of wet geraniums and roses. I dream about that evening alot.

I also dream about going shoe shopping with her. She and I wore the same size, 10AAA, not a real easy size to find anywhere. She had beautiful taste in shoes, she loved the Italian leathers in soft colors. All of her clothes were in soft colors, peaches and lilacs. At 10 she even let me try on the expensive shoes "so I would know what good shoes feel like". And she saved all of her old peach silk slips for me, because she knew how I loved them. And when my mother said" no "to Jeans, she took me shopping and bought me my very first pair of stonewashed straightlegged Lees. And she taught me how to patch them with beautiful scraps, confessing that she wished she could have been younger to wear them. She also bought me my first Carly Simon, and Beatles albums. She understood what a young soul needed.

The summer I was ten I had a bad summer full of normal childhood sufferings, and one night she came in and stroked my head and asked what was wrong. I sniffled "too much". And she continued stroking my head, "Even when Everything seems at it's darkest, it's not. And even when you feel the most alone, someone will always Reach Out, remember that." I have always wondered how she knew What to say, and that I needed to hear that.

We remember what we need and it finds us when we need it. And it reaches us even through the darkest and stormiest of nights.

[Click the title, it is Johnny Mathis singing "Chances Are"]

* [Other posts on Flo include "April 1968" and also" Grandmother Flo].

AUGUST 22, 2007, WEDNESDAY

WHEN THE TRUTH IS MILES AWAY...

* * *

I spend way too much time looking for the Truth, and especially the Truth about Iraq, and it is not just that it Miles Away, it is not being told to us properly on a Daily basis. At times I think it has merely become a Covert Mission that occasionally get propagandized for Republican Glory Events. But we aren't getting the Truth, we are being spoonfed lies daily, and most of us know it.

I was digging around on YouTube last night. I was actually looking for 911 Footage to see if Iraq is mentioned in those early days after 911? (It was to settle that question that has been rattling around my head now for monthes). And I ended up looking at 911 Footage again. And what haunts me is that the footage from that day, we really were on OUR Own, it was the First Katrina if we think about it. I mean literally for hours we had NO REAL Accurate Information. And the people that got us through that day were actually "Journalists", on CNN there was Arron Brown, and on ABC there was Peter Jennings. And what I remember is that both of them STILL even in that Castrohphic Moment, they still knew HOW to ASK Questions and they did not try to Edit or even Editoriliize the Moment. They just ran the live feed and the footage as it came and they asked questions when they could get Someone on the Phone. Even though it was painful they strove for accuracy. They aired the Reality of the Moment.

Arron Brown was just starting at CNN, matter of fact that was his first day. All day and most of that week that is who we watched on my street in

Watergate Summer

the Northwest. Arron is teaching Somewhere now. And Peter Jennings has died from Lung Cancer, but there is still a Journalistic Chasm there.

* * *

And now to my point I was thinking about Vietnam and WHAT really Brought the reality of War Home. It was not just the Statistics, or that the Draft, or that the Middle Class had had it. It was the REALITY OF IT ON TV everyday, every night for many monthes, People could NOT take IT anymore. But it was not just the Pictures, and footage, it was the Journalists Let the FACTS speak and they aired IT, ALL OF IT, even the BODY Bags,the Bodies, the Tears, and the Blood. The Government did NOT Dictate the News, Censor it, or Edit It, or Control It. They Do Now. THIS HAS TO STOP, and WE MUST STOP IT.I have some ideas in September how we can pressure the News Medias (and no not Faux, but others). It is one thing to Have Us Numbed Up, and it is another to have us Numbed Up and Dumbed Down. And we are not going to get OUR Country back and End a War until we work on Both Problems. And Also WE NEED THE MSM to start being Responsible and Accurate.

During the Week of Katrina in 2005 We had REAL News Again, and it made all of us look inside of ourselves and each other and DC alot harder, and Finally A Real Event was properly documented for the sake of History. We need More of THAT. (And the media should have learned that their Ratings Soared. And it was better when we were not told to go out and "shopping").I KNOW Keith Olbermann has had a huge Impact, but we need MORE. And we need it NOW and we need it on Iraq and we need it NOW.

And here's Why, because some parts of the Country are not much different than the 1970s'. Not everyone has cable and not everyone has the Internet. It is up to the rest of us to Help Advocate and Educate the Others. And make the Media do their Job again, instead of the Infotainment Crap, we NEED Real Journalism Again. The Reality is the Truth, and we all need it NOW.

* * *Click Title: "Gimme Shelter", Rolling Stones, and it is a historical Perspective of Vietnam.I also need to say because of the number of Iraq

Vet families that come to this site, and the Number of VETS that come I try hard NOT to post images that are painful. My blog is about many things—healing, soulfood, comfort. And yes,at times I do write about the pain and mess of ALL of this, but because We Need Change as a Country.If you are a VET don't watch this video. If you are 18 and want to enlist—watch the Video. *   *   *

SEPTEMBER 30, 2007, SUNDAY

THOUGHT FOR A NEW WEEK....

* * *

My Grandmother Flo used to say this all the time "Never Give Up".... and it got me in the habit of saying it. She would go stand on her porch and stare at the moon, and I would hear her muttering it. I said it when I ran High Hurdles on an all Boys Team, thanks to Title IX back in the Seventies. I said it when I waited tables with a less than graceful attitude. I said it as I worked and cursed Full Moons in the ER. I said it when taking care of the AIDS patients in the Seattle Hospice in the 80's and 90's. I said it when I was in labor with the world's largest watermelon. I said it when the EPA officials lied to me about "how Safe" my little Town's Drinking Water was, yet they drank canned soda at the meetings in 2002. (and the US Attorney's office called my home to make sure I had gotten home "safe").

I learned to say this phrase at the worst moments, say it quietly, say it to those around you . . . just say it.

I had a Bad Week last week. I had a bad eye Bleed that is still healing, and I guess my Invincibility Cape got torn. I don't think women that blog should have to put up with Harrassment and Death "Wishes" just for Writing a Blog, yet that is the Age we live in. But I learned something Valuable. I learned that there are still Good People in this World, and they have Courage and Wisdom they are willing to share, and that inspires me. So I am repairing that Torn Cape . . . .

BUT I am still Here. And alot of people have Bad Weeks. But This Week will be better. It is Sunday Night and I walked the Dog, and it was a beautiful moon and I could hear Grandmother Flo say" Never Give Up."

NOVEMBER 18, 2007, SUNDAY

THE KILLING FIELDS ARE HERE, OVER 100 VET SUICIDES PER WEEK HERE, GO TO CROOKS AND LIARS AND SEE THE WHOLE STORY

I have wondered for quite a while WHAT the Actual VET Suicide rate is, I read the Obits here in Ohio, and I suspected for over 3 years as I lived all over the Country that Something was Wrong. I have said this before, DEAD PEOPLE DON'T LIE, THE ANSWERS ARE ALWAYS IN THE OBITS. The Other HUGE issue attached to this Story is that we have a PTSD problem here in the US.And the VET Suicide rate for 2005 ALONE was more than 125 A WEEK Across the Country . . . . That is over 6500 for that year alone, MORE died here at Home than In Iraq, in that year alone . . . . CBS did their own Investigation, and went state by state tracking the Stats on their Own, the Federal Level failed miserably when questioned for Data and FOIA'd. Watch this story, learn More, Someone's Live May Depend on it. And Lets See if CNN has enough Balls to bring it to the Debate tonight.

[Buscho should not just be Impeached, they should indeed be Tried For Crimes Against Humanity]

*   *   *On November18th, I will have a post up about PTSD . . . . and Suicide Signs*   *   *

NOVEMBER 18, 2007, SUNDAY

VET SUICIDE RATES: PART II OF THE CBS VET SUICIDE STORY:CLICK THIS TITLE

(originally posted 11.16.07)

About Suicide:

I am posting this series here. I also have to say I did get emails about this Post and the Suicide Issue. As a nurse, I have worked Psych, and ER, and also Homecare,and with PTSD VETS, where I learned more about suicide that maybe I should share this weekend as Thanksgiving Holiday approaches. The tricky part of this is that PTSD indeed might have different suicidal patterns and warnings and clues, so please bear with me as I explore this. Please know that if Someone you love is exhibiting ANY signs that concern you or worry you, please get them help, if that means going to a local ER,or Mental Health Specialist, then do it. Many of the Reports that I have read involved Time Lapsing while someone waited to be able to have a loved one seen at the VA. If you have someone that you feel is in crisis, do not wait to take them to the ER, atleast this also sends a messege that you Value this person, that YOU would never make them Wait. There are two times when Suicide Rates are up, when VET is home on leave for holiday or vacation or when VET has returned from assignment.

*{FACTOID: Important as of 2006 there were over 100,000 Disability Claims filed for PTSD, only one third are from the Gulf War, the rest are from this era Iraq and Afganistan. That is a large number—and how many are getting propercare and support, and meds, we don't know. National Guard Troops that were there at the start only had health care for TWO years, so

most of the ones with PTSD are on the street or homeless, and I have not been able to find suicide numbers—but I am working on it.Considering 25% of all Homeless are VETS, this number is important.}*

Warning Signs:

Important: These signs are those that a nurse has noticed over 20 years, but I am not a Doctor, if you notice any of these, or more than one think about getting this peron help, and not necessarily from the VA, get to a good ER or psychiatrist that specializes in ANXIETY disorders, PTSD is NOT a Mood Disorder. VETS are being told that they have "mood Disorders", this also means that they are not being given MUCH needed Anxiety meds, and they are being told that they have a pre-exisiting condition, so that the VA actually does not feel responsible to treat the PTSD. If the Person has the symptoms below, they need help—immediately—not in 6 monthes or 4 weeks, and they need care, not a PTSD assesssment, they need meds and psychotherapy, support and professional care. (The families usually need help too).

(1) Obvious Depression Symptoms (which also can be a part of PTSD). Altered Sleep patterns (this can include too much or too little, and difficulty getting to sleep, or using substances to get to sleep).Dead Eyes, Altered eye contact. Altered sense of humor or ability to connect. Person limits contact with others,seperating or "Caves". Person seems disconnected, angers at people suggesting connection or asking too many questions. (Alternating Caving with Clinging—as one commenter has mentioned).

(2) Emotionally this person can also cry, or be quiet pensive. Atleast offer once a day, softly, and quietly without pressure "Do you want to talk?" and watch the response, but keep offering every day. If you give up trying the person sees that as you have given up on them. It can also be a rollercoaster, huge emotional swings—silence to rages, but what is noted is lack of pattern, and control. It is important that you remain calm and nonjudgemental and give unconditional support and care, remember it is not the person crying and lashing out in pain—it is the Illness, and it is a very serious illness.

(3) Patterns of care, does the person bath, care for self, and that includes eating and drinking fluids, are they connected to their own needs. This

also includes substance issues, are they only drinking or taking pills to numb themselves and forgetting to eat.

(4) Is there anything that seems odd? Are they putting everything in order, cleaning and tidying, and giving away Belongings. Apologizing to old friends, People that have planned a suicide for a long time will go to great extremes to put everything in order. Watch for this. Are they writing alot of letters and journaling excessively.

(5) Is there Reckless Behavior going on, more than usual. Sex, Drugs, or Driving, or "playing" with guns, or knives. (If you notice anything that rings a bell with this—Be Proactive—remove the Pills from home, remove the Knife or Gun Collection, don't take them hunting, and put Keys away after 9pm, LIMIT Risks).

(6) The TV clue: Are they connected to what they are watching and interested at all, or are they just staring, watch what they watch, and just note, whether it be CNN, or game shows, or Violent movies. Look for patterns.

Suicide Prevention:

IF you have concerns, please talk to another family member or friend, you will need a team and a plan to help someone that is thinking of Suicide. Remember this, the person might have been planning for quite awhile, they will not want to be confronted, they may even be angry, defensive. You can ask:" are you okay?" If they vocalize at all" I don't want to be here or I can't do this anymore", keep them talking, get them to talk as much as you can. It is about being gentle and if you keep them talking and let them know that they are loved, the chances increase considerabley to get them the help or care they need.

** { Other posts and blogs to read Lulu Maude at "Take Your Medicine", Spadoman about PTSD, and" From the Left" and also Jim over at Average American Patriot, all have revelant posts up about PTSD and VA "care".}**

If you have more suggestions or observations or need more info please email enigma4ever@earthlink.net.

NOVEMBER 22, 2007, THURSDAY

SO THANKFUL 11.22.07

* * *

"Love is a great Beautifier" Louisa May Alcott

* * *

I am so thankful . . . grateful for so much. I am thankful that my son really is a Gentle Giant, in all of his 6-6 glory, that he has a big heart and a good soul, and that even though he is a teenager, and I annoy him, he knows that I love him. I am thankful that the sick cat arrived, wandered into his life and keeps him such gentle company . . . . I am thankful that we found this old Victorian Wreck of a House that needed so much work and so much love, that has been so good for us. I am thankful for the battered old porch and the garden and fresh dirt . . . . And I guess I am happy that my Downtown Loft Building did Foreclose, as it made me find us a New Home. I am thankful for this lovely old neighborhood with such nice neighbors . . . . and all of the trees, birds, possums and skunks . . . . I am thankful that 6-6's dad got to come this past summer and stay a WHOLE month, it was heaven. I am thankful that I survived 2005 and finally recovered most of what was damaged, I am so lucky . . . I am thankful that I have made so many wonderful friends here in Blogland that have been so good to me and my son over these past 2.5 years . . . . Very Grateful . . . . very.

May your day be full of wonder, food, football, friends . . . and hugs.

So Thankful . . . for so much . . . I would love to give everyone a hug . . . .

I know there is alot wrong . . . but I also know that I am so lucky . . . . so grateful for all that I have . . . very.

I will be back on Friday.

Namaste.

DECEMBER 12, 2007, WEDNESDAY

MY OPRAH STORY 12.12.07

* * *

So this past weekend I watched the 3 day Oprah/Obama-Bonanza . . . . It was truly stunning and amazing. Crowds of people showed up in three seperate states, braving horrendous weather. What amazed me was how powerful Michelle, Barack and Oprah all were each in their own way, and that they spoke of Matters of the Heart and things that really mattered. I was stunned at how many people showed up, the crowds were so diverse full of so many different ages and backgrounds, and that moved me . . . .

The other thing that moved me was Oprah, I have linked her amazing speech to the Title, as her speech was one of the best I have ever seen. Watching that speech gave me more than Hope, it gave me Courage. It made me cry . . . . partly because I knew her when she was a Local Baltimore Celebrity on her way to bigger things, and when her life was not so wonderful. I knew her before she had a Real Voice, I knew her before everyone admired her. I knew her when her Life was Shifting. And to this day I wonder if she would remember someone like me . . . . (this is a longer post, but a inspiring story, so have some tea . . . and a good read, consider this a gift).

Oprah got much of her start in Baltimore. Many don't realize this, but she really was always meant to do Daytime Talk, it was more than a niche . . . it was her Fate. In Baltimore she worked on a show with another commentator named Richard Sher, it was an odd collaboration, and did not fully allow her skills to show or shine. I suspect that it was heavily scripted and over produced.

And I know that when Oprah worked on that show, she might not have happy or fulfilled. I think it was difficult for her, and painful at times.

Now How do I know this?

In the early 1980's as I saved for Nursing School I waited alot of tables and lifeguarded. (I have worked since I was 15 many many jobs, some stranger than other, but waitressing was just one skill). At that time I was working at Cross Keys Inn, and there was a little resturante that served all meals at the Inn, called the Roost. I worked as part of the Service Staff, so I did room service, banquets, and parties, waitressing and bartending. I liked the Roost the best, because it was a nice cozy little cafe with alot of Regulars. The Roost would be the first place that I would silently tend to the queen of Daytime, the Second Location is where I did something for her that would change a part of her life.

At the Roost, I wore my little hideous Bright Overly Cheerful Orange Uniform. I worked hard to like that horrible uniform. (Any redhead will tell you that Redheads should not ever wear Bright Orange). I worked alot of breakfast and lunches, and alot of weekend eves. I took good care of my regulars, many consistently sat in my section over and over. Oprah and her TV friends and co workers sat in my section over and over. I used to save a booth for Oprah certain days of the week, so that she could get in and out without disrupting her work schedule, she only had to ask one time. I used to do little things for my tables, like pick flowers on the way to work, or leave peppermints in a bowl. I had this theory that if I gave some ominance that my tips would improve and that people would have a nicer meal.

Oprah would come 2-3 days a week for a late lunch, and she would get the same meal everytime. She really did struggle with her weight. I admired how hard she worked on this issue, she would order a Salad Niscoise, light dressing, tuna with rye crisp melba toast, and iced tea with extra lemon wedge and 2 Sweet& Low packets. I would give her extra tuna sometimes, and always fresh cut lemons. She was always impecaably dressed, so I always made sure that there were extra napkins. She was very ladylike, with perfect makeup, and beautiful nails and hands. (When you are a tomboy like me, these ladylike qualities always impress me). And sometimes on

Fridays she would come and get a Chocolate Sunday. And there were times I noticed that even behind the bright smile, there was sadness in her eyes. And I have to say, that of all my Regulars, she was one that inspired me to take good care of her. I am not even sure why, but I felt that not enough people had appreciated or been kind to her.

I worked there at the Roost and The Inn for a couple of years, and then moved on to other jobs that paid better, and my Regulars became a thing of the past, slipping into my grey matter folds.

During Nursing School, I ended up working at a Trendy Fashion Store. I was a starving nursing student, and during those years I also did some modeling. The Trendy store partly hired me because I could model clothes for Special Clients. The Gig was that I would model Potential Clothes and then the managers would order the Clothes directly from Stores and Designers in New York City. The Special Clients included Baltimore Celebrity Women of different jobs and backgrounds. There were atleast three local Baltimore TV anchors and TV personalities. The Management would meet with the Client, and then order preliminary clothes ever season, and when they arrived, the Model would model them for the Client, and the Client would pick what they did and did not like. And then orders were placed. I was encouraged to be postive and encouraging, and for orders placed I did not get a commission, but I did get a discount if I wanted to purchase Irregulars Designer Clothes.

So this would be the Second Location that my path would cross Oprah. She was still in TV, but I did notice that she was not really happy, and to be honest I dreaded her visits, because to be honest these clothes ordering sessions made her miserable. She was polite and very quiet, but her eyes looked sad. Then during one ordering season I came to work and the Manager took me aside and showed me a collection that she had chosen with Oprah and had just arrived that they wanted me to model some of it, and also pieces of it for her to try on. I was told to be very postive, as Oprah was a facing a life changing job Interview in Chicago. That these clothes were part of her potential Daytime Hostess Audition. I was very moved by that and slightly worried.

In the early 1980's there was not much for women, especially during the daytime. There was an abundance of cooking shows, and Phil Donahue, but really not any Women Shows, and NO women of Color on during the day. I will be honest I was rooting for Oprah as soon as I heard that this Challenge was on her Path. And yes, in my gut I did, a skinny little shop girl KNEW how important that was. So I stood in the back and put the clothes together, adding accessories (scarves and jewelery). And I was more than worried, the Colors were Horrendous. I tried to talk to the Manager, but she was all swept up in the Moment and convinced that the Collection was "dramatic" and "exciting". I tried tactfully to explain to her, my Boss, that the Colors were Terrible, that it needed to be changed, evaluated and re-examined. I was told to be quiet, and not "Cause Trouble".

So Oprah arrived, nervous, and tense. So I modeled some and she modeled some. And there was much hemming and hauling about WHAT to order, what to wear. And What Accesories would look best or "highlight" each outfit. Inside I was so devastated, and sickened. Finally at the end of this grueling afternoon, I could hold it no longer, I had to say Something. So I explained as best as I could that the Electric Melon Colors in Silk were NOT flattering to her, they were dramatic, but not in a good way, I explained that it made her look well, "Clownlike, You want to be remembered, but not like this." She stared at me stunned. Probally wondering why this skinny little thing was being Soooo critical. And then she burst out laughing, and she has has great laugh. "Oh My, you're that skinny little tuna girl from that resturante aren't you??" I could have died of embarrassment, but I nodded shyly and said yes. And then I explained, "I really want you to get this job, you deserve it, they need to see how elegant you are, how strong. I don't want anyone to laugh at you. I am sorry, I am trying to help". I had brought some soft elegant scarves to the Dressing Room, for her to see the soft chenilles of pale champagne, soft elegant mauve, and soft sunset blue. She nodded quietly, said she would think on it.

I obviously caught holy hell from my Boss for being "impertinent", and within weeks I quit the Trendy Dress Shop as my school load increased and when my great Aunt Elizabeth became sick and died . . . . And I did not give a second thought to Oprah, but over the years I have wondered did she hear what I said to her, did it help her Big Moment. I like to think that it did.

* * *

Epilogue:

The Rest they say is History, Oprah went on to become so famous and so loved, as was always her due. I always knew that she was meant to shine . . . . she made a deep impression on me as a young woman in my early 20's . . . . She was more than Memorable, she was inspiring. And I am proud to say that I crossed her path . . . .

DECEMBER 29, 2007, SATURDAY

SATURDAY NIGHT POST OF 2007

* * *

No Pin Up Girls tonight . . . . just me . . . . and I have Something to say.

This Blog is many things . . . . It is a Cafe where people sit and think and talk to each other. For me it a place where I blog about the things that matter in our lives and try to give some Hope Back . . . . I like to think that in the end that I have given something back to Blogatopia, that I have created a Circle of People, maybe even a Circle of Hope . . . . that I have created a small Haven of Humanity, that I have helped us keep our Souls Intact . . . . that I have always remembered WE THE PEOPLE.

All I have ever asked here is that People be good to each other here, and that you all read what I post and listen to the Music, and listen with your heart, not just your head. This is not a Blog for Intellectual Battling it is a place to find Refuge from those kind of Blogs. I am so grateful for all that have come here and formed this Circle over the years.

It is not enough for me to blog about Bushco Criminal Crimes and these Dark Times that I do truly understand in ways that are unimagineable. I have to blog about the realities of our lives, but as a HippyChild of the Sixties, Mom, a Nurse, a Scorched WhistleBlower, I like to think that I have done it with some Heart. and with Integrity . . . . and that Soul Tending will help us all Fight On . . . . and save what is left of OUR Tattered Country. We are Living through Broken times, and our Government is Broken, my hope is that I can help Heal some of that Brokeness here on this little blog.

Allie McNeil

I am asking that you listen to this Song, the" Boxer" by Simon and Garfunkel that I have linked to the Title, I am indeed one of the Ragged People with a Story that is Seldom Told . . . . but I am using this Blog to also tell the Story of Our Times and Our People. I hope and pray that in the New Year we are able to achieve some Real Change to heal this Country and the Damage that has been created for the world under the Bush Regime. We can not rewrite History, but we can make Our Own. I am so grateful to all of you for coming and sharing and being a part of this Blog. You are the Salt of the Earth.

Namaste.

JANUARY 23, 2008, WEDNESDAY

MOONMONGERING 1.23.08

* * *

It is so beautiful out . . . . There is a beautiful Moon . . . it is sitting up there looking so inviting . . . . and there is this lovely bit a wispy veil that keeps floating across . . . So I laid on my bed this eve and looked out the window . . . . I have this amazing window . . . . (I decorated it after I took 6-6's tree down).I hung the Handmade Beaded Ice Sickle Ornaments on a Silver Ribbon and White Christmas Lights and I made lovely Snow Flakes from orgami paper that are painted with glitter and shimmery paint. But the best part in the winter is that the Moon sits right in the Middle. (In the summer it is a Treehouse Window with leaves abound). I had an amazing day with my son, the kind of day where we really really talked . . . about all kinds of things that Matter: from Unexpected Death of a young actor, to Making Really Wonderful movies (he wants to be a director), and music (why disco sucks), and WHY he wishes he could Vote in the Next Election (which he can't—he is too young.)

We watched SpidermanIII, and we talked about watching it be filmed. In 2006 It was filmed in Downtown Cleveland, at the time we lived in Downtown Cleveland, and it was filmed ON OUR STREET. It was very exciting, and we used to go get Starbucks snacks, and hit the curbs, and watch as they set up scenes and fix up the sets and FILM. It was very exciting in kind of a slow methodical way, but as 6-6 wants to make Movies it was a helluva learning experience . . . . He loved it in a quiet critical way. We moved from downtown a year ago, because our Loft Buiding got Foreclosed, we were very lucky to find another home. But we do both miss the Loft . . . and we loved seeing our old Street all gussied up for the Film.

Allie McNeil

Today we ate too much popcorn and drank too much Diet Pepsi . . . . and we laughed as we looked at our old Street. Which was the best Medicine, the laughter or the Moon. I may never know . . . . I don't think I need to know . . . . (The Moon knows it is the Boy with the Blue Eyes that makes me laugh . . . and warms my heart.)

*   *   *{ If you have children or grandchildren, this video attached to the Link will make you smile . . . . it is Snow Patrol, a song my son loves, it is about Growing Up . . . . and growing with your children . . . it is from the Soundtrack of Spiderman III, it is called Signal Fire}*   *   *

FEBRUARY 28, 2008, THURSDAY

BARACK OBAMA AND WHY HE MATTERS TO SO MANY AND TO MY SON AND ME . . . .

Originally posted 1.05.07 6am: This Post will stay at Top of Page

UPDATE: 2.23.08

I had a really really bad Day yesterday and ended up spending a huge chunk of it in the ER, and we know since I am uninsured that will be so costly.I had a really bad fall and bruised my HipBone, atleast we "think" it is not broken . . . . long story. BUT ALL I do KNOW is that I have tickets for 6-6 and I to see Obama tonight . . . and we are going . . . . Because Obama matters to Both of us, more than I can say.

* * *

{ Originally posted 1.6.08 }

* * *

{{{(Explanantion: I am just asking that people watch the Video attached to the Title, and think about What we have lost these past 7 years, and and what we need to heal. I support a Obama Team,In 2004 he gave the Speech at the Democratic Cinvention, this video is made from the speech-it is clips woven together.(I encourage you all to go see the WHOLE speech on Youtube, parts 1&2, it is about 15 minutes total on Youtube, video here is 4 minutes.) The Media has spent alot of time showing Hillary speeches, but I wanted folks to be able to see a piece of Who he is. Just for this weekend I wanted people to be able to think on this and see him. We don't have to agree . . . . that's okay . . . . as long as we all are thinking about our future. I also posted this video because many people abroad don't know about him.And they too are worried about our future.}}}

In 2004 as an Exiled Refugee Whistleblower in my own Country I was living in an old dilapitated Rooming House in California with my son.By the Time we had gotten there, we had lost Friends, a Home, pets,Meaningful Work, and a marriage of many years, ALL Under the Bush Regime.And in many ways Faith was Lost, Faith in Justice, and Faith in Our Own Government. We were just one family of Millions that have suffered under This Regime. But that summer my son was very invested in the Election, we watched Cspan, Crossfire, and read everything we could. We were Huge John Edwards Supporters in 2004 and still are today. I was trying to desperately teach my son that we were still part of Our Country . . . but Hope was beyond fragile at that point.I Like so many Other Americans, Under the Bush Regime had Lost Everything . . . . and yes, I was indeed Hung Out to Dry by my Government . . . . So I was Looking for Something . . .

Someone to say This Is Not Forever, There is Change . . . .

In 2004 Barack Obama spoke at the 2004 Democratic Convention . . . . I was standing washing dishes and I heard this Voice From the TV and this Voice spoke of E.Pluribus Unum and Unity. Out Of Many We Are One. I stopped what I was doing and with my son I watched the TV and we listened. And 6-6, barely a teen, said "He should be President". He still believes that.

I never ever forgot That Moment.

Please watch the Video in the Link, it has Highlights of that 2004 Speech. (when you go to watch it, on YouTube you can see Parts 1&2. Please watch ALL of it.) And if you have time go get the Book "The Audacity of Hope", his Book. I bought it for myself for Christmas last year . . . . That book has given my son and I something to Hold On To . . . Hope.

But Since living here since 2005, I have watched and seen so many others that need Hope and to no longer be disenfranchised and Invisible. Homeless VETS with PTSD that I worked with downtown, the people losing homes by the thousands (Slavic Village is just ONE devastated neighborhood), More than 250,000 Unemployed Factory Workers, and So Many young people whose schools are in shambles . . . . But So Much of the pain I see we have seen across the Country . . . . So many people needing Hope . . . and to feel Empowered and a part of the Country . . . again.

But this is not just about us.I tell my pieces of my tale here on this blog, because for People that Feel Left Behind, Abandoned, Disenfranchised by this Government he represents Something. I have been watching him and he Connects. He Reaches Out. He Cares.He has Vision. He Has Courage. He Has Hope.

* * *

(I wrote this post because I got many emails from so far away, Canada to Thailand asking me, WHO is Obama?This is WHO he is . . . . Spread This News and Spread the Hope.)

MAY 28, 2008, WEDNESDAY

PTSD: ATLEAST 40,000 VETS CURRENTLY SUFFERING, HUGE RISE IN PAST 3 YEARS

* * *

For many years I known this Painting is susposed to represent the Creation of Adam, yet to me I see Something totally different. I see it as a metaphor about Relationships, that at times they are fragile, so fragile that people can barely touch,barely connect. I also see the crack behind their hands, and I see that as HOPE, because even though things are fractured, cracking at the foundation, they are still able to reach, with the Hope of touch and connection.

* * *

{{UPDATE: Originally This Post was published on November 18,2007, it was to help families as Thanksgiving and Vacations and Leaves approached. PTSD Stats have been difficult at Best to locate. This Week in the News it has finally been revealed that PTSD has risen sharply, the VA is claiming that 40,000 are battling the Disorder. from Iraq alone. How accurate this is, is questionable. in 2006 it was revealed that almost 100,000 are on Disablility due to the disorder, and new stats reveal a 50% rise since 2005/2006.Hopefully the new numbers are more accurately assessing the victims suffering this from Afganistan, Iraq and first Gulf War.}}

Background of PTSD:

This Anxiety Disorder needs so much more study and serious examination and people who are willing to explore how to help those ill with it as well as their families. It is not a mood disorder, or an underlying personality disorder. The Government and the Military are funding HUGE studies right now trying to prove that it is a pre-existing condition and that it needs mood disorder or schizophrenic medications. This is a huge disservice to those suffering with it. It is also indeed a longterm disorder, not a short term or merely a temporary condition. It is an Epidemic of Crisis Proportions right now and not even being statistically monitored properly by the VA, and the National Guard that have returned home with it are only receiving healthcare for 2 years upon discharge, after that they have no Care for mental, neurological, or physical deficits or damage caused by their service to Our Country in a War Zone.

In 2006 Over 100,000 VET Disability Claims had been filed for PTSD, even though thousands went through the assessment process, many are still awaiting only limited care. the VA lacks caregivers and Trained Professionals to treat and care for the suffering. Yet they are willing to spend 38 Million to Study it and prove it is a Mood Disorder, that means VETS are being denied care so that the Govt and the Military have an opportunity to Inaccurately "prove" it is a Mood Disorder and Pre-Existing Condition. Meanwhile in 2005 alone more than (Please do see the two previous posts on Suicide below) 6500 VETS committed Suicide, I can not help but wonder HOW MANY had PTSD, how many needed desperately to get Care and Treatment? How Many had been told that they were not Ill? How Many even died waiting for an Assessment or care?) PTSD is Not a "Mood Disorder or a pre-Existing Condition", it is a Anxiety Disorder that is Triggered by Stress or Trauma.It is also to be evaluated with exposure to IED Explosions in Iraq, whether some of those that are suffering symptoms are also suffering brain trauma and neurological damage.

The other issue is that People with these symptoms or that have had head trauma as well, should be treated as though they have Neurological Damage and should not be returning to service, and should not be carrying firearms. And many of the VETS are being reordered to the Front or

Battlezones without proper care or even a proper assessment. Many that have PTSD and attempt to return to normal Homelife or Previous Work are struggling, and many can not work due to concentration problems, yet they are sent back to the Front? This may indeed have much to do with the Huge VET Suicide Rates.

If you take someone for care, be sure to look for Mental Health Professionals that specialize in Anxiety Disorders. I am not a Doctor, I am a nurse, I am merely trying to provide Public Health Information in a time of a National Healthcare Crisis.But please use this blog as a stepping stone to do more research and pursue better data. I also have to say some of this research is from being research done as a nurse, and some is learned from Downtown Cleveland Homeless VETS with PTSD. For those families living with it, please do email me enigma4ever@earthlink.net if you notice symptoms I have missed. Thank you.

* * *

SIGNS AND SYMPTOMS OF PTSD:

(1) Depression & Withdrawal:

Many people will say that the person appears withdrawn, or even barely connected, or say that their eyes were dead and there as a flat effect or even an absence of emotion.

(2) Jitters/nerves/ shakiness/nervous tics:

People have noticed that there may be tics, or shaky hands or extremities, the tic may be the eyes, or head region or their entire body. Some that have had head trauma—it is unclear which is causing the uncontrolled movement.

(3) Substance Abuse/Reckless Behavior:

Many that are showing any of the symptoms on here, and especially who are not receiving treatment or care may start to pursue self medication or anesthesia, especially ones that are having sleep difficulties. All manner of drugs may be pursued to dull senses and memories, and toleration will exceed old norms. It is not just that Drugs or Alcohol are being used as an Escape. I also include in this category, Reckless behavior (there are enough Single Car accidents here, involving trees and Alcohol, that I have been curious if this issue has been examined). Be proactive, remove excess alcohol and hide keys if needed.And the same goes for guns in home.

(4) Nightmares and Flashbacks (Effected Sleep Patterns):

Both of these occur, and sometimes simultaneously, which means also that for some people, especially if they are sleep deprived and have been for long periods it effects reality and distorts events and perceptions.

(5) Relationship Problems:

After many monthes from home, with others that may suffer or suffering, they are unable to relate to ordinary life and also feel "Alien".(What is needed is more support groups for those that have returned to encourage that they support each other and know that they are not alone, and that their feelings are "normal" and shared.)

(6) Anxiety Attacks:

Random and also ones that seem perdictable, The random ones cause more frustation and discomfort for all. There were Propananol studies ongoing, and Inderal to study the effects that these drugs had on lowering heart rate and adrenalin reactions to events(they had good effect, yet I can find no current VA studies on these drugs). but be sure to have the persons' heart rate and EKG done, as well as BP, as many are returning with High BP.

(7) Inability to pay attention(Job performance effected):

Concentration is alter, even on minor tasks, so driving and other more major tasks should be monitored with care.

(8) Mood Swings:

This runs the gamut, if you are concerned, start logging and track so that you can try to look for triggers or events or try to find things that provide comfort and stabilty. You might not. You also may have to let the VET find for himself what brings comfort, it maybe just sitting on a bench on the porch, and be sure to always offer to be there, alot of this is letting the person knowing that they are cared for, they are used to being hated and scrutinized, but you need to observe quietly and try not to ask too many questions, but just be available to talk, and be a good Listener, and be willing to listen and know that it might be hard to hear—but they need you to be willing.

* * * Also upon return or Holidays, be sure to check WHAT they want—they may want lots of rest and peace and quiet, not a ton of visitors and Parties, they may not feel up to it. (Fatigue is a part of the mood changes).

(9) Memory Problems (Short term)

There are many different kind of problems with memory, short term to long term, Short Term tends to be more common, do not be surprised if they can not remember holidays and day to day celebrations. Be patient.

This list is some of what you may see and what you can do to help. If you see more than one of these start documenting and logging (you don't have to tell them). And talk to another friend or family member and try to come up with a plan to help this person and start planning to get them supportive professional help that I mentioned above. I know the VA Assessment Wait is 6 months or longer, I recommend that you get them care, even if you have to take them to sliding scale Mental Health Clinic, and with that you are letting them know that you care, and YOU would never make them wait. You can always keep receipts and Bill the Federal Government later. And especially if they exhibit any of the Suicide symptoms below, get help right away, do not wait.

Tomorrow at this Blog: Support for the PTSD Families and Caregivers.

{Music in the title: Natlie Merchant "What's the Matter Here"}

JUNE 19, 2008, THURSDAY

KING GEORGE'S REGIME ONCE AGAIN FLOODED WITH INCOMPETENCE

{Cross Posted over at Sirens Chronicles on wed.6.18.08}

* * *

This Summer again has proven that at this rate as we all have known since 2005, we should all keep an Ax and blow up rowboat in the attic. The Current Flooding in the Midwest is one example of Disaster Unpreparedness at it's absolute worst (and I say that with no disrespect to the thousands working to sandbag and people there working to save their homes, farms and communities and businesses).

People say that the Flooding in the Midwest is not as bad Katrina. I have to disagree. There are hundreds of miles and thousands of acres effected in 6 states. Where you really see the scope of this is looking at aerials (photos and video). I find it interesting the MSM has shown very little of these aerials, if they did people would realize the staggering enormity of this situation. The Heartland is in some ways like Katrina, this is not a wealthy region, this is Middle America at it's finest, small towns and rural farms. King George should not have been on his "Farewell to Europe" tour, he should have come home and been monitoring this devastation. He should have for once been doing Flyovers and inspecting damage and Potential Damage. He should have ordered Branches of the Military to assist, including Coast Guard and even Airforce could have done aerial assessments. Mulitple crops will be effected, from soybean to corn to basic vegetables. So again Food Prices will suffer.

We have seen very little of FEMA or Chertoff (which in some ways is fine, we do not really need more Brownie Moments). We have not even seen interviews of Red Cross Administration with updates regarding sheltering needs and reports, and really not even any ads. So I am encouraging people to write to the Red Cross, if you donate Specify on your check WHERE you want it to go. Now some of the reporting that has been insufficient might just be a matter of the MSM journalistic inability to properly report other than Propaganda. I also think some of the Media, like CNN worries what Foreigners see and only show what they see fit. (You do have to admit that Katrina atleast they did show the aerials with great concern, and actually embarrassed the president to do his famous "Flyover".)

And finally National Guard and Civil Defense Management should all be in place, as ALL aspects of life there are going to be impacted for thousands of people, from the transportation issues (roads and bridge and raliway damage), to basic needs of living from sheltering to food. It is also important to note that many will be trapped inland with these massive problems. I have seen very few guard at the sandbag line photos. Another question or concern that we should all be asking, do they have enough Guard and Equipment? Or is it all over in Iraq, this is the time to ask. (Please also note that we have seen very few interviews with Governors on TV). And another thing that we can do to help our neighbors in the Midwest is to write and call the MSM and demand better coverage of this event that is not just a "weather phenom" it will impact this entire Country for many monthes to come and thousands of lives are effected.

Some of the other issues to come will be the lack of Fresh Potable water, disease risk from the muddy sewage ridden waters, and insects, as well as other contamination concerns. This also raises Medical Concerns for those in the region, during the clean up process, as well has many that are elderly and not physically up to the clean up challenge. Nothing has been said about Aid that will be there to assist these people, whether it be economic or phyiscal assistance. So once you think on this you can see that Multiple Agencies should have feet on the ground there already, CDC, NOAA, and USGS and Army Corp of Engineers.

When the Bush Regime faces justice for the War Crimes of this Regime, I do hope that one of the aspects they closely examine is the Presidents inablilty to care of Refugees within his own country. His ignorance and incompetent neglect has damaged the lives of thousands, and not all of it can be blamed on the Natural Disasters.Do what you can to help Our Neighbors in the Midwest, be creative and resourceful, they depend on us.Sadly the Sandbags will provide some protection from the waters magnitude, but it will not protect these good people from the Dangerous Incompetence of the Bush Regime.

{{{ Please see Aerial Video Footage below, about one week old. I will post newer footage over at Watergate Summer as I find it. Please know that has a Nurse that has worked Disasters with the Red Cross and had FEMA training, that this post is written with great concern,}}}

JULY 21, 2008, MONDAY

LESSONS FROM OUR CHILDREN . . . .

*   *   *(This story is a bit of a break from Politics of the Moment, but it is about How Our Children are part of teaching us how to Heal what is Broken . . . . and that seems applicable as we look forward during These Times. Originally posted July 2007 Watergate Summer and is Crossposted at PEACE TREE.}*   *   *

*   *   *

The Story of Luther

When my son was small he kept growing excessively, and this threw off his balance and coordination. So this required that he have physical therapy, and speech therapy,occupational therapy, and swimming everyday, and even therapuetic riding. Now we were not rich parents, so this was not something that we had budgeted for when he was a baby. Nurses and teachers don't make alot of money. So my Ex worked alot of overtime and the Enigma fought with the Insurance companies and tried to get things paid for.And we found ways to get the Son what he needed. So there I was in my late 30's negogiating with a Riding Program, offering to clean stalls and take care of horses so he could get the Riding lessons he so badly needed, that helped his balance and coordination. The Horses gave him confidence and touched him in a magical way.

So I learned how to care for the horses, every weekend for a couple of years, I cleaned and cared for 20 horses. I fed them what they needed, gave them pasture time, watered, brushed and yes, even cleaned out their stalls. I learned about laminititis, shoe-ing, and what they could and could not eat. Some were retired Race Horses, and a bit highstrung. So I took courses on Tellington Touch and Massage and learned that these beautiful Creatures were smarter than I and more communicative than most knew.

My Son fell in love with them all, one by one, and he knew what they ate and Who got along with Who. (This was critical when putting horses in fields.). He was 7 and he knew that sometimes they needed to play and he also knew that if we put Chantilly in the one field she would eat too many apples, but it would make her happy. He loved the one big old Black Morgan named Luther. Luther was a big easygoing fellow, and he was not doing well with the riding program because he himself was having coordination problems. My son had great compassion for Luther, because they were bonded on this issue. And in a funny way, my son knew that something was making this problem worse for Luther. And lo and behold he figured it out. One day putting Luther in the field, my son of 7 said, "Ya know, he likes this field, but it's not the plum trees or the apple tree, it's those plants down by the fence, the ones with the berries. Are you sure he can or should be eating those?" I was struck by this, and sat down with my son and watched Luther, and sure enough he beelined for the plants with the berries . . . . And over the weekend, my son was right Luther's co-ordination was definently worse in the evening.

So that weekend we did alot of research and found the Luther Plant in a book, it was Nightshade, and it was indeed poisonous, and could indeed cause Major Coordination issues for horses. So we talked to the Managers and the owners and the Vet, and what was figured out that Luther was going to need PT and OT and lots of care, and to move to another barn and be watched and cared for, and Time to get better. We mentioned to the Vet that ended up adopting Luther that we had been to see the Seattle Police Horses in their barn, on a field trip and that they got beautiful care, and she was intrigued with that idea. And she found a home for him with the Seattle Police Horses. So Luther ended up getting the care he needed, and he got better and he also ended up being a Police Horse with his gentle unflappable disposition. Everytime I see a program on Police Horses I think of this gentle Morgan with the Brown soulful eyes that touched my son's life.

Allie McNeil

My son did a Good Thing that summer . . . . he may not remember it. But I always will.

                              *   *   *

My Son 6-6 is almost grown now . . . and he sees what Trouble this Country is in, How Damaged and Broken it is . . . and he wants to be part of that, part of the repairing . . . the Healing. Many young people across the country, first time voters, want to be part of that, part of Something Bigger. We need to Embrace that . . . . It may be more important than we know.

AUGUST 13, 2008, WEDNESDAY

WE THE PEOPLE . . . .

WE THE PEOPLE . . .

These people are OUR people . . . they are US . . . . and yet we have over 5.1 Million Homeless in this country. OUR Country. this is just so wrong . . . . it is Our Greatest Shame . . . . This video was made with Mandt of Agitdiaries,it was a collaboration . . . . I have been collecting photos of Homeless for over 3 years, so some of these are from all over LA, SF, Portland, Seattle, Cleveland, NOLA and NY and DC . . . . the Song is "Teardrop" written and sung by Liz Frazer and performed by Massive Attack . . . It is a sobering video about People in our own country . . . for me it was about taking photos of my neighbors when I lived in Downtown Cleveland.

(Still live in Downtown—about 2 miles from the heart of the Downtown area . . . but my old loft apt building got foreclosed . . . . so I had to move in winter 2007) . . . But they are still my neighbors.

The Video was a collaboration with Mandt of Agitdiaries, it was a wonderful collaboration . . . . the Photos are from all over, NY, SF, DC,LA, Portland, Seattle,NOLA and yes, Cleveland. The Song is called "TearDrop" by Massive Attack, written by Liz Frazer.

*   *   *

There is more posted over at Peace Tree about Homelessness, and also Sirens Chronicles if you want to read and learn more.

AUGUST 24, 2008, SUNDAY

BALTIMORE . . . . (OR HOW RANDY NEWMAN STOPPED A RIOT DURING A SNOWSTORM)

The Story Behind the Song . . . .

I was telling my son about Baltimore, I have many stories from that era of my life . . . . and I was telling him about my First Randy Newman Concert. It was winter, many years ago and it was bitter cold and snowing . . . . It was in an old Dance Hall, and people showed up mostly for the Main Act which was the Nitty Gritty Dirt Band. Now This was the same year that "Short People" came out and believe it or not Little People would come and protest at Randy's Concerts.

So outside waiting in the snowstorm was the Nitty Gritty Dirt Band Fans (alot of Bikers) and then the Protesting Midgets and Dwarves. And I am not sure why, but they were not getting along. So then the Parrotheads arrived, somehow they were there to see both bands. So they were in their Full Margauritaville Gear with Hawaii Shirts and funny hats. So The Management let all of us in. I was with my sister who was in a DISCO phase and really pissed at me for dragging her to "this dumass circus of a concert". There I sat in my Hippy gear, patched jeans, Indian top, and 2nd hand coat and clogs smoking clove cigarettes. It was not a Sisterly loving event. (I invited her because her date cancelled and I had an extra ticket.)

So the Dance Hall is packed every old battered wooden theater seat is full and Everyone has made their way in, the Pissed Off Little People, the Rowdy Bikers, and the Parrotheads . . . . So the waiting begins.

Well, it turns out that the Nitty Gritty Dirt Band was not coming . . . and would not be coming. And that supposedly their Bus had broken down somewhere. Now the Audience had to be told this . . . . So there are Pissed off Little People marching up and down the aisles, and then now the Bikers were about to be given a bad blow. So a little tiny wisp of a man came out to deliver the bad news . . . .

"I have some troubling news, I am not sure when or if the Nitty Gritty Dirt Band is coming. But if you want to wait for them, because they had some bus trouble, then I am sure they will be here when Randy Finishes playing, Maybe"

His voice cracked and rose off and on, sweat ran down his little face. By the time he was done the Bikers were on their feet yelling "We want our Godamn Money Back NOW!!!!

Meanwhile the Parrotheads have all settled in to watch the show—and are getting stoned and blowing up HUGE Beachballs and bouncing them around the audience. Meanwhile the angry little people are still stomping around the aisles.And the Bikers are now stamping their feet and Yelling and getting ready to Break Something.

My sister sitting there in her leather pants and her Donna Summer tube top was looking disgusted, and "I wish I was anywhere else!!". Someone handed her a Flask and told her "Here Darlin' have some Courage", She mellowed considerably.

And while the Tension rose and the Noise got louder, the Little Man on the stage said, "Without Further ado—I give you Randy Newman" . . . .

So out comes Randy, still putting on his jacket, looking a bit rumpled like he just fell off the bus . . . . He quickly gauged the room . . . and came out on stage and sat at the Piano and started talking . . . . as soothing as a Fine Southern Gentleman, telling the Bikers not to worry that he would keep them happy until The Band arrived, and apologizing to the Little People, and even making nice jokes about his gratitude to the Mysterious Parrotheads and their doobies and beach balls. (No one was even sure why they were there . . .). He had a rambling style like a traveling Medicine Man offering some sweet bottled Sunshine and promises out the back of a wagon as he stroked the piano keys.

He sang it all Blues, Ray Charles, Some Jimmy Buffet, and some Willie Nelson . . . . all of it . . . He used his music to make peace that snowy night . . . .

And this Song was how he began his show . . . .".Baltimore" . . . . a much longer version . . . .

And no the Nitty Gritty Dirt Band never showed . . . . but 20 minutes into Randy telling stories and singing songs Something Wonderful happened . . . .

SEPTEMBER 26, 2008, FRIDAY

THE WASHINGTON MUTUAL BANK DEMISE, A SUMMARY OF ARTICLES AND WHAT IT MEANS. AND WHAT HAPPENS NOW . . .

As many of us had perdicted and worried all summer, Washington Mutual hit the skids on Thursday Night, and was quietly seized by the FEDS FDIC and then sold at Firesale Price to JP Morgan. What happens to all of it's shareholders? investors? mortgages? and it's employees time will tell. One of the Biggest and Oldest Banks in America (read the WIKI article linked to the title). More Information down below about the History of this collapse and longterm implications. I will post more when I have it.

* * *

A Snippet from the Wikipedia:

On September 25, 2008 (the 119th anniversary of WaMu's founding) the United States Office of Thrift Supervision (OTS) announced that it had closed the bank, and had placed it into the receivership of the Federal Deposit Insurance Corporation (FDIC).[3] The FDIC announced that it had sold most of the bank's assets and liabilities, including covered bonds and other secured debt to JPMorgan Chase for $1.9 billion. Claims of equity holders, senior and subordinated debt holders were not acquired by JP Morgan Chase.[4][5] Washington Mutual's government takeover is the largest bank failure in American financial history.[6] Before the collapse, it was the sixth-largest bank in the United States.[7] According to Washington Mutual's 2007 SEC filing, it held assets valued at $327.9 billion. However, its stock declined from a high of $45 per share in 2007 to 16 cents per share on September 25, 2008.

* * *

More on the Actual Collapse and how the Bank fell.

More on the Actual Acquisition by JP Morgan and what it means.

The World Wide Implications are staggering . . . Read this Article in Taiwan Paper it is time to better understand Global Problems that are being triggered from America.

Sadly the Golden Parachutes are still being given out, read about this 13 Million Dollar one (for 18 days of work) he just came in Sept and NOW he is leaving with alot of money weeks later.

SEPTEMBER 28, 2008, SUNDAY

BAILOUT STILL BEING WORKED ON . . . . SUNDAY EVE.

* * *

Still waiting for the Congress and Senate to Work the Bailout Details out . . . . Click the title to read the Entire Current Proposal as of 5PM Sunday there is a "tenative" agreement . . . . Still very unclear When the Vote will occur and if this Plan is Being Agreed to . . . Caucusing right now . . . Watch the Asian markets tonight . . . . This bailout is also about our futures, school loans, and home loans, and mortgages and retirement accounts and funds . . . It is too late to protect us as Mainstreet—we already are vulnerable . . . . The Unraveling has already started, at this point it is about protecting us further. There are NO Good solutions at this point . . . It's like asking a Fireman how you want to throw water on the fire? Big Buckets or a hose?

This Plan effects all of us . . . and the Repugs of the House are NOT looking out for you and me they are looking out for Wallstreet trying to buy them Time and a "Insurance" plan (that would be like people of the 9th ward being Offered Flood Insurance August 29th, 2005 . . . . if you get my point.) They also have Lobbyists to make happy, they don't want Regulations and Oversight and Investigations and Monitoring . . . . I will post updates through the Night, but Huffpost really is doing a good job, but I will add updates from Reuters, WSJ and Bloomberg . . . .

* * * Click the Title for More Information and IT DOES LINK TO HUFFPOST AND THE ACTUAL 130 PG PROPOSAL, BUT IS

Allie McNeil

NOT DOWNLOADABLE—BUT IT DOES LINK—DO ENLARGE TO FULL SCREEN TO READ BETTER .... *   *   *

*   *   *Large European Bank Fails: Fortis .... more to come. More on on Fortis ... and their bailout.

*   *   * I am still looking back through my posts for the Link to the 32 Page Dodd Plan—if anyone has it please leave it on the Comment thread—thanks.

*   *   * More about effects on World Markets and banks abroad as of 9.28.08

Another Bank in Trouble—Britian's Biggest Lender ... critical.

And More about Wachovia which is noew facing being bought out ...

9:30PM two links to try to read the Bailout Huffpost one is 130pgs ... and the Politico is 106? the first version, and the Huffpost version is longer.

12:30 AM HOUSE HEARINGS ON THE BAILOUT BILL ON CSPAN .... interesting ... Slaughter, Dreier, and now Kaptur speaking ...

SEPTEMBER 30, 2008, TUESDAY

AN APOLOGY AND AN EXPLANATION FROM ENIGMA . . . . ME.

I love this photo from the Depression, because the LOOK in the Mother's Eyes, I know too well (Dorthea Lange photo was with the post) . . . If I seem to be blogging my heart out this month . . . . I am. I am partly doing it because the Election, and I am partly doing it because I live on the Edge . . . If you read my post on Sept.29th at 11am you understand . . . my living situation is more than precarious. My work situation is not stable, and I live very frugally simply trying to raise a teenage son, who I want more than anything to send to College and Film School. I worry about all of us, and his Future.

I have no Financial Expertise, I am just a nurse. I am merely watching and blogging these events as best I can so that I can better understand and grasp what is happening. And yes, the Bigger picture for you, me and yes, globally. We have Neighbors in the World. And yes, I know alot of people are like me Living On This Edge, so yes, I blog and share that information. I am not trying to make anyone worry more. I am trying to make certain that we all are better Educated. That we have the information we need to feel strong, informed and never be fearful. Knowledge is Power. Always.

So I just ask for your patience . . . . and know that I blog because I care and yes worry . . . . But I will not ever offer False hope or sugar coat when things are Beyond Rough . . . I would rather be Truthful even in Dark Times. And I am always looking for the Shaft of Light, no matter how Dim, how thin . . . how Precious. I also believe that we are a Community that we prevail as we take care of each other . . . . In Dark times we just hand each other Another Candle . . . and pass it Person to Person . . . .

Beautiful song "These Days" by Natalie Merchant . . . about being on The Edge . . . and still having Hope. (if you click the Title, you can see the Lyrics).

* * *

From Sept.29th post:

On the HomeFront:

More about National City For Ohio Folks to follow.Say a little prayer for 6-6 and me . . . . This is my landlord's bank . . . in January 2007 I moved because our Previous Landlord got foreclosed (we had been living in our Downtown Loft that we loved behind Jacob's Field). So in the Middle of winter, I went searching for a place, in snow and ice, ... and found this battered old house, it was Ten Below Zero, but I got us all moved in. I negotiated the rent and Fixed Every Blessed Inch of it, the Floors, the broken stairs, the holes in the walls, the pee stained walls,fixed up the porch. I even painted the Kitchen Floor Black and white . . . . I made it a Home . . . And this past winter he finally fixed the Heat . . . . It has been nice to have a dining room and here is the Cat Chair . . . . and yeah, I even made a garden out back . . . . but I will go collect boxes today and pray that I don't need to use them, (but here in Ohio if your landlord gets foreclosed, you have 3 days to be out) . . . I hope and pray that 6-6 and I can stay here until he goes to Film School Next year,(we were planning to stay until then) . . . and that we get to use that new Heater . . . . I worry about everyone . . . getting through this, . . . I really do . . . . Home is a Precious Thing . . . .

* * *

"And as we let our own light shine,we unconsciously give other people permission to do the same."

Nelson Mandela

OCTOBER 06, 2008, MONDAY

MONDAY VOTING UPDATE FOR ENIGMA . . . . (YES, MY STORY HAS A HAPPY ENDING . . . SO FAR)

5 PM Update Monday:

Brief History of Enigma's Voting Situation.

So as of 3 am Last Night, I was not registered on the Online Sites (MoveOn, RocktheVote, or the Obama site) . . . . SO at 3am DK came up with Checking the State Site, Ohio Secretary of State, which did have me registered . . . . BUT the County site did not . . . . (which I found after she crashed . . .) NOW . . . . As I said Earlier I have been registered here since early 2006, and at this address since Spring 2007 (after my downtown address got foreclosed—and we moved winter 2007 I did re-register in person at the County Board of Elections.) I voted here in 2006 and the Primary 2008 (with an early vote at the County Election Center). I voted early for Obama. I have a new registration card that was mailed to me January of 2008.

Previous History: (MY Caged Voting Story)

I voted in 2000 for Gore, along with my neighborhood, we all stood in line for hours. Mr,Enigma (my Ex) was in front of me in the line about a 100 people and he voted first. We were in line long enough, that someone had Pizza sent to us . . . . and we watched the sun go down . . . . So we voted and then we all watched that Election Night . . . . and we all know it was stolen . . . . So then in 2004, I was living in a different state, California, and when I went to register they could not find My Vote or previous registration in Northwest Washington State. I had voted in every election since I was 18 . . . . A LONG TIME . . . . And once I was a mom . . . I always took my son with me . . . even as a Baby. (he swears he remembers helping to Vote for Clinton and playing under the polling booth.) . . . . So in California this Justice Dept Person calls me from Diane Feinstein's office and asked me questions about my Voting History, and I said I voted and told her about 2000, that is what she had Questions about. Then she asked more about my neighborhood, how many people voted, were they poor, elderly or college students. I said, they are ALL of those, so when they looked up my street, there was only ONE recorded Vote . . . . She read the Name . . . . it was Mr.Enigma's name . . . HIS VOTE was the ONLY Vote for the WHOLE Street for three blocks . . . . It made me ill, realizing that I had stood there for hours with my friends, and neighbors and NONE of us had been counted . . . . NONE.

(Needless to say I filed all the reports with ALL the right people, Diane Feinstiens Office, Human Rights Watch and ACLU . . . . and they were all very nice . . . and they said there 1000's of such reports from people like me . . . . they did also ask if I worked as an activist, lifelong Democrat etc . . . . I said yes . . . to all. They also asked questions about my neighborhoods etc. Which have always been the same . . . . poorer, elderly, college students etc. I never heard more, and at one point I heard on the news or cspan that the situation /investigation was dropped?)

2004 I voted with special Ballot after all of this . . . and went and voted in person that fateful day . . . .

THEN in Late 2005 I moved here to C-Town . . . and did not register to vote until late that fall, and received paperwork January 2006 . . . . and at that point we could not locate my previous Vote of 2004 in California . . . . again . . .

So NOW you can see that I am Wanting to Make Certain that THIS Vote is Counted . . . .

UPDATE OF TODAY:

So at 2PM I am driving to the Board of Elections . . . and the Obama People called me . . . . From Franklin County, and they were very nice . . . . they let me know I am NOT alone, that there are many going through this and that the Obama Campaign is there to help. They said if I ran into ANY problems, they would send a lawyer over. I was speechless . . . . They said just call and let them know . . . . For the First time in 8 very long years . . . . I drove to the Center finally not feeling Abandoned or Invisible. I thanked him . . . profusely . . . . really choked me up . . . WOW . . . they KNOW that Cleveland and Ohio really does have problems . . . the Voters do Matter . . . .

So I arrived at the center . . . I had to park over a mile away . . . . there was no parking or lots open near the Election Center . . . . People were excited and cheerful . . . there was even a rep. outside of the Center helping people and guiding them how to register. Then inside everybody was very nice . . . . even the Security Guards were very nice . . . . The lines for voting were winding through the building but very calm and not stressed. There were also Church Vans helping the elderly and disabled vote . . . . that was nice to see . . . . So I went talked with them now everything is fixed in the computer, I am NOW registered at the County and the State Level and I have a NEW Laminated Card . . . So as of right now 4 PM I AM REGISTERED . . . . Phew . . . .

Thank you ONE and ALL for all of your advice and support and good thoughts and helpful advice . . . be sure to see the post below about HOW to check your vote and your registration . . . . and get ready to vote . . . and Just Do It . . . and take lots of photos and post them on your blog and tell your story . . . We should ALL Document OUR Votes . . .

* * * And yes, I am going to vote, but I promised 6-6 that he could be there when I vote . . . . like always . . . we will take lots of photos . . . .

* * *

Allie McNeil

10.09.08 Update:
Report: Voter purges in 6 states may violate law
October 08, 2008 10:48 PM EDT

NEW YORK—The New York Times reports that tens of thousands of eligible voters have been removed from rolls or blocked from registering in at least six swing states, and the voters' exclusion appears to violate federal law. The newspaper says its findings are based on reviews of state records and Social Security data.

The Times says voters appear to have been purged by mistake, not because of any intentional violations by election officials or coordinated efforts by any party. The newspaper says it identified apparent problems in Colorado, Indiana, Ohio, Michigan, Nevada and North Carolina. It says some states are improperly using Social Security data to verify new voters' registration applications, and others may have broken rules that govern removing voters from the rolls within 90 days of a federal election.

*   *   * Considering it took me TWO years to get the Social Security Administration to get MY card with MY Number and My Name right . . . this little tidbit that came in my email tonight might explain Some of the problems . . .

OCTOBER 09, 2008, THURSDAY

TO A FRIEND ....
HAPPY BIRTHDAY ...

* * *

Many years ago I made a friend . . . . We met at a Coffee Shop in the Northwest . . . I was immediately aware of his humor, his wisdom, his sensitivity, and his ability to read situations. Before we ever met I watched him at the Coffee Shop how kind he was to others, the way he would offer a chair, or a better muffin, or a joke when it was needed. He taught me the value of Empathy and Listening. This week he turns 50 and he is thousands of miles away . . .

We have spent many hours talking . . . . over the years . . . . walking in the rain, sitting on my porch at all hours . . . . making pancakes . . . . and drinking Chai Tea . . . and reading . . . . and yes dissecting American Politics . . . and reviewing the Culture of America and other Places . . . . and he has helped me learn many things about my son . . . . and raising a boy . . . . he helped me keep anchored when life became more than rocky . . . there is no way I can let him know how much richer and better he has made my life . . . . He has been a Gift . . . . In many ways he is the Brother I never had . . . and he knows it . . . . I can only say Namaste . . . .

The two songs below always remind me of him and how blessed . . . truly lucky I have been to have him as a friend . . . and that I always carry him in my heart . . . . and that there is always a place on my porch just for him . . . always . . .

Allie McNeil

If you were here my friend we would go sit and have tea and coffee and muffins . . . . These two songs always came on in the car when I was driving around digging through boxes of toxic documents, "Name "by GooGoo Dolls and "Iris" . . . . I would drive home pondering the documents and the FOIAS and how the trail of paper led to our sick friends and obituaries of neighbors . . . and as I write Silent Fallout I know that somewhere I will always be grateful to you, no matter where you are.

DECEMBER 05, 2008, FRIDAY

THE LIST . . . . CLICK ON THE ONES THAT YOU HAVE DONE . . . AND THEN DO THE LIST OF THINGS YOU WANT TO DO . . .

While you sip some warm coffee . . . ponder this 100 List . . . and see How Many of these you have done . . . great list Stolen from DK at Redheaded Wisdom . . . .

I HAVE . . . **{{ means I did it}}**

1. Started my own blog **
2. Slept under the stars**
3. Played in a band** {{Did Lights, and also tamborine and back up}}
4. Visited Hawaii
5. Watched a meteor shower ** {{ many times}}
6. Given more than I can afford to charity **{{{yup . . . over and over}}}**
7. Been to Disneyland/world ** {{{disney world}}}**
8. Climbed a mountain **{{{ yup . . .}}**
9. Held a praying mantis *   *   * {{{ son had pet one, also walkingstick and pet slug too}}}**
10. Sung a solo *   *   * {{don't ask—it was totally embarrassing}}}}*   *   *
11. Bungee jumped
12. Visited Paris

13. Watched lightning at sea * * * {{{had a sailor boyfriend}}}* * *
14. Taught myself an art from scratch * * *{{many jewelery, caligraphy,chinese painting etc}}* * *
15. Adopted a child * * * {{{ fostered two girls,sisters one year}}}* * *
16. Had food poisoning * * * {{many times}}}* * *
17. Walked to the top of the Statue of Liberty * * *{{{went pretty high—not sure how high}}}**
18. Grown my own vegetables * * * {{many many times}}}* * *
19. Seen the Mona Lisa in France
20. Slept on an overnight train* * *{{many times}}* * *
21. Had a pillow fight* * *{{{ many times}}**
22. Hitchhiked* * * {{ as a dumb teen}}}* * *
23. Taken a sick day when you're not ill * * *{{{ gulp. yup}}* * *
24. Built a snow fort * * *{{{ yup . . . }}* * *
25. Held a lamb* * *{{{ yup}}* * *
26. Gone skinny dipping * * *{{{ yup many times}}}* * *
27. Run a Marathon* * * {{{ used to run half marathons in college}}**
28. Ridden in a gondola in Venice
29. Seen a total eclipse * * * {{{yup}}* * *
30. Watched a sunrise or sunset * * *{{{ both many times}}}* * *
31. Hit a home run * * * {{{ long time ago}}}* * *
32. Been on a cruise * * *{{ gone on overnight sailing trips . . . not sure that counts}}}* * *
33. Seen Niagara Falls in person
34. Visited the birthplace of my ancestors* * *{{{ In UK and also in Kentuckey and West Va.}}}**
35. Seen an Amish community **{{ many times}}}* * *
36. Taught myself a new language * * * {{ some french, some thai,some spanish }}* * *
37. Had enough money to be truly satisfied * * *{{sometimes}}**
38. Seen the Leaning Tower of Pisa in person
39. Gone rock climbing * * * {{{ yup, and I sucked }}* * *

40. Seen Michelangelo's David
41. Sung karaoke *   *   * {{ don't ask}}}*   *   *
42. Seen Old Faithful geyser erupt
43. Bought a stranger a meal at a restaurant *   *   *{{{yup}**
44. Visited Africa
45. Walked on a beach by moonlight **{{{ many times}}}*   *   *
46. Been transported in an ambulance*   *   * {{{ also worked on one, son had bad asthma attack went with him}}*   *
47. Had my portrait painted *   *   * {{{ had photos taken for a friends photo class, and he did also paint it . . . ugh}}*   *   *
48. Gone deep sea fishing *   *   *{{{ kind of, we went but did not catch much }}}*   *   *
49. Seen the Sistine Chapel in person
50. Been to the top of the Eiffel Tower in Paris
51. Gone scuba diving or snorkeling *   *   * {{{ as a teen snorkeling, also swam with dolphins }}}}*   *   *
52. Kissed in the rain *   *   * {{yup}}*   *   *
53. Played in the mud *   *   * {{{yup with son}}}*   *   *
54. Gone to a drive-in **{{ long ago}}}*   *   *
55. Been in a movie *   *   * {{ son and I were Extra's in Singles, I was asked to Extra in Spiderman filmed in 2006—turned down}}}**
56. Visited the Great Wall of China
57. Started a business *   *   * {{yup}*   *   *
58. Taken a martial arts class
59. Visited Russia
60. Served at a soup kitchen*   *   *{{{ yup}*   *   *
61. Sold Girl Scout Cookies *   *   * {{ and bought}}**
62. Gone whale watching *   *   *{{{ many times}}*   *   *
63. Got flowers for no reason *   *   * {{{not in a long time}}}*   *   *
64. Donated blood, platelets or plasma *   *   * {{{not recently}}**
65. Gone sky diving
66. Visited a Nazi Concentration Camp
67. Bounced a check **{{{ ooooops by accident, rare}}**
68. Flown in a helicopter *   *   * {{ ex was a fight nurse, I begged for a fly, but watched him alot}}}**
69. Saved a favorite childhood toy *   *   * {{ yup}}*   *   *

70. Visited the Lincoln Memorial *   *   *{{many times}}**
71. Eaten Caviar *   *   *{{ yup . . . rare}}**
72. Pieced a quilt **{{ many }}**
73. Stood in Times Square **{{yup, long ago}}}**
74. Toured the Everglades **{{ long ago}}*   *   *
75. Been fired from a job *   *   * {{ got in a fight with a big company—about AIDS care}}*   *   *
76. Seen the Changing of the Guards in London **{{yup}}}**
77. Broken a bone *   *   *{{many}*   *   *
78. Been on a speeding motorcycle *   *   *{{{ not sure if it was going too fast}}}*   *   *
79. Seen the Grand Canyon in person
80. Published a book*   *   * {{long ago}}}*   *   *
81. Visited the Vatican
82. Bought a brand new car **{{long ago}}}*   *   *
83. Walked in Jerusalem
84. Had my picture in the newspaper **{{{embarrassing}}}**
85. Read the entire Bible
86. Visited the White House *   *   * {{not the inside}}}*   *   *
87. Killed and prepared an animal for eating *   *   *{{{ it was a fish, does that count}}}*   *   *
88. Had chickenpox**{{{ yup}}*   *   *
89. Saved someone's life *   *   * {{{yup 1st time I was 11, a drowning, and then as a nurse}}}*   *   *
90. Sat on a jury
91. Met someone famous *   *   * {{{{ a few }}}*   *   *
92. Joined a book club **{{joined a few}}**
93. Lost a loved one **{{{yup}}**
94. Had a baby *   *   *{{yup}}**
95. Seen the Alamo in person
96. Swam in the Great Salt Lake **{{{did not swim in it—did see—it's gross}}**
97. Been involved in a law suit **{{yup}}}*   *   *
98. Owned a cell phone *   *   * {{{{ yup . . . . since 1999}*   *   *
99. Been stung by a bee *   *   *{{{ a few times, I am allergic . . . not good.}}}*   *   *
100. Ridden an elephant *   *   * {{ I was little won a contest, I was 5—or 6 . . . . it was wonderful, it was a baby}}}*   *   *

234

DECEMBER 12, 2008, FRIDAY

A NEW LIST . . . . JOB LIST.

So here is my theory . . . that we all can get through these times if we just adapt . . . . and change and flow with it . . . What kind of jobs have you had? has it shaped your life?

* * *

This is a List of Jobs I have had . . . Some I worked for pay . . . some I worked for trades, I worked a barn so my son could ride and learn to ride, etc . . . . so bartering is in a way a useful skill . . . .

1. waitress (over and over)
2. worked concert halls and political events (coat checks, and service for events)
3. Stage crew for plays
4. Lighting for bands at a Baltimore Bar
5. Lifeguard,
6. Pool Manager
7. Swimming Instructor
8. Stall Cleaner and care of 20 Horse Barn (trade for lessons for son)
9. Horse Therapy/grooming and Massage (Tellington Touch)
10. Research for a News Station in College
11. nurse's aid.volunteer (highschool and junior High, Special Olympics and Childrens Hospital, also was a Reader and did puppet shows . . . .)
12. Hospice Volunteer (started when 17, before that volunteered)
13. Parking Lot Attendent at Harbor Construction Site

14. Bartending
15. Taught HIV/AIDS Classes for years in Seattle 1988-1998
16. Cofounded a Environmental Health Non Profit
17. Red Cross Disaster Volunteer
18. Reader for Blind College Students
19. tutoring
20. housecleaning
21. Pet Care
22. volunteer at Nature Center (rehabing Wild Animals—bears to baby squirrels)
23. Market Checkout
24. Rickshaw Driver in Baltimore (first female one in early 80's Harbor)
25. Inventory Bookeeping at a resturante
26. Personal Trainer (taught eexercise classes at gym for free membership)
27. Worked at 2nd Hand Store
28. worked in Special Dress Shop In Baltimore (where I met Oprah . . . .)
29. And yes, I am still a nurse an RN . . . . (PEDS, Hospice, PICU, ER, AIDS Nursing . . . .)

DECEMBER 31, 2008, WEDNESDAY

REFLECTIONS ON THE END OF 2008 . . . .

In Many Ways . . . .

I look at the Migrant Mother photo . . . it haunts me . . . because I see that Woman in my eyes . . . and other mom's eyes and I carry it in my heart . . . . it is WHY I blog . . . and blog so much . . . We are living through an important part of Our History . . . . the most difficult Challenging ever . . . . for many of us . . . it is Up to Us HOW we get through this . . . about Adapting, Learning and Taking Care of Each Other . . . . Empathy is part of Survival.

But really I am the Gold Dust Woman . . . . because I am always looking for the Golden Moments . . . mining for it . . . . in small moments and trying to share it, songs, music, photos, art and even stories, anything to Stoke Our Humanity . . . to help us come through This Time Intact, I am part Gypsy, Part Nurse, Part Appalachian Mama, part worried librarian . . . so of course I look for the Gold . . . . it is my way of Hopemongering . . . .

It started long ago . . . in the Seventies when I was in Highschool I studied Wildflowering . . . . (in Appalachia that is the study and collecting of Herbs to heal . . . . my parents were not impressed with my Herbal Studies . . .) But it taught me that What we need to Heal and Care for Each Other is around us . . . . we just have to look . . . . and open our Hearts . . .

So I will be here . . . . writing it all . . . trying to capture it writing Our History with Heart and Hope . . . . and yes, with Honesty and Empathy . . . . Happy New Year . . . .

JANUARY 23, 2008, WEDNESDAY

MOONMONGERING 1.23.08

* * *

It is so beautiful out . . . . There is a beautiful Moon . . . it is sitting up there looking so inviting . . . . and there is this lovely bit a wispy veil that keeps floating across . . . So I laid on my bed this eve and looked out the window . . . . I have this amazing window . . . . (I decorated it after I took 6-6's tree down).I hung the Handmade Beaded Ice Sickle Ornaments on a Silver Ribbon and White Christmas Lights and I made lovely Snow Flakes from orgami paper that are painted with glitter and shimmery paint. But the best part in the winter is that the Moon sits right in the Middle. (In the summer it is a Treehouse Window with leaves abound). I had an amazing day with my son, the kind of day where we really really talked . . . about all kinds of things that Matter: from Unexpected Death of a young actor, to Making Really Wonderful movies (he wants to be a director), and music (why disco sucks), and WHY he wishes he could Vote in the Next Election (which he can't—he is too young.)

We watched SpidermanIII, and we talked about watching it be filmed. In 2006 It was filmed in Downtown Cleveland, at the time we lived in Downtown Cleveland, and it was filmed ON OUR STREET. It was very exciting, and we used to go get Starbucks snacks, and hit the curbs, and watch as they set up scenes and fix up the sets and FILM. It was very exciting in kind of a slow methodical way, but as 6-6 wants to make Movies it was a helluva learning experience . . . . He loved it in a quiet critical way. We moved from downtown a year ago, because our Loft Buiding got Foreclosed, we were very lucky to find another home. But we do both miss the Loft . . . and we loved seeing our old Street all gussied up for the Film.

Today we ate too much popcorn and drank too much Diet Pepsi . . . . and we laughed as we looked at our old Street. Which was the best Medicine, the laughter or the Moon. I may never know . . . . I don't think I need to know . . . . (The Moon knows it is the Boy with the Blue Eyes that makes me laugh . . . and warms my heart.)

JANUARY 13, 2009, TUESDAY

BUSH IS STILL DELUDED ABOUT KATRINA.... HE THINKS THAT HISTORY WILL REMEMBER IT DIFFERENTLY—BUT THE PEOPLE KNOW THE TRUTH.

So the Deluded King gave his LAST Presser today and he was questioned about Katrina.... and this is how he responded (Huffpo):

> "On another issue destined to figure prominently in his legacy, Bush said he disagrees with those who say the federal response to Hurricane Katrina was slow.

> "Don't tell me the federal response was slow when there were 30,000 people pulled off roofs right after the storm passed.... Could things been done better? Absolutely. But when I hear people say the federal response was slow, what are they going to say to those chopper drivers or the 30,000 who got pulled off the roof?" he said.

* * *

Just to be really clear—there were Thousands of Victims due to Katrina, but NOT just due to the Storm, Many were Victims of Bush's Criminal Negligence, that he did NOTHING for over FIVE DAYS, and then the "aid" he provided was pathetic and meager. There are International Laws that mandate that National Leadership take care of Natural Disaster Refugees.

And Just to Correct Bush, he is wrong about the Numbers Rescued and WHO rescued them, it was the Coast Guard, Who did so WITHOUT Orders, because they had to, and the MIlitary was NOT activated, even the Navy sat idle, because Busb would not and did NOT give the orders. Even Gore helped Bring Private Planes in to remove Hospital Victims. The UN sent Disaster Assessment Teams . . . The Devastation and Neglect was seen World Wide, there is hundreds of hours of Footage and Photos.

So When there are Trials held About the Bush Regime's Crimes Against Humanity, let us not forget that it is NOT just Gitmo and Illegal War and Illegal Torture where Bush as a Leader harmed His People and Humanity . . . . there is Katrina.

* * *

He has not a clue about the Devastation, even now, or What was Lost and Damaged Forever or his role in it. Maybe Someone Should sit him down and make him watch this Documentary, "The Drive" about NOLA, and what was Lost there in 2005 . . . While he was on Vacation and Eating Cake with McCain . . . .

* * *

Bush had the "Help" of the Homeland Security Dept to add to Mishandling and Negligence of Katrina (Chertoff and Brownie both have blood on their hands as well . . . .) NOW Knowing that—please do read this HOW HLS NOW wants to have a 3.4 BILLION Dollar Facility Built in these Hard Economic Times does Anyone really need to wonder at the Level of Incompetence of the Bush Regime? It's Downright Criminal . . . .

JANUARY 17, 2009, SATURDAY

TO RESTORE JUSTICE, THERE MUST BE TRIALS FOR THE WAR CRIMES AND TORTURE COMMITTED IN OUR NAMES.

* * *

This man was tortured at GITMO in Our Name for 6 years. (photo)

* * *

Dear President Obama and Attorney General Eric Holder,

I am writing to you about Crimes, War Crimes and Crimes Against Humanity that were committed in OUR Name by the Bush Regime. I am respectfully requesting that Your Administration Investigate and Prosecute the Crimes that were Ordered and Knowingly Carried out against Individuals that involved various levels of Torture and Causation of Inhumane Discomfort and Pain, this includes Renditioning of Individuals to Countries where they could suffer under Foreign laws, as well as Renditioning to Secret Prisons and Black Prisons where they could be held away from Scrutiny and Red Cross Observation. There were many Individuals that went to great trouble to attempt to subvert or re-write Our National Laws and International Laws and Treaties, as well as Defiance of The Geneva Conventions.

The Leadership that Gave the Orders must face Legal Justice, and that includes John Ashcroft, Alberto Gonzales, Donald Rumsfeld, and Mr.Bush and Mr.Cheney. These Crimes were ordered by them, and the laws were flagrantly violated, in Prisons, Abu Gahrib, Other Iraqi Prisons, and Gitmo, and other Foreign Prisons that have been established in clandestine Illegal Gulag System. The FBI, CIA and Military and Private Contractors were Ordered to Follow Orders from the Whitehouse that were in violation of Existing Laws and violating Providing Humane Prisoner Care as well as Basic Rights and going as far as to Torture. At Gitmo some of the these orders were even carried out on Minors. Orders were carried out even leading to Causation of Physical and Psychological damage.

Always in History when there have been War Crimes Committed, there have been Trials. In World War II, and even after Vietnam there were Trials against those that Committed Torture. In these Times there can be NO Exception, or break from Our History, even though Our Own Laws were and have been Violated. The Previous President attempted to Make Laws to Protect his Administration, not to Protect Our Safety. This would also require that the Patriot Act be Fully Dissected and Re-evaluated, as all laws that justify the Interrogation and Torture in Our Names are indeed still part of the Problem and Violation of Rights.

As a Nurse I am also concerned that Medical Personnel in the Military were used to institute or as a part of the Interrogation Techniques and as passive and active participants in a knowingly harmful process. This would also explain why Detainees were hidden from the International Red Cross as they experienced harmful care and treatment. At this point is Also Medically Necessary that ALL Remaining Prisoners and Detainees have Full Medical Exams By Civilian Medical Personnel and be finally accessible to the International Red Cross.

I also respectfully ask that if there is a War Crimes and Crimes Against Humanity Investigation that Katrina must be included in the Investigation and Prosecution, as the President Knowingly Neglected Thousands of Natural Disaster Refugees that under International Laws should have been fully protected and cared for under his Leadership.

(per Standards and Laws explained by the U.N, and they did send an Disaster Assessment Team to NOLA in September 2005). It is also revelant that Our National Guard Troops were deployed illegally to War Zone based on Lies, and that left Our Home Disaster Stricken Areas without Enough National Guard to Render Care, Aid, and Shelter perpetuating a Cycle of Criminal Negligence.

I am respectfully asking that you appoint a Special Prosecutor, as well as Form a Special Investigatory Review Panel to examine those that have been harmed and mistreated by the Previous Regime, that it be based on the Investigatory panels that were put in place to work on the Nuremberg Trials. Senator Dodd's Father worked on the Nuremberg Trials, expertise on these trials should be willingly pursued and consulted. It also must be noted that the International Community also must be allowed to see that this Process is being carried forward. It is to be noted that Other Countries also have Concerns about War Crimes and Crimes against Humanity. They should be allowed some way to see that Justice is being restored in Our Country, whether it be with Public Hearings or Written Reports. American Citizens also must be given Transparency as well, with Hearings to be seen on CSPAN or some other Public TV or Youtube. American Citizens suffered 8 years of Lies and Propaganda, and many fear that there have been even worse Crimes committed in Our Names that we must Know.

Full Truth and Justice are needed to Heal Our Nation, turning Our Backs on Crimes will lead to Continued Damage and Pain in this Country.

Thank you for reading this letter and hearing my concerns. We place our Trust and Faith in your Constitutional Law Knowledge and Skills, and that we again have a Leader with a Moral Code and Integrity.

* * *

(click title for BBC article about why Gitmo must be closed . . . . and torture.)

FEBRUARY 19, 2009, THURSDAY

BUSH'S EXECUTIVE CIA DIRECTOR FACES SENTENCING THIS WEEK.... DUSTY FOGGO'S FATE...

Part of the DC Examiner article....

"Kyle "Dusty" Foggo, the highest-ranking member of a federal intelligence or law enforcement agency convicted of a federal crime, is expected to be sentenced in Alexandria's federal court today, where federal secrets could be made public.

Foggo, 53, admitted in September that he used his position as the third-highest-ranking member of the CIA to steer government contracts to his good friend Brent R. Wilkes. In return, Wilkes offered Foggo a job with his company upon leaving government service, sent Foggo and his family on a $30,000 vacation and took Foggo out to high-priced dinners in the Washington area.

Foggo was the CIA's executive director from November 2004 until May 2006, when he resigned after the federal investigation became public. During his time overseeing the CIA's daily operations and budget, Foggo gave Wilkes lucrative contracts marked up by as much as 60 percent over the going rate. One contract for supplying water to CIA outposts in Afghanistan and Iraq caused the government to pay $1.8 million more than was justified.

In the months before his September guilty plea, Foggo's attorneys threatened to expose classified government secrets during the trial. The move pushed prosecutors to drop 27 of the 28 charges against Foggo. When Foggo pleaded guilty to one count of wire fraud, Judge James C. Cacheris told Foggo his attorneys "have done a good job for you in this case."

* * *

Interesting . . . . Bush did not even attempt to pardon Duke Cunningham or Foggo or Wilkes . . . .

MARCH 02, 2009, MONDAY

ROVE IS NOW ATTEMPTING TO RE-WRITE KATRINA HISTORY ABOUT HOW BUSH HANDLED IT . . . .

* * *

Dear Karl the Criminal-

I saved hundreds of photos of Katrina Damage, because the Photos don't lie . . . . Dead Bodies never do. We The People will NEVER forget how you and the Bush Administration in genocidal fashion Ignored the Plight of the Storm Victims before and during and after the Hurricane . . . . because in true Caligula Fashion you all were on Vacation . . . Shame on you. YOU are as guilty as Bush and Cheney . . . . You should read International Laws . . . . Citizens of a Country who are suffering from a Natural Disaster, must be treated as Refugees, provided care and shelter by their Leadership In Power . . . . It is a Crime when these This Humane treatment is not provided . . . . the UN Investigates . . . . Did you know that? Did you know that the UN sent Assessment team in September 2005 to NOLA?

* * * Click the title to read more of the Delusional Turd Blossom . . . . and how Bush did a Heckuva Job with Katrina . . . .

MARCH 08, 2009, SUNDAY

MORE THAN 700 APPLY FOR SCHOOL JANITOR JOB IN OHIO . . . (CLICK TITLE TO READ MORE)

Ohio school gets 700 applicants for janitorial job

March 08, 2009 11:06 AM EDT

MASSILON, Ohio—Evidence of the slumping economy is stacking up at an Ohio school which has nearly 700 applications for one open janitorial job. Officials at Perry Local Schools near Canton in northeast Ohio say they've extended the deadline until Monday to accommodate the overwhelming response to the week-old posting. The full-time position at Edison Junior High School pays $15 to $16 an hour plus benefits. Superintendent John Richard says many applicants are laid-off workers with heart-wrenching stories about the tough economic times. Forty-nine-year-old Donna Croston says she applied after losing jobs at two nearby factories that closed. Croston says her chances of being hired amid the hundreds of applicants are slim, but she's hoping to get lucky.

* * *

News Update: They are holding the position open and accepting more applications . . . . it is over 800 as of tonight.

MARCH 11, 2009, WEDNESDAY

ONE IN FIFTY CHILDREN ARE HOMELESS... FOR CHILDREN IT'S AS BAD AS THE THIRTIES.... BUT WE ALL KNEW THAT....

* * *

Snippet from Raw Story Article.... click the title to read the rest...

"One in 50 American children is homeless and the economic crisis hitting the United States will make the problem worse, a report released Tuesday said." Without a voice, more than 1.5 million of our nation's children go to sleep without a home each year," said the "America's Young Outcasts" report by the National Center on Family Homelessness. The child homelessness crisis is the worst since the Great Depression, says the report, which looked at the years 2005-06—or before the economic slump had fully hit the United States. Children without homes are twice as likely to go hungry, more than twice as likely as middle class children to have health problems, and run twice the risk of other children of repeating a grade at school, being expelled or suspended, or not finishing high school, the report said."

* * *

Now the awful thing about this report is that it was done in 2005 and 2006, BEFORE the Economic Meltdown hit so many families, now with so many Jobs Lost (MILLIONS) and Homes Lost (Millions Foreclosed), We can only estimate how bad is this number? The 2010 Census may the only way to truly gather all the needed data on the Crisis hurting our Children and Families . . . .

MARCH 20, 2009, FRIDAY

SACRAMENTO TENT CITY UPDATE:::MAYOR OF SACRAMENTO HAS PROMISED TO FIND SHELTER FOR HIS LARGEST TENT CITY....

* * *

I read this story last night that the Tent City in Sacramento is about to be facing changes, and it is inspiring that the Mayor realizes that this is an intolerable situation and is trying to remedy it.... I hope the Media publicizes it as it would inspire Other Mayors to also create safe haven for People that have lost Everything. Tent Cities are imerging because many shelters are Single Gender and do not allow families or families with pets. Another problem is that many that are homeless are still trying to work and save money to find an apartment or home to rent. But for folks living in shelters, they have to wander from shelter to shelter during the day to claim a "sleeping spot". Tent Cities also allow people to keep their possessions and cook for themselves, it allows some independence. For women and children and families Tent Cities also offer some limited degree of Community and safety. We must watch this and see what happens to these families.

Click the Title to read Reuters Article on it, here is a snippet:::

"Tent city residents and police say the camp had existed for at least a year and had expanded after several smaller clusters of homeless settlements were shut down. Johnson said his plan included enlarging existing shelters, opening a short-term tented shelter area at a fairground, and creating "permanent housing opportunities" for an additional 40 homeless individuals. He said city officials would meet individually with each of the tent dwellers to discuss options, and a special task force would finish devising a long-term strategy for all the city's known homeless. The plan, which will be financed from various public funds, will be submitted to the City Council for approval next week."

* * *

March 9th Video of the Sacramento Tent City(NBC) shows the economic plight of these Families.

* * *

Previous Video this month posted Down Below, raises Questions is the Sacramento Tent City being closed due to Embarrassment, or are they really acting in good faith to help these Homeless Families and provide better shelter. In the Video the City Attorney speaks of "cleaning" the area, and that the area is "Private" Land, someone needs to ask WHO owns the Land. I think in some ways, maybe their tented Community should be respected and proper water and bath facilities provided . . . . What will happen to the Tent City Residents, are they going to be merely "removed" by Law Enforcement . . . . Remember this is their "HOME", their Community—Hundreds have lived there for monthes . . . . It is true during the day many of the Tent Residents do travel during the day, either to work, or job hunt, or yes some do panhandle. People in these Tent Cities are doing what they need to do to do to survive, or attempt to survive. They are not "druggies" or vagrants or lazy people, they are people who have suffered an Economic Devastation . . . . and they need to be Remembered as People. Real people . . . and maybe once Our Neighbors not long ago.

3.20.09 4 PM Update and new video from the Mercury News . . . .

* * *

A Video about The People of Tent City in Sacramento . . . .

* * *

The Governor visited the site March 19th, yesterday, the same day the President came to California. (I wonder if Arnold shared this story with Obama on the Place back to DC last night?). I am still hoping that all the attention to this Tent City will show America and DC How Bad the problem is . . . .

* * *ABC 20/20 Tonight is Covering People losing their Homes, Hotel Families and Shelter Families, I will post the Video when I find it.It was called "Life on the Edge: the New Homeless" by David Muir.

* * *Chris Janson is also doing more followup on People Losing their Homes on Sunday on NBC Dateline.

* * *

On a Personal Note:

I first saw this Sacramento Tent City in 2005—it is visible by Train, and it was smaller about 100 tents/occupants. Now it is up to about 400 people, and perhaps 40% are "Recession Refugees" that have arrived this year. The Tent cities are not new, merely growing—silently and at an increased alarming rate.

* * *

MARCH 25, 2009, WEDNESDAY

US POSTAL SERVICE TO CUT JOBS, THOUSANDS FACING JOB LOSS.... CLICK THE TITLE.

From Reuters:

Posted 2009/03/20 at 2:13 pm EDT . . . Mar. 20, 2009 (Reuters)—"The U.S. Postal Service said on Friday it is closing six of its 80 district offices. In addition, administrative staff positions at district level nationwide are being reduced by 15 percent and nearly 150,000 employees nationwide being given opportunity to take an early retirement."

* * *

150,000 facing EARLY retirement?????? An "Opportunity"??? Or Pink Slip? This story has barely gotten mentioned in the news, and yet it impacts so many thousands. I am wondering have ALL options been examined to help this situation? Reduced hours? Different schedules? Merging Offices.

AND YET The Bonus Question Once again Rears it's ugly head . . . . Postal General is still (getting?) giving Bonuses even in these Economically struggling times . . . . In this February 19th article we learn that even though the Post Service has lost over 2 Billion dollars the Management rewarded themselves with Bonuses . . . . even though there is No Performance that deserves Rewarding? Read the snippet below . . .

"As the U.S. Postal Service considers cutting delivery service in the face of dwindling mail volume and rising costs, the postmaster general received a big pay raise and a performance bonus last year, all authorized by Congress. Postmaster General John Potter's base salary climbed to $265,000 last year from $186,000 in 2007. He also received a performance bonus of $135,000. In all his total compensation—salary, bonuses, retirement benefits and other perks—topped $850,000, a spokesman with the U.S. Postal Service told FOXNews.com on Wednesday.

At the same time, the Postal Service, an independent federal agency, is crumbling alongside the economy and as online communications increase competition. The Postal Service lost $2.8 billion last year when total mail volume recorded 202 billion pieces of mail, its largest single drop in history—down more than 9 billion pieces from a year earlier."

APRIL 22, 2009, WEDNESDAY

FREDDIE MAC ACCOUNTING EXEC: "APPARENT" SUICIDE . . . .

Reuters:

"RESTON, Va., April 22 (Reuters)—David Kellermann, acting chief financial officer of troubled U.S. mortgage giant Freddie Mac (FRE.P) (FRE.N), was found dead on Wednesday in his suburban Virginia home after apparently committing suicide, a local police source said. Kellermann, 41, was named Freddie Mac's acting CFO last September after the Treasury Department seized the company, and its sibling mortgage agency Fannie Mae FNM.N., as the agencies faced deep losses on a crashing U.S. housing market that was rapidly engulfing other financial institutions. A police source said that Kellermann was found hanging in the basement of his home in Reston, outside Washington. A 16-year veteran of Freddie Mac, Kellermann had played a key role in helping the firm navigate accounting scandals and answer questions from regulators and investors who put the company under intense scrutiny as the U.S. housing market ended a five-year boom in 2006."

* * *

Updates will be posted . . . .

More the New York Times.

More about the Police Investigation that is ongoing.

APRIL 06, 2009, MONDAY

HOMELESSNESS UPDATES FOR APRIL: RAPID RISES IN LOWER MIDDLE INCOME FAMILIES EFFECTED....

* * *

From the USA article today:

"Cities and counties are reporting a sharp increase in homeless families as the economic crisis leads to job loss and makes housing unaffordable. In Seattle, 40% more people are living on suburban streets. In Miami, calls from people with eviction notices have quadrupled." The demand from families with children has increased dramatically," says Robert Hess of New York City's Department of Homeless Services. Each month since September, shelter requests have been at least 20% higher than they were a year ago. The Department of Housing and Urban Development requires a one-day count in January of people living on the street, in shelters or in transitional housing. National figures have not been compiled."

**(Okay—someone will have to explain to me WHY the DHHS only does ONE ONE Day Count??? I do know in the Beginning of January I went to the DHHS website for Information on Homelessness—and there was ONLY one page—and NO Stats had been updated since .... wait for it .... yes, the 2000 Census .... So that means that NO ONE has Counted Real People—the Homeless for NINE years ....)*   *   *

Of 56 places where figures were available, 35 reported an increase in homelessness; 12 had a drop.

*   *   * (For anyone that reads about Shelter Numbers, remember these are numbers of those at the Shelters, what we really need is how many are turned away.)*   *   *

FIND MORE STORIES IN: Boston | Seattle | Phoenix | Los Angeles | Minneapolis | Urban Development | Miami-Dade County |

"People who were on the edge can't hold on anymore," says Cathy ten Broeke homelessness project coordinator in Minneapolis and Hennepin County. She says 1,251 families sought emergency shelter last year, up from 1,032 in 2007.

- In Chicago, calls to a homelessness prevention hotline were 59% higher in February than a year earlier, says Nancy Radner, head of the Chicago Alliance to End Homelessness. "We're getting requests from people earning more than $30,000 a year, even $65,000. That's unprecedented."

- In Los Angeles, 620 families used the winter shelter program this winter, compared with 330 families a year earlier, manager David Martel says.

- In the Phoenix area, 230 people in families were living on the street in January; there were 49 a year ago. There were 139 children younger than 18 living on the street on their own, according to the Maricopa Association of Governments.

- In Miami-Dade County, the number of people calling for help after getting an eviction notice jumped from 1,000 in 2007 to 4,000 last year, David Raymond of the county's Homeless Trust says. "We've beefed up our prevention efforts," he says, so fewer people become homeless.

- In the Seattle area, street homelessness increased 2% overall but 40% in the suburbs, where the number living in cars rose from 229 last year to 339, homelessness project director Bill Block says.

*   *   * (Seattle is where the Mayor has been less than gracious about Homeless Issues and harsh on the Tent Cities, so they now name they Nickelsville's to honor his "compassion")*   *   *

JULY 13, 2009, MONDAY

POVERTY INDICATORS FOR CHILDREN CONTINUE TO RISE....

Snippet from Article:

"A growing number of American children are living in poverty and with unemployed parents, and are facing the threat of hunger, according to a federal report released yesterday. According to the report, "America's Children: Key National Indicators of Well-Being," 18 percent of all children 17 and younger were living in poverty in 2007, up from 17 percent in 2006. The percentage of children with at least one parent working full time was 77 percent in 2007, down from 78 percent in 2006. Those living in households where parents described children as being hungry, having skipped a meal or having gone without eating for an entire day increased from 0.6 percent in 2006 to 0.9percent in 2007, the report said.

Federal officials said the statistics predate the current economic downturn, and forecast harder times for some of the country's 74 million children 17 and younger. "It foreshadows greater changes we'll see when we look at these figures next year," said Duane Alexander, director of the Eunice Kennedy Shriver National Institute of Child Health and Human Development at the National Institutes of Heath, one of the government agencies that participated in the study."

* * *

There are other issues that this is not addressing yet .... Malnutrition, Medical Care, Education, and yes even child abuse issues as the economic stress continues to rise. (There are statistic correlations between domestic abuse and economic downfalls).I have yet to hear the DHHS raise any of these issues, or the MSM to cover any of these issues. The Economic Crisis has real impact on real people, wealth should be measured against the Human Condition . . . and how we treat our young and care for them and nurture them says much about us as People, as a Nation. A year ago we had a President who could not even say the "R" word, because it made him uncomfortable, and the media coddled him and wallstreet as the Economy Plummeted.

Children should never be the Consequence of Arrogance and Abuse of Power . . . .

Why would I write such a harsh endightment? Have you ever seen people sleeping in cars? Families? It changes your perspective . . . .

* * *

WHAT can you do?

Give to your local foodbank, especially in the summer when school meal programs are not providing meals. In many states the meal programs and Summer school programs have been drastically cut. These are children that normally would get meals at school and now are home for the summer. Give Child friendly foods, cookies, mac&cheese, baked beans, juices, canned fruit and pudding. And also check and see if the Food banks needs Formula and Diapers. Thank you.

JULY 29, 2009, WEDNESDAY

ATLEAST 52 MILLION AMERICANS HAVE NO HEALTHCARE . . . . I AM JUST ONE PERSON WHO TRULY NEEDS THE PUBLIC OPTION. NOW.

This is Not Rocket Science . . . . click the article and learn talking points and facts that will help you make calls to your reps . . . be sure to emphasize that the Public Option would Save Lives. (read this article for more infor and learn more.

* * *

My Healthcare Story . . . . DC and the MSM need to Cover ALL of Our Stories . . . The Reality of this Crisis. Both to some degree are Enabling the Insurance Industry. We do Not need Insurance Reform, we need Healthcare Reform. The Public Option would save Lives.

* * *

I am an RN of 20+ Years. I have worked to take care of hundreds,maybe even more. I have never ever refused anyone care for anything, I have worked it all from Community Health, to AIDS to ER to Hospice . . . . Homecare to Hospital Care. I took an Oath to care for people, to deny No One Care and to do No Harm. As a Nurse I have always tried to teach others to be proactive and take good care of themselves.I never thought I would be UnInsured or not able to have access to care I need. I have been Uninsured since 2006, this is my story of why and how it happened . . . .

and it is personal, and I am sharing it because it matters . . . it is Reality. It is a Reality for me, and 52 Million other Americans. Below is merely a piece of my Healthcare-Less story . . .

In 2005 I went through a Divorce, and therefore needed to find Insurance on my own as a single mom. My son still did and does have coverage, and that was my top priority. I set off to find a job that would offer benefits and also to find Health Insurance. The Cheapest Single Payer plan I could find was $480/month. I contacted more than 14 companies, and only ONE would take me. I was denied coverage by 6 of them for having MVP (Mitral Valve Prolapse—a simple heart valve deformity that millions of Americans have and it is a structural issue). That was the beginning of seeing the dimensions of the ability of Insurance Companies to deny care. I called the Insurance Company and learned that many conditions are Exclusion worthy it was a long list. Even someone being ordered for an EKG or an Echo or other test that indicates Heart Monitoring would have people be cancelled. So also Doctors can not properly monitor for Heart Disease without restrictions and being over powered by the Insurance Companies. So people with Insurance could also be cancelled at any time for a test or Xray being ordered, without warning or notice. What bothers me about this process is that Insurance companies don't have to follow or abide by any HIPPA laws, they can do demand access to your Health History and records BEFORE they agree to accept you. It is like a Club that does not have to follow ANY laws?

(By the way—that is just part of the Heart Story . . . . but it was the beginning of learning about being Denied care . . . . I do have valve issues, BUT the bigger picture is that I take good care of myself, I walk everyday, use a treadmill, and don't smoke or drink . . . . I am proactive, but no one ever asked me that. Bottemline someone with an enlarged heart and valve issues SHOULD have Monitoring and Regular Screening, ie EKG'S etc.)

So that was the beginning of the struggle. So Finally after many monthes, I found a company that would cover me, and I was willing to pay the 480/month until I could get a job with benefits. So I paid for the insurance for 3 monthes, then I went to get my first Breast exam in many years, thinking I was going for a routine mammogram. I got there and there was a lump, actually a cyst the size of a small plum. So there was ultrasounds done and the cyst was aspirated (9 cc's . . . .). And I was sent to a follow up to a Breast Expert. He was very thorough. He did a History, he asked about my family. I explained that my grandmom had died of Breast Cancer and Lung Cancer. I also explained because she encouraged me, that before I had gotten pregnant with my son I had had the BRCA test when I lived in another state. He asked me to try to get those records, so I did, and could not—they were archived or lost by the Institution. So he did what any doctor would do, he ordered the important blood work be redone because it is important for monitoring and screening for breast cancer. I asked him not to, I told him when it was ordered that it would cause me Insurance Problems. he said it was worth the risk.

So within weeks, I was Cancelled for not providing a FULL Medical History, and ALL of the care for the Breast Appointments I had to cover myself, over $1500.

Now it is 3 years later. I am underemployed, with 3 part time jobs. The One job that is not even a Nurse job is at a market,I took it because I was told that within a year I could be Eligible for Health Insurance. NOW for the Truth, the Market Job will review my situation at one year and submit my name, and start paying in, but that is a Probation period, and THEN the Actual Plan review is Not Until Spring 2010 (though I have worked there since 2008). And then at that time I can and still could potentially be denied, even after paying in during the Probation period. The Nursing work here is all part time or per diem with NO Access to ANY coverage—so that is my ONLY Option. (The Hospitals here have a Freeze or only are hiring per diem or part time if at all, and this has been the case since 2007).

So here is where it gets very interesting.

For the past year I have been battling 98% of the Symptoms of MS, thankfully, my Brain is fine and working at same speed. BUT my muscles are failing, and I am losing strength and coordination.I have constant pain and muscle spasm and stiffness and my gait is effected. I have NO meds for this. I have received some free medical "advice" and guidance about what I "need", (which vitamins and supplements to try). I need a Neurologist, but can not find one single one that is willing to take me Without Insurance.

I have contacted all the right people and organizations. I even found one group willing to donate an $2000 MRI for me, but without a doctor or someone to offer me care, it is a meaningless gift. MS means that for work I get up 3 hours early so that I can get "Unstiff". I do have a Doc In the Box I go to when I am desperate for care, but I can not go there for this. I have only been there this year when the Recalled Cookie Dough left me so sick and dehydrated, but I had to pay out of pocket for everything. Another time when I needed antibiotics for a respiratory infection I ordered Fish Antibiotics from a Pet Company. And this winter I had a stress fracture in my foot I used Duct tape to treat it. And about the Breast Cancer Risks and History, there was never a follow up or another test done. I did try to get care at the Free Clinic and was denied because they are not taking ANY new patients, they are full. Other low income clinics would not take me without Insurance or MediCaid. I am out of Options.

So there is a Piece of my Medical Story . . . . Beyond Broken . . . and I am just one of 52 Million that has such a Story . . . . I am one of 52 Million Americans that Needs a Public Option . . . . Now.

AUGUST 12, 2009. WEDNESDAY

CONGRESSWOMAN MARCIA FUDGE TOWN HALL MEETING: FORD AUDITOREUM CASE WESTERN AUGUST 2009

This is the shortened version of the 11 PM Channel 3 News. It does show some of what happened at the Town Hall Meeting. It does show some of the tension and rude people who were attempting to disrupt. They are clearly not there to discuss or learn or look at options, they randomly would yell out and in the beginning would yell things that were hateful and senseless. The police were very organized and quick to remove anyone that was problematic. Marcia Fudge was amazing, strong and clear that it was HER meeting and she was in charge and that Rudeness would not be tolerated. She was brave and determined to have her meeting, period. The Disrupters only want to shut the meeting down, they were not successful tonight. The Crowd also did a good job supporting her and clapping loudly over the Disrupters, and it worked. The Disrupters were mostly middle-aged white men well dressed, looking like they left a golf game early in their Dockers and sport shirts. They sat in the middle and yelled at random. People around them yelled them down, and photographed and filmed them. The Auditoreum held approximately 500, I am not sure of number of Disrupters, maybe 20?

Marcia did get the Facts out about the Financial Burden of this situation. She explained that "rationing' is already happening and being done by the Insurance Companies deciding what they will pay for. She also explained that premiums are already high to pay for the un-insured. She also explained about the Bankruptcy Numbers and people losing homes for Care. And that 14,000 a day are losing Healthcare.

Her Statement from her site that she repeated.

"Dr. Martin Luther King Jr. said, "Of all the forms of inequality, injustice in healthcare is the most shocking and inhumane." Forty years after Dr. King made this statement, injustice persists.

America has suffered an escalating healthcare crisis for decades. Those who say our system is sufficient have avoided the truth. Truly, there is something wrong when healthcare is more reactive than proactive. There is something wrong when healthcare costs rise more rapidly than individual income. There is something wrong when where you are born or the neighborhood you live in determines your quality of care. All of these wrongs can be found in our current healthcare system.

Within Congress, I will advocate for every American to have healthcare. Whether the citizen is rich or poor, schooled or unschooled, black or white, America must ensure all her citizens have care that is preventive, cost-effective and humane.

Government's job is to take care of its people. Caring for citizens includes facilitating their access to healthcare. Congress is currently discussing healthcare reform and I will use my vote to advocate for true healthcare reform for all Americans."

About My Question and What I asked Marcia Fudge?

And it shows some of the Questions, I was Number 5. I did explain that I am a Nurse, and have been for over 20 years. That I took an oath to take care of people, all people, and that I had never denied care to anyone for any reason, or if they had insurance or money. I explained that I had gone through hell trying to get insurance, and due to Family history was cancelled and now I have no insurance and no care. I asked the People in the Audience, and I turned to face them, I asked them to remember someone sitting near them has no health Insurance and no healthcare, and that no one should be ashamed or embarrassed that they have been denied or cancelled, or can not afford it. (Channel 3 said I was tearful—which is not true—I was nervous and a bit pale from the flu,and scrubs are less than flattering, but I wanted people to understand I am a Nurse. Channel 4,and 19 also filmed the meeting and yes, my question made it on their channels too).

I asked Marcia Fudge if she would promise to fight for people like me, 52 Million Americans and do all she could to make certain that the Public Option was in the Final Bill?

Her Response . . . .

She explained that she would do all she could to make sure it was in the Bill, and that she would not Vote for the Bill unless it was in the Bill.

(I am trying to locate the video of her Response—because it was amazing and did get thunderous applause and many were standing).

* * *

Questions that did come up in the Q&A period, the most important ones

(1) The Death Panel Question (she explained that it made no sense, that she has a mom that she loves).
(2) WHO and HOW will we pay for it (the but our grandchildren will pay for it?)She explained that is still being worked on, but that they are trying to do it in a way that does not contribute to debt or deficit.
(3) What is the Rush?(She reminded folks that America has been working on this since Teddy Roosevelt).
(4) Two people asked if Single Payer was off the table (it clearly is,and she did explain that we have working Government programs, from VA to medicare).
(5) A disabled woman did ask if there was any way she could get insurance and work and get off disability. (it sounded like that is not addressed in this bill).

(6) She did admit that she has not read the whole bill, that she has staff to do that (HR 3200 was up to 1400 pages so that is an absurd question, I think).

(7) A Med student explained that the financial costs were huge, and she agreed and said they are trying to work that in the bill to pay for increased education and then have increased care in areas of need.

* * *

Okay, so I did take cellphone photos—but they did not turn out well . . . sorry, looking for better ones . . . . Please also if Anyone has video, I would love to see, I know someone from Daily Kos was supposed to be there, so please let me know.

* * *

Final thoughts and Reflections

I was very proud of Marcia Fudge and her staff and of the Reform Supporters there. I don't know what to think after seeing the Disrupters in person. It was a lesson that there is Hate in this country, and it was palpable and worrisome. It was also a lesson that we need to stand up for people, all people. There were people there braver than me, a woman in wheelchair and elderly and people with disease who need us to stand up and ask for Better Care in this Country. Marcia Fudge was also a wonderful example of Some Capable of Stating the Facts and being clear about what we are facing, but also willing to listen and talk. At one point she yelled back to Hecklers that THIS was HER meeting and she was in Charge, and that really set the Rules. I loved that she also told some stories and used humor to diffuse the tension. I know that somewhere tonight Stephanie Tubbs Jones is proud tonight of Clevelanders and of Marcia Fudge . . . .

I also want to thanks the people there . . . for their courage and solidarity. I also think the Police and Security were very calm and watchful and that helped. And also Marcia's staff were very much there and a calming presence.

AUGUST 21, 2009, FRIDAY

STATISTICS TELL THE STORY . . . OF THE HEALTHCARE CRISIS IN AMERICA

The horrible part of looking at these numbers, that is so worrisome is that it does address the 6 Million People that have undergone job changes in the past 18 monthes, or the 14,000 a day that are losing Health Insurance and Healthcare. As much as no one wants to admit this, Dems and Repugs are Losing Jobs and Healthcare, and the Numbers are already bad and now they are getting worse.

* * *

More Stats,of UnInsured and how bad is the Situation, More from NCHC that will make you see how grim the picture really is . . . .

"Several studies estimate the number of uninsured Americans. According to the U.S. Census Bureau, nearly 46 million Americans, or 18 percent of the population under the age of 65, were without health insurance in 2007, their latest data available.1

The Agency for Healthcare Research and Quality, using the Medical Expenditure Panel Survey (MEPS) estimated that the percentage of uninsured Americans under age 65 represented 27 percent of the population. According to the MEPS data, nearly 54 million Americans under the age of 65 were uninsured in the first-half of 2007. 2

A recent study shows that based on the effects of the recession alone (not job loss), it is projected that nearly seven (7) million Americans will lose their health insurance coverage between 2008 and 2010. 3 Urban Institute researchers estimate that if unemployment reaches 10 percent, another six (6) million Americans will lose their health insurance coverage. Taking these numbers together, it is conceivable that by next year, 57 to 60 million Americans will be uninsured.

The Urban Institute estimates that under a worse case scenario, 66 million Americans will be uninsured by 2019. 4

Nearly 90 million people—about one-third of the population below the age of 65 spent a portion of either 2007 or 2008 without health coverage."

* * *

More from the CDC, correlates with this data, but is from 2004/2005

AUGUST 25, 2009, TUESDAY

URBAN INSTITUTE PUTS THE MORTALITY STATS OF UNINSURED OVER 100,000 IN PAST 8 YEARS.... READ MORE BELOW

{Originally posted 8.19.09}

Urban Institute, puts number between 18-22,000 per year, past 8 years, 137,000. (Click the link for the downloaded Research, here, http://www.urban.org/UploadedPDF/411588_uninsured_dying.pdf)

page 1 of Urban Institute Report:

Summary

"The absence of health insurance creates a range of consequences, including lower quality of life, increased morbidity and mortality, and higher financial burdens. This paper focuses on just one aspect of this harm—namely, greater risk of death—and seeks to illustrate its general order of magnitude. In 2002, the Institute of Medicine (IOM) estimated that 18,000 Americans died in 2000 because they were uninsured. Since then, the number of uninsured has grown. Based on the IOM's methodology and subsequent Census Bureau estimates of insurance coverage, 137,000 people died from 2000 through 2006 because they lacked health insurance, including 22,000 people in 2006."

* * *

Enigma's thoughts on this:

In the last two years we have seen massive layoffs and people lose homes and jobs, these numbers above only go to 2006. I would be very curious about what they really are at this point. From another post below, I did tabulate the loss of life under the Bush Years well over 167,000 from lack of Healthcare, and I think it is a horrific statement to our Country, worse yet, that No One has said a word about it . . . The Guardian did do an article below about people Dying for affordable Care . . . but MSM has not said a word . . .

NOVEMBER 03, 2009, TUESDAY

A KILLER AMOUNG US, AND HOW IT HAPPENED ... MEET CLEVELAND'S SERIAL KILLER. AND PRAY IT GETS BETTER NEWS COVERAGE ...

* * *

Anyone looking at this house in a East Side lower middle class neighborhood would never know that it was a house of horrors . . . . Last Friday that all changed . . . forever.

Here in Cleveland we have some problems, joblessness, poverty, foreclosured homes rampant on the East Side. We now have a problem that may have gone under the radar, but now is about to get National Attention . . . We Hope. Because Something Smells Here in Cleveland, more than just the Rotting Bodies at Imperial Ave. And while we still have Backhoes there, we need National Coverage of this mess that went Under-reported by Police and Media and while Countless Women are still Missing.

Did the Police Fail to Protect an Entire Community from a Sexual Criminal?

The facts broke Halloween Weekend just like a grisly Stephen King novel leaked . . . Bodies found at an East Side Residence after Police came to talk to the resident about Sexual Assault Complaints were filed against the Owner. The Owner is a 50 year old man who served time for Sexual Assault& rape, 15 years in Prison. In 1989 he assaulted, strangled and raped a woman, he was arrested for this crime and then served 15 years in prison for this crime. In 2005 he left prison he was only required to register his address to his parole officer. Periodically the Police would check that he did live at address he gave Authorities. Meanwhile the Neighborhood had NO idea that a Convicted Rapist was living in their neighborhood these past 4 years. The families and women in that Hood should have been warned. Also one has to wonder were there ANY complaints by women while he lived there? According to news stations various reports interviewing neighbors, there were calls and complaints about actiivity at that house.

The Women Go Missing . . . . And No One Knows?

Over the past few years women started disappearing from the neighborhood. Yet it was not reported on the Local News. Now this week, finally we have seen fliers of these Missing Women and we hear their stories, many are young women with families and children. Yet until this week we knew NOTHING of their Vanishings? As a woman, a mom, I am outraged. How and Why this happened. Was the Silence about these Missing Women because it is an impoverished area of the East Side? Was it because the Women are Black? Because they were poor? Or because Police Services were cut to that district? WHY didn't the Police publicize the Missing Women and take their photos and names to the Local Media? Would the Media Have Covered their Situation? Down Below I will post their photos and information I can find on them. At this point We need to know how many are actually missing. Within a one block radius of the House on Imperial supposedly it is up to 8 women Missing. Didn't the Police Map out the Missing Women and Wonder WHY a Cluster of Missing women are from the same area?

Police had been to Sowell's Home 4 times this past year, Why was he not arrested or Foul Odors Investigated?

Mr. Sowell was arrested on Saturday Afternoon after Police and Federal Marshalls searched all night for him. They began their search after arriving at him home to speak to him about a woman that claimed she was sexually assaulted at his home on Sept 22nd. (The Public is mystified WHY it took over a month to arrive at his home and question him, much less arrest him for these allegations that involved sexual assault, rape and strangulation with an electrical cord.) During recent days we have learned Police visited his home in December 2008, March2009, June 2009 and September 2009. We learned that supposedly they did not enter home or investigate the foul odors coming from the home. They also did not arrest him or take him for questioning. One other women supposedly filed charges this year, but then dropped her charges due to "Intimidation", and even that was not investigated. On Friday Evening October30th, he was not at the home, but this time the Police did enter and they at first found 2 decomposed Bodies on an upper floor. Over the next 24 hours they would find another partially buried in the basement, and then one in the yard and then two in the backyard. Six Bodies were found by Sunday, in various states of Decomposition, and beyond recognition. By Sunday the Museum of Natural History was contacted by the Police and Coroners Office to help identify bodies, date the decomposition and gender of the bodies. All six so far are women and 5 are known strangulation (local news reports, there still has been NO formal report or press conference by Police or Coroner's office).

What we learned from watching the Vigil on Monday Nov2nd. About the Missing Women.

Monday Night Clevelanders watched the local news and a Vigil had been planned to be held on Imperial Ave. More than a hundred showed up and not only grieved but shared information about the Missing Women. From local news reports it looks that there are atleast 8 Missing Women from that area of the location. The Families shared fliers and outrage as they realized that none of them knew about Sowell in their area, a Known Rapist, or of the other missing women. And yes, questions started to swirl as People started asking HOW did this happen and How Many are really missing?

The Issue of the Odors in the Neighborhood

So even Friday Night when the News Crews showed up when questioning people in the neighborhood about Sowell, most did not know him or the house, but many reported a Foul Odor in the Neighborhood." Oh, so bodies were found there, THAT must be the Odor" I saw three separate interviews on different stations where people reported the Odor. On another station a person reported that Neighbors had always thought the Odors Originated from the Sausage Factory. On Monday Channel 5 went and interviewed Sausage Workers, and they too had smelled the Odors and said they did not know the smell came from. All described it as a "Rotting Animal Smell", one Sausage worker said "I thought maybe some animal had died in the Sewer".

Sowells History: Scraping and Many Boxes of Large Garbage bags

On Monday Nov2 Channel5 News Ron Reagon went and interviewed the local Grocer in the Neighborhood, and the owner admitted that yes he knew Sowell quite well," because he was frequently in buying LARGE BOXES OF LARGE STURDY HEFTY GARBAGE BAGS". Tuesday November3 the street was closed and Excavation equipment and Cadaver Dogs were brought to the Imperial Street Address.

Channel 4 (Nov3) interviewed the man, Don Laster, that had helped rescue a woman that was found outside naked on the ground by the home in September, supposedly she was not clothed barely conscious and bystanders called 911 and gave a tshirt, supposedly medics came and took her to hospital. No Police reports from that day have been found or released to the public. One of the men that tended to her said she was barely conscious and was under debris in the yard and he took photos of her under a pile of debris. Sowell was naked in the yard and yelled, begging not to have Police Called. It is unclear WHY police did not come to this event, even though Sowell yelled to bystanders that she was his wife (like that would justify her being thrown off a porch nude?) Why wasn't he picked up and questioned about this injured woman? EMS supposedly did go to home—where are the reports from that day?

Tuesday November 3rd Updates:

News Crews have been by home all day, 3 Coroner Vans have been to home today, and cadaver dogs. Atleast More Body Bags have been removed. Police today are saying they do not know how many are there. Excavation equipment is still there. Many are concerned that this man was a known Scraper, going to East Side neighborhoods looking for scrape metal. Very concerning is that this man might have been looking for empty houses. Today digging continued at the houses, the basement, the garage.

FIRST OFFICIAL POLICE NEWS CONFERENCE IS ON AT 6PM

There are more Questions than Answers here in Cleveland....

* * *

More Articles on this.

(1) Nov3: Channel 19 NEWS now has a LIVE feed and Camera Set up and Hourly updates
(2) Philip Morris's Excellent post in Cleveland Plain Dealer explores more of the issues involved with this case.
(3) More from the Examiner on this case.

* * *

PLEASE SEE MORE DAILY UPDATES IN COMMENTS.

Channel 19 has POSTERS of Many of the MISSING WOMEN

* * *

Thursday November 5th Update:

Three Bodies have been Identified.

Tuesday Tonia Carmicheal (53) first one identified from Backyard remains.

Thursday Nov5th, Telacia Fortson missing since Junest, and Tishana Culver 31 (resident of Imperial Ave) both identified.

(* The "T" names—Coinicidence)

*   *   *

(Am attending site on Friday will post more at that time from the Missing Wall—as no MSM station has posted All the MISSING WOMEN Posters that are on Wall there) 123rd)

DECEMBER 03, 2009, THURSDAY

ABOUT MS....
THE PRICE OF REALITY...

* * *

The Leaves have fallen now . . . all of them . . . . and It is up to me to face some harsh Realities.

First off I need to say I am very very grateful that my son is growing up to be a Fine Young man and that he talks to me . . . . and that he is a Thinking Caring Compassionate wise soul . . . . and that he is and has been patient through all of this . . . . and that his dad has been helping us get through a pretty miserable time . . . . I am very thankful . . . and that is why I hate that my gratitude is so tarnished . . . .

At some point I need to write about this . . . . I need to let it out of my head . . . my heart . . . I need to find a way to fight it but still make peace with it . . . I need to find a way to have hope but make my way with this miserable companion. I have not a clue how to do any of those things . . . I have been the caregiver too long, I have no idea how to be anything else. How many years can I justify this lack of care? Four? Five? How long is too long? 2005 seems like yesterday, it seems like 20 years ago.

The sad yet silly truth of it is—I have NO way to take care of it or deal with "It"—or even try to fight it. Not because I am not wise enough or brave enough, but because Corporate Entities have dictated my circumstances . . . . I am UnInsured, Cancelled, soiled, spent, set aside like rotting garbage at a curb in my own country. How do I pretend to

Understand or Explain THAT? Or that it is happening to Millions of us? How Can I say that it does not anger me?

During this Healthcare Battle I have been forced to examine much of my life has been manipulated and manhandled by Insurance Companies . . . . and while working as a Nurse caring for hundreds of people, my own care was always rationed sparingly . . . It is senseless, demeaning, mind boggling. It means all that care I Gave meant Nothing in the scheme of things, that Giving Care is only meant for others, it has no value to the Bean Counters. Watching the DC Sausage Machine I was humiliated that suddenly the Costs of Healthcare were flung about the chambers like rotted vegetables. One GOP lawmaker said "that the Dems wanting to care for people was like watching a Wife let loose with a credit Card". And I watched Grassley quote Andrew Jackson—yes, the one president who died in 1845, and It gave new perspective to the phrase "Out of Touch". But the Corporations and the Lawmakers have Abandoned Humanity. And yes, abandoned millions of people just like me.

Can I face the next four years with No Insurance?No real Medical Care? and No Chance of Insurance? Is it right that I stay up night after night with THAT question banging through my brain,numbing my senses and wishing praying for another reality? How many of us stay up night after night staring at a clock,listening to it tick, stealing time . . . . the Worry Gift that it is. Time is no longer measured in Hours, it is measured in Dollars, and Lawmakers and Corporate Powers measure us in Dollars, not Life or Quality of Life. These past six months can not heal that perverse Reality . . . .

And I can not change that this reality hit after many monthes of watching HCR be haggled over like a grown hog . . . . And hate mail that was beyond civilized,letters from those abroad questioning our Broken Country ("What Kind of Country does not take care of it's People?" Your Healthcare System is like watching Katrina again" said a wise Scot) . . . . I can not change that I had this Reality Correction during Thanksgiving, a time when I should be so grateful, and usually am . . . . And I am left here angry,confused, dissillusioned . . . . like Millions of Americans . . . . and deep down I think that What is Happening is Very UnAmerican.

DECEMBER 14, 2009, MONDAY

MY FAVORITE MARKET THAT I STILL EVEN DREAM ABOUT ... AND OTHER BEACH DREAMS

Back in 2004 for 18 months my son and I lived in Pacific Grove California, and it was an amazing experience. In Many ways it was the hardest time of my life and in other ways it was the greatest adventure. We lived in a dilapitated old Victorian Rooming House and we shared a room. I had a window over the little Corner Kitchen Sink. I could stand in the mornings and make Tea and smell the Ocean and taste the breeze. At nigh the Deer would come munch on the bushes and shrubs at the bottom of the stairs, and my basset Abby would look at them softly with her big brown eyes. (Abby had spent her early years on a farm, so we thought that maybe she viewed them as goats.) And at night the seals would bark down at the Beach mere blocks away—So Abby would yodel back to them. My son and I boogied boarded and got wet suits and explored the Tide Pools and located Sandwich shops. And we figured out whenever the Power went out due to Storms, which was often, that many little shops halfpriced their goods.

And we found the Pacific Grove Market, that was full of Wonders, British Teas and cookies, and fresh fruits and vegetables. And we became "Fun Doo" Experts dipping vegis and fruit and bagels in the warm gooey crockpot of cheese. And we made Noodles with all kinds of vegetables. And we read many books and newspapers blissfully. And the Library turned out to be a wonderful find, walking there to treasure hunt . . . . it is those Memories I wrap around me late at night when it is cold and snowing . . . . It is why I still wear my Flip Flops in the house . . . . all year . . . It is why I dream about the Market at night . . . .

JANUARY 19, 2010, TUESDAY

A POST FOR MEDICAL WORKERS CONSIDERING TRAVELING TO WORK IN HAITI

Many of us that are Medical, especially Doctors or Nurses are wrestling with the decision to go to Haiti, I have been getting emails about this, so I decided to write a post about the actual decision process.And remember above all else, you can give from here and it does matter, and does help. Please see this list to get ideas how to help (Relief list compiled by Faydra Deon), this list has many ways to help and WHO to give to to help the Haiti Survivors. There are many fine medical Organizations that are doing an amazing job in Haiti, from the Red Cross to Doctors Without Borders, or Medicine Sans Frontiers, to Partners in Health, who have set up a Haiti Page to UNICEF. Please give what you can.

* * *

Introduction About Rendering Aid in a Diaster Zone

As a nurse of over 20 years I have worked disasters, and also rendered aid during Disasters. But all of my experience was on American Soil, and working with Groups such as the Red Cross or a Medical Group. I am an RN that has ER/PICU/PEDS/NICU/AIDS experience.l am also EMT trained and have work on an ambulance in a rural area, as well as worked and trained in an Urban setting(including crush and severe injuries and gunshot wounds).But even with all of these experiences, if I was to consider going I would ask myself many questions. {{ As I am living,caring for a teenage son, I am not planning to go at this point, I am working on twitter/cellphone as an intermediary connecting messages to aid.In 2005 with the Tsunami and Katrina I did the same thing to help the Disaster Refugees.}} But as someone who has worked Disasters I do want to help those planning or thinking of going to Haiti. (Please do follow my twitter page @watergatesummer to learn more about Haiti on the ground).

* * *

Part One: What the Medical Needs are In Haiti?

At this point most of the injured are severe, Many broken bones, head injuries, crush injuries.People that have experience in Orthopedics, Surgery, Neurology are all severely needed at this time. The work in the Tent Clinics is brutal, guerrilla medicine.People that have worked in this kind of setting or in dire circumstances need to be aware that meds,equipment, and supplies are all limited.Dehydration and Wound Care are only part of what is being provided and with limited resources.(2.5 Million People are without shelter, this includes the people caring for them, there is limited Shelter, Those caring for the patients are sleeping with the Tent Facilities,and there is limited Relief Staff).The staff at these facilities are not just providing care, they are providing comfort,food and water. There is limited food,water and such necessities as IV equipment,pain meds,surgical equipment,antibiotics,and sterilization processes.There are at this point 5-7 operating Hospital Facilities (these are mostly open air Clinics near Damaged Hospitals at this point). The USS Comfort has arrived as of tonight, which can care for 350Beds,7 Operating Rooms. Medical Care is also being provided at Sea by the USS Vinson,and Critical patients are being transferred to Miami as well.

* * *

Part Two: What do you ask yourself if you want to go?

(1) Have you ever done guerialla Medical Care, Street Care, or worked in an urban or rural setting that lacks resources? Do you consider yourself creative? Can you MacGuyver yourself if you are in need? IE. Have you ever made a splint out of a cardboard box?

or cared for an injury on a Hike or a car accident? (with limited resources?)
(2) Have you ever worked Trauma? ER? Surgery? Neuro? ALL of these areas are needed in Haiti—and will be for months.
(3) Have you ever worked 24 hour days, with limited rest or relief for days on end?
(4) Have you ever had to share a setting with your patients?
(5) Have your ever worked mass trauma with Thousands of grieving families?
(6) Are you physically strong enough to go? (You might even want to consider getting a physical before you go, and make sure all of your meds are up to date, do take extra Antibiotics—ie, Month supply of cipro for wounds or Stomach ailments).
(7) Are you spiritually strong enough to deal with such devastation and loss and also chaos? Are you strong under pressure?

Ask yourself what is the worst even you ever went through and how you got through it?(Remember you will mostly be with people that you do not know in a different culture).

(8) Do you speak any other languages? There is French and Creole, some spanish there as well. French especially would be helpful.

* * *

What to take and how to prepare if you plan to go to Haiti

There are many fine organizations in Haiti. Doctors without Borders (MSF) is there, and has been there for many years, even though their facilities were heavily damaged they have set up mobile facilities, and tent clinics and hospitals. Partners in Health and Red Cross are also there, and you can call them as well and offer your services and ask questions.

If you do go do check with the Organization you go with, and check if you are aloud to bring Blackberry or Iphone so you can communicate. Do bring extra meds for self. Protein Bars,Peanut Butter,Dried Fruit. Do bring Sturdy Shoes or boots,like hiking boots. Spare Contacts or glasses.

Do bring a bible, 80% of the Injured are Catholic, you will need to pray with them. Do be prepared to sing with them and pray with them, regardless of their religion. Their culture does also embrace voodooism, which means they are very spiritual and seek comfort from the earth and animals around them, you will have to be open to their beliefs.

If you do decide to go to help the Disaster Refugees and Quake Survivors, and need any more information please do email me if I can help more.

*   *   *

Photo by Soledad O'brien

*   *   *

Update 1.20.09

The Guardian has latest update on 6.1 aftershock/Quake this am. BBC and The Guardian are still doing an amazing job covering the quake, and CNN has huge team there as well. Reuters is also doing a good job.

MAY 16, 2010, SUNDAY

WHY THE GULF MATTERS TO ME . . . .

I have been trying to Blog and Tweet about the Gulf and the Oil Disaster, I have been trying to post Information, Science, Facts, videos and updates. I have tried to approach it clinically like a very sick patient, keeping my emotions to a minimum. Yet as it is now Day 32, my emotions are getting in the way. My Memories are getting in the way. My Longings and those memories are now haunting me and distracting me from my mission of blogging with clarity.

As a nerdish liberal child I grew up in a VERY Republican family. Yet the year I turned 11 we started spending much time in Florida on the Gulf of Mexico. Partly because my grandmother was moving there due to health problems. It was partly because my parents bought a condo at a bargain price and all vacations and summers were then spent there. By the summer I was 12 I was grossly absorbed with the Watergate Break In and then the following summer it was the Watergate Hearings. I was absorbed with spending hours walking the white sands and watching tide pools and touching shells and hermit crabs and other Sea Wonders. I was spellbound by the wonders of the Gulf, the beautiful azure waters against the White Sands with the number of Birds swooping overhead and Sunsets that transformed my soul.

Going to the Gulf was my Escape, but it was also very much where I found myself as I moved from childhood to Adulthood. It was where I was allowed to have compassion and hope. I sat on the Beach watching the Birds and wrote. I participated in Turtle Counts and Bird Counts. Where silent observations was a valuable gift. The Island where were, Sanibel was devoted to the Preservation of so many animals,buildings limited in a height and a Preserve (Ding Darling) that was beautiful. Every year the Turtles come to lay their eggs and then the eggs hatch and the Turtles would return to the Sea. As a young teen I hollowed out a hole on the beach with another Teen and with special Goggles and Binoculars we observed this Beautiful Event. And we sat and wrote our notes in the Dark of the Night. And in the Morning we touched the gentle trails left in the sand with awe.

When I was 12 my mother went out and told us to stay home and read. But the Gulf was beautiful and I had just passed my LifeSaving classes. So I did what an obstinate lonely teen would do, I went swimming. And on the 3rd Sand bar I stood up and admired the beautiful gleaming sea. When I stood up I felt the water move not far from me and realized there were "Finned Fish" moving my me. Three of them. My first thought was "Oh no, My mother will be right and I will be eaten by Sharks because she was right." I didn't have my glasses on, I am legally blind without glasses, so I really had to breath deep and calm down and try to assess the situation. I stood very still barely breathing and then I realized as one got very close that it was a Dolphin and that up close they really do look like they are smiling . . . . And I did the Unthinkable, I reached out very slowly and very gently and tenderly touched the closest one. It was so smooth, gentle and cool to my hand. It did not back off or go away but circled around again. They circled about and dove with each other clearly playing and clearly enjoying showing off. It was the most mystical magical moment I have ever had. It took my breath away.

To this day, the memory is so clear even though I had impaired vision I can close my eyes and still see them and their dipping and diving and beautiful graceful swimming. It moved me and inspired me in way that I can not explain. Through the years up until I was married I would return to the Island when I need respite or a break from School or Nursing Life or Wretched Boyfriends. It was where I sought solace. The Island and the Gulf was magical . . . . It was healing. Grounding. It would be where I would lifeguard, write, read too much and learn to sail. It would be where I would learn so much.

There would later be other trips to other parts of the Gulf and the Coast, And in many ways it is true that I am Home when I am by the

Sea—Always. But the Gulf and Sanibel was where I wanted to take my son one day, so I could show him the Wonders. And these past few years as I lost so many skills and physical strength I have always wanted to go back, as it is the one place that remains Home, accepting and full of Light. I am mad at myself now that I did not get my son there now. I am worried about the Fishermen and all of the Creatures . . . . the birds . . . the Turtles and the Dolphins and so many more . . . . I have learned over these past few years that Time is a Gift. But I did not realize how fragile Something so beautiful could be . . . and now it may be out of Time.

Allie McNeil

MAY 22, 2010, SATURDAY

DEAR PRESIDENT OBAMA, A LETTER ABOUT THE GULF DISASTER.

"We are tied to the ocean and when we go back to the Sea, whether it is to sail or to watch, we are going back from whence we came."~ John F. Kennedy

* * *

Dear Mr. President,

Millions of us worked to get you elected. We worked for you because we believed that you were the kind of man that when Trouble came Knocking you would be up to the challenge. A man of wisdom, integrity, and a Man wise enough to have the Integrity to listen to Wisdom. There is Wisdom knocking on your door, and I worry you are not listening. Millions of Americans are watching the Disaster in the Gulf unfold. Many are Scientists who are worried about the Situation because they have the Wisdom to see what is going on and what it holds in the Future.

Millions of People need answers and assurances that your Leadership is committed to them, but placing BP in charge of the Disaster the message to the People is that BP a Corporation is more important than them. For the Gulf residents that were abandoned, shunned, lied to, exploited and mistreated during and after Katrina, your Leadership is Critical at this time. Instead they have been given a BP hotline for everything for Dead Oiled

Carcasses, Fume Reports and Questions about Seafood. And they have watched BP lie about the Gusher and yet they are supposed to call BP for wounded animals? And they see that EPA is working with BP while hundreds of thousands of gallons of Toxic Dispersant are poured into their gulf. Yet has your administration reached out to the Fishermen, the Shrimpers, the Workers in the Gulf? Have you offered them relief and Programs for this situation? (Again FEMA, National Guard, HLS have been sparingly sparsely committed and silently deployed) This is your moment to historically provide Aid and relief.

So far those Scientists have had no avenue to share their concerns and their skills. They have merely been tossed the BP phone number and told to leave a message. In this kind of Crisis Energy, Vision and Scientific Expertise should be harnessed and utilized. There are Scientists who have worked to protect the Gulf for years and now they would problem solve to save it or try to save what is left of it. (Woodshole, Oceanography Programs across the Country, Engineering Programs).Scientists who work with National Geographic and Sierra Club, NWF, NRDC etc all have people who have studied and prepared and protected Ecosystems for years they are not compromised by Greed of Oil Laden ambitions.

You have been given your first American Disaster of Epic Proportions and it was created by Corporate greed and mistakes. Yet the Company that is Responsible for the Disaster is still controlling the Crime Scene. 11 Good Men died in an Explosion and yet instead of hearing that the Justice Department is Investigating Americans are told that BP is now in charge of the Disaster. Can you see how unjust and corrupt that appears to Americans? I have read the Justice Department is in NOLA, but you as President need to Announce that the Justice Department is investigating this Event and the Oil Slick.

Your Administration and even you should be giving Daily or bi-daily Briefings with NOAA, Coast Guard and EPA and DHHS issuing accurate Unbiased Uncompromised information regarding this Oil Slick. Hurricane Season is fast upon us, and this is your chance to help people prepare and work together to prevent panic and distress.

Mr.Gibbs has been mishandling the Pressers, mocking and dismissing Reporters concerns.Yet the Press Corps has been asking the same questions as millions of Americans have been asking. You need to acknowledge this anger, this frustration and angst. Americans watched on their TVs on May 18th when a CBS reporter was threatened with arrest for photographing Marshland Slime. The Reporter was told by a Coast Guard official that "BP is in charge". In that moment millions of Americans had their worst fear confirmed. BP not only owns the Disaster, they own the Gulf and Our Government Supports and Condones BP being in charge of this Disaster. The Message was that the Government has submitted Power to BP. And the Presser with Gibbs on the 20th and 21st confirmed this fear.

The Press needs to be able to report, interview Scientists, Fishermen, Residents and to take photos of the Dead Animals, the Damaged Gulf. This Crisis needs transparency and honesty and action. Silence will only be construed as part of the BP Coverup at this point. After numerous Coverups under the Bush Administration and 8 years of Lies, Americans are smart enough to KNOW they want Honesty and Leadership during this Disaster. We need you to do the Right Thing Now, Declare it a National Emergency.

Signed,
Just a Mom, Nurse, ...

(mailed and posted to White House Blog May 22,2010 Day 32 of the Gulf Disaster)

MAY 24, 2010, MONDAY

OIL DISASTER UPDATE: DAY 35: MONDAY MAY 24TH GUSHER STILL GOING STRONG, NOAA ISSUES 1ST HURRICANE UPDATE

Scientists found this oil-coated adult loggerhead turtle Thursday off the coast of Venice after an aerial survey directed from Houma. (From the HoumaNewsBlog, please see Turtle Update in the Wildlife Update Section below).

* * *

Quick Enigma Note: This post was put together late last night, with many helping to gather information via Internet and Twitter of Weekend Gulf Updates as the Oil Slick hit the Shores and Marshlands. I am so grateful for the many helping hands and minds of Twitter. Thank you. I will try to not post Dead Oiled Animals, but I did want to post this Oiled Turtle being rescued and cared for. Do see More at Boston Globe's BIG PICTURE.

* * *

* * ***WEEKEND UPDATES FROM THE GULF**

* * *

Saturday May 22nd Eve news:

CBS More of the Slick moves on shore, Concerns about the Government's role continues . . .
Watch CBS News Videos Online

* * *

NBC evening News (Saturday May 22):

Visit msnbc.com for breaking news, world news, and news about the economy

* * *

HURRICANE UPDATES (now to be included with Oil Slick Updates

We have been waiting for NOAA to issue it's first Hurricane Updates, with Maps, Images and projections, that was due to come out June 1st. I did read last week that USGS, NOAA and others were meeting to assemble data and examine this situation (Twitter). Late Last Night NOAA issued first Hurricane Update (not Storm, but Hurricane forming in the Atlantic that bears watching at this point, solely because of the gulf Situation). NOAA issued this first update and it shows the storm formation out past Bermuda, and it looks to be moving in that direction, hopefully it will not move into Gulf. The reason this season is of such concern is that like 2005 there are Warmest Temperatures on record, which impacts the Hurricane Season. People have been asking why do Hurricanes impact the gulf Situation, it is because with large underwater Oil Cloud formations in the Sea combined with the Current, it sets up a very complicated situation for the entire Gulf Coastline.

To read more and understand better Times Picayune (NOLA.com) has first article up about this Atlantic Storm forming, and explains why it matters for those in the Gulf.

CRITICAL: From another perspective it would be and is important that the NASA Sat Photos be analyzed and overlaid with the NOAA Hurricane Images and Trajectory Maps, especially comparing the SE

LOOP Currents and the Storm Maps in the Gulf. This would help to estimate where the Oil Slick could impact Shorelines on Gulf Coasts during Hurricanes.

* * *

GUSHERCAM WEBSITES FOR LIVE COVERAGE FROM SPILLZONE

BP's own site: LIVE Webcam

(NYT/CNN) LIVE CAM

*{ This is the Cam Link that was finally posted after Markey and Boxer worked so hard demanding BP let Experts and Public SEE the actual Flow from the Site. Now a Panel of experts has been assembled to examine footage and estimate Daily Flow. Please see Friday's post below to learn more. Sunday Night there were problems with the LiveCam—which we are hoping was Camera Malfunction. Today both cameras are up, people on Twitter are monitoring for increased plumage and more debris falling at site. People on Twitter are also watching trying to ascertain that the feed is not LOOPED.}

* * *

Times Picayune has more this morning regarding BP's plan to attempt the TOP KILL Project to Cap leak, at the earliest the Process has been made to start on Wednesday (it has been delayed twice, not sure why).It is important to recognize that this Process has never been done in Deep Water region, or underwater in these conditions, and with such presence of Methane and Hydrates or with an active gusher like this one. (This will be the forth attempt by BP to stop Leak. It is also to be noted that according to reports, the Siphon is not working as well as of Sunday night and is siphoning "less".) (Sunday morning is when BP admitted that the Siphoning Process was not working as effectively, you can read more here.)

Allie McNeil

* * *

WildLife and EcoSystem Updates:

(1) Over Weekend Washington Post posted this graphic which helps educate what Oil does to salt marsh ecosystems and its effects on birds and all wildlife. This post is especially important as now Grand Isle, many Barrier Island off Louisana and 54 Miles of Louisiana Coastline is Directly impacted with the Oily Goo of the Oil Slick

* * *

(2) US Fish & Wildlife Service reports 32 Nat'l Wildlife Refuges are at risk from the the BP Oil Slick. This is a critical issue, because as the Recovery and Rescue of the injured wildlife continues, it raises questions of where to release them, but also the future fate for thousands, maybe millions of creatures.

* * *

(3) Local Louisiana Stations are reporting of the Slick and the Pelican Nesting Grounds, especially on Cat Island. Please click the link to learn more about this.(I won't post oily Pelican photos-sorry-it's too graphic) If you want to learn more about the Risk of Oil to the Nesting Areas please do read this attached post.

* * *

Biologists find more oiled sea turtles. The number of Dead Turtles total is over 166 as of now, but the oiled Turtles that are found are not all dead, there are Rescue operations ongoing. The Turtles are of different kinds, Kemp Ridley, Loggerheads and Sea Turtles are all sensitive to this oil in the Gulf, as they have to swim in it, and they are Deep Swimmers as they look for food. The Effects of the Dispersant are a huge risk to them as well

* * *

Health Issues

I am still passing this OSHA FactSheet around Twitter and the Internet because it has Facts regarding being exposed to the Oilspill and FUMES. HLS and DHHS are still not issuing any warnings or Facts sheets-we are now 32 days into this crisis, so I don't know what they are waiting for at this point. If you want to share the info I will put it in comments so you can Twitter. Meanwhile the Fishermen that are assisting in the Clean Up Operations are having health effects and problems that they are not sure if they are related to Oils or Dispersant. EdBlizzard's huffpo post on GulfWorkers feeling effects is a must read. OSHA is involved, but there is no care or agency for the Residents yet. Volunteers for America is going down this week to set up help centers for the Gulf and assist with psychological care and other needs. But as of yet there is still No Hotlines for the Physical Symptoms of the fumes reaching shore. ((As a Nurse I am encouraging people with existing Conditions, Immune disorders, Heart and respiratory conditions to limit time outside and spend time indoors if they smell fumes, and to use AC and filtered air.)

* * *

More MUST READS from the Weekend:

* * *

From @Unclo he points out that if People want to boycott BP, they need to boycott other entities as well, ARCO, and AM/PM shops as well, you can read more from the post he sent me. Please think on it.

* * *

As this Disaster unfold it is important to recognize that it is being watched Worldwide.(I am grateful I got emails and links sent to me from all over—from Indonesia, Japan, UK and Australia to name a few.) This attached article is from the UK, from The Independent "The Black Hole in the Gulf."

Allie McNeil

* * *

Tom Foreman CCN writes Letter to the President that is much better than mine down below, I hope more and more do write to the President about this Disaster.

* * *

"Kevin Costner and His Brother Helping to Clean Up the Oil Spill" Is a Must read. BP is listening and working with this actor who spent 20 years investing in the Oil Seperator Technology that might help this situation. For those of us that went to see WaterWorld, we now know that our going to his movies was actually a good investment to help this Disaster. It's Ironic and poignant.

* * *

Oil spill video: Times-Picayune reporters give latest updates and coverage.

* * *

Audobon Magazine has update on sealife, Spill update: Oil might've killed 87 sea turtles, 18 birds, 6 dolphins; oil industry tax hike; leak video.

* * *

Once again Huffington Post has devoted a whole page to this situation. It is to be noted that Think Progress and Truthout and Raw Story and many other blogs have really been tracking Whistleblower concerns, Animal damage and reports from the Gulf States.

* * *

Seafood Resturantes and Suppliers have already started to Sue BP, this has not been reported by Big Media, but local media on the Gulf is starting to Report.

Watergate Summer

*   *   *

If you want to help, Volunteer or Donate you can still read more of this post. Thank you for caring for the Gulf.

*   *   *

Please do scroll down as all the posts below explain about the Volume and the Sat photos explain about the Oil Spill Entering the SE Loop.

*   *   *

Many Other Blogs, Internet News are doing great job with Updates: Truthout, SkyTruth, HuffingtonPost, Think Progress, and the Times Picayune, and @GOHSEP are Daily Greats.

*   *   *

More Updates later . . . . taking break for now . . .

AUGUST 04, 2010, WEDNESDAY

WHEN THERE ARE NO WORDS . . . .

* * *

I look at this woman . . . . The Tension, the Fatigue, the Fight, the Spirit, the Question of "When Does this End?" . . . the Look in her eyes . . . It could be a mirror . . . . It could be me . . . . (It's not me . . . it's a Migrant Worker from the Depression . . . . captured in time by Dorthea Lange).

I have always tried to be hopeful, even when blogging, writing about about the Worst of Anything. Even blogging all through the Titannical Bush Years. I tried to keep Perspective and even a sense of humor . . . and even tried to keep my wits . . . tried to stay strong . . . When you live with a Teenager you worry that you will set the wrong example, you realize What you do teaches irreplacable Life Lessons. When my son and I lived in one room in a rooming house in California, and our clothes were stolen from the Laundry Mat, I tried to explain to my son that Someone Must be in worst Straights than Us.And if the Pipes broke and flooded the Basement in the 1894 Rental . . . I tried to use that as yet another "Fix It" Lesson with my "Tool Purse". (At this point I could write books on "Why Redheads should Not be Plumbers"). When our rented Loft downtown got Foreclosed and we had 2 weeks to move and it was Zero Degrees and January, I made awful jokes about Why Siberians Don't even Move in Winter . . . . I even made jokes about how ludicrous a Nurse should work at a grocery store in an attempt to get Health Insurance . . . . I even made jokes when the said grocery store made us wear coats and fingerless gloves, rather than spend money on Fixing the Heater.(I called that the Bush Repair Program).

Watergate Summer

When my son and I left the Downtown Loft we moved into an old Battered Side By Side in an old tree-lined street in an older neighborhood 2 miles from the heart of DownTown. An 1894 Trolley House that is full of challenges.My hood was originally full of working class families and College and grad students. But months after coming here slowly things started to change . . . . I know that we have been told that the "Recession" started in 2008. But it started long before that, in 2006 or 2007. I am haunted that Bush could not even say the "R" word, and the Media let him get away with it. While he could not say the "R" word, people in my hood were losing Homes, and jobs and cars and yes, Hope and Dreams.

Over the years I have blogged about watching furniture being dragged to the Curb and watching men restlessly do yard work and quietly and with shameladen faces use Food Stamps at the little market. And Old People from my hood pay for meager soup meals with change in coffee cans. I have made brownies for families as I said goodbye and helped them pack. I have watched students move home, because they could not find jobs.I have taken soup to families sleeping in cars at end of street.I have cared for stray animals left behind.I have met most of the Metal Men who scavenge our streets on Sunday night. I have watched other students move home because there were no loans and not enough money . . . . I too am living with a son who should be in college, but financially there is not a path right now, he knows the realities, yet he keeps reading and studying, and that tugs at my heart. And I know that there are thousands of young people who have been effected by this, their lives changed.

I have watched two neighbors die without Health Insurance and without Care, the one lady died alone. I still have trouble walking by those houses. The one house they lost the house because they had a reverse mortgage, that had been set up in case they had a medical emergency. And over time, there have been more and more houses. I even lost neighbors who were renting, because their landlords got foreclosed. And over time it got be that I would walk my dog and listen to Music or watch birds and squirrels because there was no one to greet or talk to. And the Empty Houses looked as lonely as I felt . . . .

Allie McNeil

* * *

{*Depression Photo Russell Lee-did not want to post photos of homes from hood, as it might embarass struggling neighbors}

And I thought I was OK.... working perdiem and odd jobs and keeping the routine of taking care of my son, walking the dog, applying for jobs every week and even keeping my house tidy, that the routines would shield me from the Reality....

Now in the Midst of all this I lost two jobs.... and while everything was busy breaking in June (Car, Computer, the Thugs that took apart my railing.... etc.... etc...)

Then The Census Worker came.... and she said that she was having trouble getting people to answer the doors to finish our Street. So we walked the street and I explained House by House the situation. "That was where a Teacher lived-he got laid off and foreclosed". "That is where a nurse and medtech lived-but they lost their house-it's been foreclosed, or for sale for over 2 years." (If they take the Mail box off the house that is a good hint that the family is gone). She was stunned, "I had no idea that so many homes had been lost". We talked about the level of Loss of Homes and jobs and how they were intertwined, and how they were all hardworking families, living in old homes, none were living beyond their means. We talked about how it was all intertwined, the jobs, the healthcare crisis, the Economy that has hurt so many. I told her that I had canvassed for Obama so I knew my hood really well, that it had seemed to slowly change, but that I now realized that so much had changed since that Winter when homes still had families....

I watched her write down the information, house by house carefully Documenting the Damage and we both silently wondered if the devastation can really be documented fully? What was it like in the 30's? It's hard to document the Damage and the quiet desolation of the Empty Houses is deafening....

* * *

And in the midst of this Vast Emptiness . . . . the Street of Goodbyes, And the Summer of Broken Things . . . . I also have had to face Myself. That the MS is not going away . . . . it's Real, it's part of my life . . . in a Broken Frustrating way . . . . There are things I can not do, and that are getting too hard and harder by the day and just like facing the Empty Houses I have to admit that Rickety Old Stairs and a Huge Hill are making my life miserable. And that I can not "fix" it . . . or me. And that does not mean I am weak or whining . . . it means that things Change . . . . I need to find other ways to be Strong, that means live in a different place and yes even look at NonNursing Jobs as a Reality . . . . it means giving up . . . and letting go. It means finding other ways to reach dreams and goals. It means that sometimes being Broken effects others . . . . and saying I am sorry to my son in a 1000 different ways . . . . That I will still help him reach his goals and dreams . . . but we need to do it Another Way . . . .

And it took me two months of Silence to make Peace with That Reality . . . . There were No Words . . . .

* * *

To all of those that offered to listen to talk and were and are so kind I can only say thank you. I just had to get through it alone, it is how I cope and work through things, especially when the struggle is at it's heaviest, I can not bear to burden others with my problems. I also in some ways guilty for posting this when so many others are suffering, especially those in the Gulf and Haiti, but I know others are also struggling during these times. I also need to say I am sorry but if you emailed me in May or June I was hacked and didn't get alot of my mail . . . so again I apologize . . . . But I remain grateful to all . . . . very much so. I continue to try to find my grace during this period . . . thank you and I apologize . . .

SEPTEMBER 22, 2010, WEDNESDAY

INDIAN SUMMER BRINGS CHANGES: ENIGMA UPDATE

* * *

Hope is that thing with feathers that perches in the soul and sings the tune without the words and never stops . . . at all. ~Emily Dickinson

* * *

Hope begins in the dark, the stubborn hope that if you just show up and try to do the right thing, the dawn will come. ~Anne Lamott

* * *

So many of you wrote and offered support and kindness and compassion, I am more than grateful. So summer was hot and full of turmoil, as I wrestled with the Job Situation and the Hell Hill. 29 Steps became my the main refrain of my days, and it was making me my life something that was constantly measured in steps. It became humorous too, at times I would be so tired I would fall up the stairs, not down. The landlord never did get the railing fixed,but he did something that was very kind, he offered me another rental that was not on a hill, it is on Flat Ground and a Flat street near a Market. And I can walk 3 steps into the house, and it has a driveway where I can park and take my groceries into the kitchen. And for me that is bliss.

The House is a sideby side again, but not 1894 . . . newer. Which means the stairs are more even and less steep . . . . It is in a hood full of houses and college kids and old hippies. There are people on porches grilling, playing guitars, and singing, College kids playing RISK, and young families our walking and a Community Pea patch and so many dogs all kinds and sizes. And it smells of candles and incense and grilling and Basil. And NO Foreclosed homes-not one. (My old house I was surrounded on all sides, and it made me so sad, especially when they were empty).

So I spent most of August and part of September getting Son and I moved, I cleaned out both places, I scrubbed and painted and tidied and even laid one tile floor and stripped another of carpet and tile to get to the hardwood. It was hot and withering . . . and I worked and I knew that I wanted to be moved by the time the seasons changed. I did it frantically because every fall has brought changes. Where I am so stiff and sore and weak I can not do things in the same way, this has happened for the past 3 falls. Where I drop things and break things as the temperature shifts, and the tingling is worse and the spasms are like knifes. I wanted to be ready this year. And I wanted to have everything taken care of. And the new place does have stairs, but for now I can still do them, some days better than others. And we will have to see how it goes . . . . for now.

And the Ex came and we had a long talk and I explained that I NEED a job where I am not on my feet and where I can sit, it is not being lazy, that MS is real and damaging and a battle and I need another way to fight it. So this month I am working on my Resume and will be looking for jobs that embrace my Research Skills and if I have to be using a cane I will interview with a Cane. So be it. I am done lying and trying to "act fine". I am exhausted and tired. I was diagnosed in Fall 2004 and have had no Healthcare, that is NOT my fault. That shows we are a Broken Country.

Now about HCR. I did receive a Call back from the High Risk Pool chosen Insurance Company in August. They said that my NEW insurance that I could apply for would cost 1200/month and that there would be a 10,000 deductible.I can not afford 1200 /month, that is more than my rent, WHO could afford THAT? And the joke, it is the SAME company that canceled me in 2006 for having Breast Cancer in my family History. I told the lady on the phone that the Rate was "Unrealistic, that NO ONE could pay that, that it would again limit care and access.She had no response.Silence when confronted with the Truth" . . . . So for now it looks like I am waiting to get HealthCare in 2014 . . . Or hoping and praying that I get a job with Insurance. I would love a job that allows me to still be a Nurse, maybe Psych nursing or something like that . . . or more research. But no standing, no running around . . . . But Time will tell.

For now Son and I are staying here, in Cleveland by Lake Erie, and hoping and praying that we find our way this year to get to NYC and trying to come up with a Better Plan. So if you have ideas I am still listening . . . Always.

And I am going to add PayPal to my blog because maybe I could allow people to support and appreciate my writing. I also am going to start blogging again everyday,because it helps keep me focused and connected.

* * *

This tub is my heaven . . . it has a Window overlooking tall old trees and the curtains are made from an old dotted swiss dress and I have candles and sunchimes that I made out of wires and marbles . . . (6-6 has the 2nd floor to himself and I live in the attic, it's all good and we don't share the Bathroom anymore, he has his . . . and I have mine, so neither has to rush now.And his OCD has it's own space . . . . I have a little bit of heaven . . .)

* * *

This is the Floor in the attic-I have two rooms to myself . . . and I had to strip the carpet . . . and then I found there was tile . . . UGH. I had to remove all the carpet-it was pet stained and bugridden-so off it went. But this floor really challenged me, as I sat and picked the tile-that chipped off in tiny pieces I had lots of time to reflect and think and pray . . . . Patience and Strength are taught by Circumstances and Problems . . . . that is is the way of it.

JANUARY 06, 2011, THURSDAY

UNHEALTHY NEWS .... UPDATES ON OUR HEALTH CARE CRISIS (INSURANCE GREED TO GOP IDIOTS)

* * *

(1) Dailykos posted the first story (via National Nurses Union) about how the CEOs make sickening Bonuses while all of us are Dying for care . . . I want Someone to tell me WHAT they do that deserves Millions of Dollars while I have friends and neighbors with NO Healthcare at all . . . . dying in their homes . . . . How can that be OK with Anyone????

(2) Here is the actual Link from Kaiser Health News that has the actual information about the Bonuses and who and how it effects us . . . .

(3) Meanwhile Blue Cross of California jumps on the Greed Wagon and decides that it is now planning a 59% Increase for Individual Policies that will surely make sure that MORE people go UnInsured or unable to afford even just basic care. It is amazing after watching the Economic hell that so many are experiencing that Big Companies find more and more ways to screw Middle Class Working Poor in this country . . . . Stunning.

(4) Meanwhile Wendell Potter tweeted this great Eugene Robinson Article that is a Must Read about the HCR battle that Dems SHOULD want to take on . . . .

(5) And now adding to the Health Care Mess we have in this Country, the Repugs want to REPEAL the HCR, and low and behold they say it is to Save Money, but the joke is their actual Repeal will cost

well over 230 Billion Dollars by CBO estimates . . . . (TPM story linked here)

*   *   *

Enigma Note: For those that are new Followers, I am an RN of over 20+ years and I also am UnInsured due to being cancelled in 2006 due to family Cancer History (Breast Cancer), and I worked for over 2 years blogging and trying to educate all of us about our Health Care Crisis, and worked very hard on HCR. I am not happy with the Bill we got, but it is a Start . . . . in the End I know as many do that we NEED HCR for ALL, Medicare for All, even a Buy In Program would benifit the more than 60 Million that are uninsured. More than 47,000 People die each year with NO health Insurance and No healthcare . . . . So yeah, as an UnInsured RN, I am rather Opinionated about this issue, No One should be dying for healthcare . . . . No One.

January 11, 2011

Bear with me . . . . Sometimes I feel small in All of this . . . this is only my 4th Blogpost on M.S. in many years of blogging . . . .

* * *

It's pretty isn't it? (Photo of Cane) I love that you can tell someone carved it and painted it, worked the wood with love. I love that a friend gave it to me, that she bought it at Zoo in California and that it is made by a woman . . . . I love that it is from a Baobab tree of Kenya . . . I love that it is to look like a Zebra . . . . Which for me is so horse like . . . I love that it is a gift,but somehow it is the exact height for me, even though my lovely friend is an online friend and she was not so sure how tall I was . . . I love that it is So Arty . . . So well crafted . . . . that it is so strong and so sturdy . . . I even named it . . . KENNY . . . (from Kenya . . .) . . . . And in Winter I am so grateful to have Kenny . . . because well . . . Getting through Heavy Snow is like Tap Dancing through Wet Cement . . . But.

BUT . . . .

But I wish it was for Someone Else . . . I wish it was not for me . . . .

In 2004 I was first diagnosed with MS when a disturbing pattern of symptoms collided in on me . . . actually it turned out to be a Multiple Diagnosis . . . but that is a much longer story for another time. Suffice it to say . . . . A lovely neurologist on West Coast, said that she was concerned I had MS, perhaps ALS. She wanted to order Another MRI and she wanted to do Tests. But my Insurance at the time said no. I had had an MRI in 2002, and that was recent enough, that they would only cover one every 5 years. And yes there was some concerning "things" on it, some "spots", and yes it did warrant followup, but not another $1500 MRI they said. I remember joking well, Homer Simpson had crayon in his head, so maybe we should make sure of What the Said Spot was, make sure it was not a crayon . . . I was desperately trying to not have to really know what the Spot was . . . But . . . . (She didn't share my sense of humor . . .) If one wakes up with numb gripless hands and trouble swallowing one clings to Humor . . . and prays that their Insurance Company will do the Right Thing . . . But . . . .

And about the Insurance Company . . . . Gee it's not like I was asking to buy myself something of a Luxory, a damn Cruise or ill deserved Prada Shoes . . . . this was a Real Doctor asking to Look further at my Innerds because there was Something Wrong . . . And Since I had other symptoms the Doctor said it would be good to be evaluated further. And the Insurance Company said "Well if that is the case . . . We need you to go to one of our Centers of Excellence for further evaluation, we have Eight Hospitals in the Country you can choose." (Yeah., because we know that when someone is Really sick they really want to travel???) Long story short, for anyone who cares THIS is part of How I ended up in Cleveland . . . .

Longer Story within 14 months of seeing her I was canceled by Insurance, not because of the MS, but because of Breast Cancer in my family. Yup . . . . totally screwed over by TWO different companies . . . It amazes me . . . a Nurse what Crappy Insurance Companies we have Determining Level of Care and access of Care in this country . . . . A Thorough Doctor ordered some bloodwork related to Family History (BRCA testing) and Voila, within 4 weeks canceled . . . . *POOF* No More Insurance, No More Medical Care . . . $440 dollars /month . . . . swept away . . . (Which is damn ironic, because if anything Someone with a gene situation, a family history should be getting screened and checked and monitored . . . NOT Cancelled . . . and frankly damnit I think millions of Women are being discriminated against . . . . but that is a Beef for another day . . . .)

So I have coped quietly with it . . . Ignored it, cursing it ever so silently. Other times fighting it . . . or even trying to Make Nice with it . . . But the last few years it has not been something I could ignore, not something I could curse so silently. I feel like I have the flu, all the time. "Fatigue" Is a REAL thing . . . I feel like I am drowning in it . . . its all encompassing . . . like a bed of quicksand a cold heavy sensation that requires a wrestling match to get out of bed . . . . And I don't cope with Temperature changes well, if

I get Cold, I can not get warm. And if I wake up and my leg is "Numb" I know it will be like that all day, that I will drag it around like an old rotted piece of luggage.

And other nights, especially when I have been working that I will have leg cramps all night. And Stiffness, I wake up in the morning and give orders out to my limbs and Nothing happens, I lay there like a giant lump of Stale Playdough. I move through the day like the Tinman from the Wizard of Oz, creaking and getting stuck . . . Except there is no magic Oil Can . . . . Other times I have fallen asleep and then when I wake up my arm is trapped underneath and I can't roll to get it out. It sounds almost comical, but it isn't . . . . And My Brain seems fine, ticking along and I know it still gives orders" Get up the Stairs" . . . . but there are little dendrites down there ignoring the Orders . . .

But my brain is still ok . . . It is Still ME . . . still Thinking too much . . . Worrying too much . . . Reading too much . . . . But on another level I know I am too sensitive . . . about ALL of THIS . . . . A Friend sent me a video of a Model or a Beauty Queen falling . . . . and I know she thought it was funny . . . but for me it hit . . . it hit hard . . . it made me cry . . . . It reminded me of that Sensation of falling . . . that OH NO sensation . . . . and then the announcer on the video laughing too loudly . . . it felt Cruel . . . it felt Real . . . . for me I have fallen and people laugh . . . . and been the Only One not laughing . . . . So yeah, I guess my Sense of Humor is now damaged . . . and I tried to explain it to the friend . . . . but I was left feeling empty and More Alone . . . off in the distance with my lack of Humor . . . my fear of falling . . .

Now back to The Cane. I don't use it all the time, only when I have to. So I wake up and I look out the window and there is new fresh snow,and it looks ever so pretty . . . . but I also know there is old snow and ice underneath Lurking. I use the cane because I know if I start to fall I have no way to get up. And I fall more now, even inside I fall. It happens when I am really tired, for no reason. It is like Someone came up and pulled the rug out from under me . . . KaPAM . . . Boom . . . down I go before I can think or stop it. and then getting up depends on what is near by, what I can use to leverage myself. It becomes a Process thinking it all through . . . And I even joke with my son asking if I should yell Timber . . . .

I used to have this amazing "Walk", I had this way of walking that people would look at. It was this way of entering a room. A way of being Strong even if doing so silently. I really miss that . . . Miss having people look at me when I enter the room, miss feeling that buoyant . . . that Strong . . . that Indestructible. In my dreams . . . sleeping i still have that Look, that Walk . . . . and the cane is never in the Dreams . . . .

And I know that there are times I am really really tired and I know Stairs are getting harder and harder . . . and I know that someday I won't be able to do them. Even now there are certain days I start limiting the trips up and down the stairs, because if I get too tired I know I fall more, on the stairs, up or down . . . . it doesn't even matter. And yes for anyone who knows it's true I moved this year because we lived on a house on a Hill. I called it Hell Hill 29 steps to the Front Door . . . . it was too much . . . So Now I am on a flat street and 5 steps to the front door. Even Steps, and NO Hill.

It is so funny . . . . No one would know I used to run Half Marathons or that I swam and was a lifeguard. I stare at my legs or my arms and I don't see any of that anymore. I see??? Mashed Potatoes? I think what happened to the Tone, where did it go? From 2004 on I tried to work with hand weights, and that became laughable, from 3 to 2 to 1 pound. Now I use a Bean Can . . . .

When you don't have insurance you get Creative. You do things like a bean can as PT. You order antibiotics from Vet Companies (for fish). And you go to the Doc in the Box for basic meds, and pray you are self medicating properly. When I sprained my ankle working at the market I used Duct Tape, and it worked like a charm . . . . But it all becomes like a bad movie . . . . except it is your life . . .

I know this is about Letting Go and Control and Letting the Changes come and Coping and Still trying to have some dignity and some grace and Learning to Cope and that Everyone has Something they are trying to Cope with . . . . But I don't know ME anymore or my body . . . and I feel like I am letting go of pieces of me . . . in 20 directions . . . vision and hearing and coordination and I miss going for LONG walks and I hate always looking . . . SEARCHING for benches when I go for a walk . . . .

I hate that I feel like I have just run 14 miles . . . all the time . . . . that I wake up feeling like that . . . .

I hate that I can't run anymore . . . . and that I can't even dance . . . and yoga . . . well trying to hold poses is almost impossible . . . definitely something I can't do around others . . . . that everything has become Watching . . . That I am too sensitive now . . . That Someone posts a Crass Joke about "Scooters" and I can't laugh . . . because I KNOW there is a scooter waiting for my in my future., . . . just around the corner . . . . And that I will have to move again to a place with no stairs . . . . but I have to get my son to NYC . . . so that can't happen yet . . . not yet . . . .

And people say . . . well . . . can you still Nurse, and I say, only certain kinds . . . I can't be a Floor nurse any more . . . no more ER . . . . I was a great ER nurse . . . . really . . . but now everything revolves in planning how long I can stand . . . . I even worked at a grocery store for a while, attempting to get Health Insurance . . . . and the bottom line is that all of that lifting and bending and standing was so so painful and I would get stiff and stuck . . . I could barely make it home at night . . . . I would walk home and try to figure out how to get into the house without doing the 29 steps, and I finally found a way to crawl through the backyard bushes . . . I can laugh at it now . . . It all sounds so absurd . . . a Nurse working as a checker to try to get healthcare . . . . and then crawling through the yard to escape THE Evil Hill.

And people say well Apply for Disability . . . . But if I do that I lose so so much . . . I lose my Nursing License . . . ME . . . I lose ME the Nurse and I lose even my driving License . . . So I am NOT willing to do that . . . Not yet . . . . Because even if I am weak and "Stuck" . . . and laying in bed I can still help someone get the Hospice Care they need or diagnose my best friend's friend 6000 miles away with Typhoid . . . . I still have ALL my nursing skills intact, I have cared for hundreds and hundreds and I am now supposed to LOSE THAT because I have trouble lifting a bag of groceries? or standing for more than 20 minutes? that just isn't right . . . . sorry . . . . but it isn't . . . .

JANUARY 18, 2011, TUESDAY

ESTIMATES OF 50 MILLION UP TO 129 MILLION HAVE PRE-EXISTING CONDITIONS (WAPO) ABOUT SOON TO BE RELEASED DHHS STUDY . . .

(Photo: RAM Free Health Clinic in LA 2008: This photo symbolizes the Thousands that have had to line up for access to any Free Needed Health Care . . . .)

So late Monday Night it came across the wires that up to 129 Million People have Health Conditions that can be considered Pre-Existing Conditions by Insurance Companies. DHHS is to release this Study this week . . . . The Washington Post snuck it out while we were sleeping, like leaving a Toad on my pillow. Waking it and finding it and yelling out, "Ouch". This number as shocking as it is also shows Why Health Care Reform, even in it's most basic form, must begin now as these Numbers Unfold.

From the Article::

(((Or WHO you may ask qualifys as a Pre-Existing Condition?)))

> "The study found that one-fifth to one-half of non-elderly people in the United States have ailments that trigger rejection or higher prices in the individual insurance market. They range from cancer to chronic illnesses such as heart disease, asthma and high blood pressure."

And here's More to Consider:

> "The study found that one-fifth to one-half of non-elderly people in the United States have ailments that trigger rejection or higher prices in the individual insurance market. They range from cancer to chronic illnesses such as heart disease, asthma and high blood pressure.

The smaller estimate, by Health and Human Services Department researchers, is based on the number of Americans whose medical problems would make them eligible for states' high-risk pools—special coverage for people denied insurance because of their medical history. The researchers arrived at the larger figure by adding in other ailments that major insurers consider a basis to charge customers higher prices or to exclude coverage for some of the care they need."

*   *   *The Important sentence to note, DHHS arrived at that figure when adding in data from Insurance Companies, Major Insurers.*   *   *

Other Toads from the HCR Battle that are already Known Facts . . . .

According to Harvard Studies in 2007/2008 More than 45,000 die per year with NO Health Insurance and No Health Care. (Please do share the Sept 2009 Harvard Study)

It was estimated that at least 51 Million have No Health Insurance and No Health Care and that Wretched Number was estimated before The Huge Economic Collapse and millions more lost jobs and homes. . . and Insurance.

More than 42% of ALL Bankruptcies of People Losing Homes are directly related to Medical Debt. (Studies say 42-62% depending on which study is used).People literally losing it all for their Health. And once they are have suffered Financial Damage, they then go on to be considered a Credit Risk, so then they can not qualify for Health Insurance either.

The bottom line is that all along, all during the Health Care Battle of the past two years there were so many of us saying that alot more People than the Estimated 30 Million proposed during the Health Care Reform era have Pre-Existing Conditions. Millions have been denied Care and Insurance and Cancelled.

Now as the HCR goes into effect it is being implemented State by State to provide changes to Care Provision. Yet each State is handling certain issues differently. Each state is setting up the High Risk Pools. Yet in many states High Risk Pools are determined by Insurance Companies setting the new parameters and the Costs and the Plans of Care. So once again they are controlling the Access of Care, for the very people they already denied, cancelled or over Charged.

And as interesting as this Study is supposed to be, WHY would Sebelius wait until the last Final Hours before the Republican Vote to repeal HCR??? I am left with more questions than answers . . . . (as of 1PM it is still not Publicly Available.)

* * *

((Enigma Footnote:::: Personal little story regarding Being Cancelled. I was cancelled in early 2006, I was cancelled after a Doctor ordered BRCA blood work due to Family History: Breast Cancer. I was cancelled because I supposedly did not properly disclose all family History to said company, even though I am pretty sure I did. So low and behold in August I called the State to inquire as to the High Risk Pool. And within Days the High Risk Provider called me back. Ironically the Company that has the Contract is the same Company that Cancelled me. I was paying 440/month in 2006 (which yes is VERY high for a single mom . . . .) And they "offered" me Insurance this past August "$1150 /month, not including deductibles and Capped Care . . . . blah blah blah . . . ." At come point during that Conversation I hung up the phone before I heaved it . . . . Everyone who comes to this Blog knows for over 2 years I blogged we have a Health Care Crisis in this Country. $1150 is too much, it is more than Rent and Heat Combined . . . It is Highway Robbery . . . . And if you like you are welcome to read about my Life as a UnInsured Nurse No Healthcare and No Insurance and M.S, ... just my story, one of Millions.))

REMEMBERING
MARTIN LUTHER KING . . .

[This was originally posted on Watergate Summer 2006/2007, in honor of MLK I am reposting and honoring those of us that grew up in the Sixties and remember having Leaders violently taken . . . . Remembering how we as children had Dreams.]

Whenever I think of the year that Martin Luther King and Robert Kennedy were taken from us, I also think of my Aunts. In particular my Aunt May. She lived in downtown Baltimore on Eutaw Street in a mammoth old brownstone during the 1960's, her last decade.

She was my great great Aunt. Her real name was Margaret May, her stage name was Margeurite.She had lived quite a life by the time I stumbled band aids and chewing gum, into her historic living room. Her house was like a museum, full of trinkets and precious relics from around the world and a lifetime of adventures and secrets. She was born after the Civil War in Kentucky. She spent her early years wandering with her dad, from Virginia to DC to Kentucky. And as she grew older she would help carry his supplies. Her mother died when she was small, and she was always blaming that for a lack of ladylike manners.

Her dad was one of Lincoln's photographers, he traveled with the Brady Pack. He didn't make alot of money, but he did get to keep the rejected plates and the faulted pictures. (And in case you are wondering—Lincoln was NOT photogenic, and he really did have a good side, and a not so good side). The old photographs were kept up on the 3rd floor, lined up around the walls. They told of a Lincoln that we never saw in the History books. They showed him dozing in a chair, playing cards in a tent with Union troops, and hugging one of his sons. There were none with his wife "And Don't that about say IT All, although I heard she didn't photograph so well." Aunt May used to say. There were also photographs of battle scenes, bloody carnage and singed buildings that remained stained with blood, even though they were not in color. These graphic pictures fascinated me. Even shots from surgery tents. "Whelp, she is fascinated with the bloody medical stuff, she will be a surgeon or a Killer" Aunt May would joke to my grandmother. Flo would tell her to shush.

I would go to visit my Aunt May with my grandmother, especially that particular April as my mom's Dad was in the hospital at Hopkins that spring, and we had just moved back from Indiana that winter, and she needed my sister and I out of her hair. Aunt May's museum was my first choice, my sister went to a friend's house. Aunt May had pictures from around the world, places she had traveled and sang. Her house was big lumbering Brownstone it was a Museum that you could smell and touch the past. When you opened the door it hit you in waves, the aromas, dusty books, Strong Black Tea, French Perfume, Myr and Patchouli from India, and Okra Gumbo steeping on the back stove. She was an Opera Singer and Actress in the early 1900's. Her stage name had been Marguerite. Her old programs were also in a box in the 3rd floor. She was a beauty, she sang, danced, acted and did Vaudeville. She had long flowing hair and beautiful eyes. She was even painted by some pretty famous painters in Europe, in some very interesting outfits. And yet when she spoke she still had a Kentucky lilt. She told amazing stories that were all her own.

She would come up to the 3rd floor with me and sit on an old velvet stool and show me the old photos from all over that her dad had taken, of the South after the war, freed slaves, and coal miners, and also urban pictures of life in downtown Baltimore in the Victorian Era, and even of the Baltimore Fire (when her dad ran out to get the pictures and almost lost his house in his own fiery enthusiasm.). She had saved them all, the plates were carefully separated with felt and tissue. She also had her Entire collection of National Geographic, she had been one of the First Women to join the "Society", and she was proud of that. She also was one of the first women to vote in Baltimore. She gave me my first Brownie camera and said I was going to be a photojournalist. (I used to wonder if she knew I became a nurse, and was she disappointed.) She and my grandmother would give me little notebooks and I would question people at the family events and write down their stories. (My pictures never quite turned out).

Now the funny thing was that some of the other peripheral Aunties, that I was not close to, but who did come to the Family events used to say that she was a "Lesbian", in that loud hushed falsetto whisper that would make any one cringe. She used to laugh about it. One day we were cleaning her room and she said with a bold "Do you want to meet my men?" I of course said "sure".

She brought out a huge old hat box, inside were photos and love letters and it was pretty full. My grandmother walked in, right when I was asking "But Granny Ethel says that you like Women better than Men?" She and my grandmother both laughed.

"Well, I have never been able to know what to do about That, I guess I should have told the truth. Ethel is my cousin and she is a good godfearing Christian, and I was afraid if she knew that I had had affairs with quite a few married men, that all my holidays would have been spent listening to how fast I was going to Hell. And for some reason the Women story was just easier, it rendered her speechless. She had Jesus and I had my men."

We were at her house the night that Martin Luther King was shot dead and Robert Kennedy spoke about it, and the radio replayed it. (At this point in my life I always picture the video we see of Bobby Kennedy speaking on the back of the truck to the crowds in Indianapolis). Aunt May said "Now the Trouble will Begin." I didn't know what she meant, and I didn't know why she was so upset, I only knew that I had chills and a deep emptiness. She hustled into the Kitchen and began making soup, this she did whenever she was troubled. She would chop, dump and stir, and the pot would boil and hiss. Flo said "Now May you don't know that . . . for certain". "Oh, Yes I do." Flo didn't say another word. She used to say that May had a way of Knowing Things. I asked her was it like fortune telling. I needed to Know. She said it was more like predicting weather, and that of all the Aunties, May always Knew things first. Things that Mattered.

I remember watching Robert Kennedy that night, and I asked" Aunt May if he was Hated too? ""or did people fear him? "She shook her head and cried as she stirred the soup witb rage, angst and sorrow. She was 90 years old. I was almost eight, just days away. And that night there was singing outside, hymns and gospel songs and Aunt May went and got candles to put in the windows. She was too upset to sing. We stayed and then went home late. It rained as we drove home. Flo said "Maybe God was crying with us". I remember hearing the wipers squeak and handing her Kleenex and lifesavers out of the box on the seat. It was a sad rain. And the lifesavers tasted salty.

Later that spring as summer came Aunt May explained that she had had voice pupils that now were grown and taught in Boston and that they told her about Coretta Scott King, and how she went to Boston, and that she had the Voice of an Angel. And that she fell in love with Martin in the early 1950's and he fell in love with her. Aunt May talked about how they loved each other and how they Believed in each other. She said, now that isn't Romance, that is true Love. They Marched together. They shared a Cause. She said" Now, yes, if I had found That, I would have been married." She also explained that she Knew that Coretta would Never remarry. She talked about their Love, and trying to raise children with bombs and threats and Martin being taken to Jail. She used to talk to me about it, because she said she was worried that I wasn't get "Taught Right at school. They keep everything too Damn Polite".

Aunt May lived in an all Black section of downtown Baltimore, but she had lived in the house, and owned it herself for over 50 years. My grandmother was always trying to talk her into moving uptown with her and Ted, but she would shush her pretty fast. She was very stubborn. "This is MY Home and these are my neighbors, and we all know each other. They don't treat me like some fragile old person, they treat me with respect. They don't care what color I am. You go home and tell Ted that." (Ted was granny Ethel's eldest son and he had some strong feelings about the eccentric old aunt that refused to leave downtown). And later that summer The Riots happened after Robert Kennedy was killed and we came to her house one day and found Baseball bats behind her door. Flo was not happy about this find. "May???". Aunt May shook her head. "Please, please think about coming Uptown with us?"

"They are grieving, angry. They are my neighbors. I will not abandon my neighbors during times of Trouble. This is my Home."

It turned out that each evening the Men of the neighborhood would come and sit with Missy May, and guard her house. And yes, they were black, and it didn't matter to her, and it didn't matter to them. They were neighbors. She would serve them soup and they would talk as Downtown Burned. And yes a bottle of best bourbon was shared for strength and they sat there in the dark with baseball bats. And she would sing softly. She got through the Baltimore Riots with not so much as a broken window.

She used to sing "This Old Man" and "Where Have all the Flowers Gone"," Amazing Grace" and brush my hair, and later when I had a baby of my own I realized how grateful I was that she taught me that lullabies are for Troubled Times and Troubled Souls. Once again we are living in Troubled Times.

May Coretta be remembered as the Brave Wise Woman that Marched with Martin by his side, and sang to his Soul, and carried on his Work and his Love, and The Dream.

JUNE 01, 2010, TUESDAY

GULF OIL DISASTER: DAY 43 MONDAY JUNE 1ST (CLEAN UP WORKER ISSUES: DISPERSANT EXPOSURE, BP'S PLANNED CLEAN UP CAMPS)

* * *

"When one tugs at a single thing in nature, he finds it attached to rest of the world." - John Muir

* * *

We all are connected to this Event in the Gulf, as it unfolds I encourage that there is much Media /blog coverage worth seeing: Think Progress, @TheOilDrum, @GOHSEP, @IRBBC, Truthout, LA TImes, NOLA. com and NYT, Mother Jones, Miami Herald, The Guardian and Huffington Post.

* * *

As of today after a long weekend, BP is pursuing their new Capping Method, LMRP, which will possibly raise the amount of oil coming from the broken rise by as much as 20%. The Robotic work continues and the spill continues. Yesterday Scientists latest data is that at conservative estimates, 12,000—19,000 barrels/day, which translates to more than 510,000 gallons a day, atleast. Over the weekend Carol Browner came on Meet The Press and called this our Worst Environmental Disaster ever.

But the issue that makes it so much more stressful is that disaster is not over, it is ongoing, on growing.

Over Memorial Day Weekend the reality of watching this gusher livecam all summer hit alot of folks hard, especially the Gulf residents. Many are devastated, and we need to have compassion for what they are facing and recognize they are looking at a grim summer, but also dire situation. I heard people on Blogs and on Twitter saying "well it is not an Apocalypse". It does not matter what those of us in other states feel, it is their Reality we have to comprehend. These are strong people, but these are also people that have been abandoned before. Katrina has left deep scars and many are still recovering from that wretched year. Others who live there have even voiced concern that Katrina PTSD is a real concern.

* * *

Sadly if anyone says that this is not a Crisis, please do share these photos with them, NYT posted these nine photos over the weekend. The ones that are disturbing are especially slides 6 and 7 that show the FishKills in Waveland Mississippi of massive amounts of fish on the beaches. I have seen Fishkills in the Northwest, and I have never seen photos like this before. If we look at those photos and think of the impact of this disaster on the FoodChain it is staggering and can not be diminished by BP. Just for reference I did also check NOAA Fishing zones, and that area has already been closed off. On another note as the Oil Slick grows, and is over 29,000 Sq.Miles now, it is hard for some to fathom, a wonderful artists named Andy came up with the Map that is mobile, allowing any of us to visualize the Slick in our own Region, Our Home, just go to the Beowulfe site and type in your address or City and see the full impact of the Spill. People around the world are now using this tool to see how big it really is.@Unclo (or Larry) of Twitter deserves so much credit for educating so many with this tool.

* * *

I had mentioned in earlier posts that the we need more Science and Marine Scientists there studying this situation. The Costeau family is there doing dives, studying the water and filming. This Video was by JM Costeau and posted to twitter and is a Must See, so do click this link.(Ocean Futures

Society is their family organization if you want to support their work). The Costeaus are exploring the damage to the ecosystem and the marine life caused by the oil and dispersants in the water column. They too are worried about the plumes causing damage and lowered oxygen levels, and the effects on the food chain.

* * *

@GOHSEP—The Governor's Office of Louisiana issues daily reports on Spill Sitings but also of the expanded NOAA maps. This is Link to May 31 Report on new Oil Spill sightings throughout coastal Louisiana. NOAA and GOHSEP have done an amazing job tracking all of the oil and fishing zones and GOHSEP has been an amazing source of all information related to Louisiana.

* * *

For anyone that has not understood the importance of the Maps that NOAA and GOHSEP are issuing. We need to remember that many that fish and Shrimp and maintain the oyster beds are effected by these closures. They face uncertain futures at this point. I have attached this amazing Article here that explains the Shrimping Industry and History of the Gulf. This is a Culture, a way of life, but families that fish and shrimp in region have carried on for generations. So far BP has been more than stingy with what and how they are paying for the damage to the region. To see how contorted this situation is this weekend the LA Times did a post on a Fisherman who tried to file his claim with BP and it is disturbing and raises questions as to how the Fishing men will be reimbursed. More than 40% of All shrimp and fish for North America comes from this fragile region, and that means also thousands of jobs are at stake. As these men face loss of work, it makes sense that they also will pursue working on the BP Clean Up Crews, but this can not be looked at as viable long term work or replacement of their current or past income.

* * *

Health Information: This weekend on Day 42 finally Federal Government,

Watergate Summer

DHHS did bring forth the first Mobile Unit to assist and meet the Medical Needs of this situation. As Clean Up workers in the Region have been experiencing symptoms and some have been hospitalized, it was time to set up a system to care for them and the residents, hopefully this is the first step. Do click the link to learn more, especially if you live near Venice. (Please also do see posts below regarding Dispersant and also regarding the Sick workers that BP has tried to blame their illnesses on Heat and also foodpoisoning.)

* * *

This Weekend is when Tony Hayward spoke about the Illnesses of the workers and tried to blame it on "Food Poisoning". It was filmed and CNN posted the video, and it remarkable and worrisome.

* * *

LA TIMES has an article up last night regarding Suttles and Haywards plan of "Floating Clean Up Camps" and "Tent Cities", (see post below) it turns out that the Plan is NOW to use Trailers that look like Semi Containers? or Box Cars. They contain bunk beds. and some bathing facilities, although these workers will need FULL Showers if they are working near or around chemicals and oil. Also it is unclear from this article if OSHA has approved this plan as it means the Workers will be working 12 hour shifts and then sleeping in the Contaminated zones which does present Safety issues.

* * *

Post from the Weekend with Suttles explaining the BP plan for Floating Worker Camps and "Tent Cities". (We now know Trailers were also part of the plan).

* * *

Shrimpers working as Cleanup Workers got sick after Corexit sprayed by low flying planes overhead, this was reported by local Media, but not by MSM. Dr.Gupta will be doing special on CNN Tuesday Night on this Dispersant and it's possible relationship to Workers complaints and hospitalizations. Nine—12 have been hospitalized so far. Wives of the workers are reporting to media worried about their husbands, who are feeling intimidated or harassed to not report problems for fear of loss of work.This just became an issue over weekend, we will see if it improves. BP's Worker Camps we can hope that OSHA makes them set up Medical Care as well.

* * *

As a nurse I have concerns for the Workers and residents there regarding the Exposure to the Dispersant COREXIT in such huge volumes, now being pumped in at well site, entering directly to the Water Column.This post I wrote earlier in the Month is regarding this Compound being used. OSHA has issued Precaution fact sheet for workers and residents regarding the Oil, but there is no monitoring or precautions issued regarding the COREXIT.EPA had told BP to cease using it, but for some reason BP is still using it, and now putting it directly at wellsite. The Literature has not information on that usage, it did have information on diluted spray form on limited small spills, early on after a spill. I have tried to write to OSHA, EPA and CDC regarding this chemical and have gotten no response. EPA and OSHA also were not present at the weekend pressers where the Work Camps were discussed by BP.

* * *

Another source of discussion that has been ongoing on the Internet and Twitter is the Hurricane concern. I continue to encourage people to check Weather Underground for updates. Scientists and Weather experts are worried as NOAA has predicted up to 23 Storms, with 14 Hurricanes. Please do click this link to learn more. And to answer anyone's questions, the Hurricane with the Oil Slick poses huge risks due to the Surge issue. Another aspect of this is BP plans to set up Flotillas, Floating Clean Up Camps, which also raises questions about their safety in Hurricanes.(please see posts below regarding floating camps).

* * *

The Guardian has this excellent post from the weekend exploring Scientists concerns regarding the giant Plumes forming under the sea from the Oil, and the ongoing battle with BP regarding the Damage. BP has continued to argue with Scientists regarding assessing ecological damage, but also the ongoing amounts of oil as well.

* * *

Enigma Note: I am still reporting information what I find from the Internet and Twitter and reports from the region. I do raise questions of concern. I think all of us should question what is going on there, but also be trying to employ critical thinking and problem solve. Problemsolving can be done with compassion and vision. To help the Gulf we will need to be creative and supportive. I am not an engineer or a oil person, but I post what I can so we can all learn more. I after all these days will only be checking Gushercam sporadically. Most of my focus will be on Gulf Residents Health, Wellbeing and also the Clean Up Workers. I will continue to post Science related to the situation from a variety of sources. This blog will continue to document the damage to the region, and chronicle this Disaster, which is what it is, Our Greatest Environmental Ecological Disaster. My main focus, as always for this blog is the Humanitarian Aspect of this Crisis. If you live in the Gulf and want to be interviewed regarding your concerns, I would be happy to post your story or photos here as well.

* * *

More Updates Later today . . . .

* * * **As I continue doing research on COREXIT and dispersants, I learned of a National Academy of Sciences Study of Dispersants in 2005 that supposedly is very illuminating, if anyone has the link I would be grateful.**

JULY 19, 2011, TUESDAY

REMEMBERING WATERGATE SUMMER AND WATCHING HACKGATE....

For over 6 years I have Blogged at Watergate Summer. I originally set up this blog and named it such because those of us living through the Bush Years were hoping for a Moment of Truth Breaking Clarity. As a nerdy kid, I watched the Watergate Mess unfold, it shaped me, it made me a News Junkie. I was hooked on the Washington Post and Baltimore Sun and I followed all of this when I was 12 years old. I would weed gardens and babysit and mow lawns so I would have money to buy newspapers and books. The First Summer I read the Story of the Break In at the Watergate and then the next summer I watched with interest the actual Watergate Hearings.

I would sit and watch and read the Papers. We were spending the Summer in Florida and my mom was furious that I was wasting my days sitting inside watching the Hearings Day after Day. She didn't understand that I was hungry for the Truth, that I wanted to KNOW if Nixon broke the Laws. I wanted to know if the Journalists were investigating a Moment in our History that would Change History. That summer was amazing, for me it woke me up to Such things as Corruption and Crime in High Places.

And yes within 30 days of the Resignation of Nixon, sadly Ford would basically shut the door on the Search for the Truth and Nixon was pardoned. It left many of us bitter, confused and angry. A few years later I dated a Lifeguard who worked at the Watergate. We would sneak in in off Hours and I was haunted by the stinky moldy carpet. (To this day the smell of Moldy Carpet, the stink would remind me of The Watergate.) We would "borrow" towels and sell them as "souvenirs", and swim late night laps in the Pool of Shame . . . . We would make bad jokes about plumbers . . . . We remained haunted by the Watergate Summer.

So yes, in 2005 I named my Blog Watergate Summer because I was hoping for another Watergate Summer, A summer where the Truth would Unravel Big Lies. But sadly It never happened under the Bush years, the Lies persisted and yet the Unraveling ever happened, even though Big Lies were told that led to Crimes and an Illegal War.

I am watching Hackgate because It is a Historic Situation where a very powerful man and his family are being confronted with Something Awful that went on in their Papers. It is about Journalistic Integrity and how What happens when Journalism collides with A Broken Moral Compass, Too much Power, Too Much Money and Political Lust and Hubris . . . . It is ugly, it is fascinating . . . it is Historic. And even though some Horrendous things were done in the name of "Journalism", there is some amazing Journalism now going on with Reporting from the Guardian, BBC, The Globe and the Telegraph and others showing true integrity. And once again a Political Leader is over his head, possibly compromised on his path to Leadership. Cameron made a dangerous liaison with both Brooks and Coulson. And as in any dangerously crafted Criminal Mess with too many tentacles, a Whistleblower has turned up dead on Monday within hours of Brooks Arrest. This Situation is Dirty, and ugly, I would not be shocked if there were not more incidents or accidents. It is also sad that the Police and even Scotland Yard are dirtied by this Scandal and involved in despicable ways.

4000 People were hacked, spied on, violated. All kinds of people. Even the phone of a little girl, a murder victim. 911 Families, Military families. There is something evil that made all of that happen, and too many people were involved in such activity for the shock and revulsion of this being revealed to go away.

Will the Hackgate Hearings reach across the Ocean to our shores? Will it reveal more about FOX? and will it reveal more about WSJ? Was there

Allie McNeil

hacking in the United States? Will it wake up our Journalistic Void? Will it bring back Journalistic Integrity? . . . . There is much more to come . . . .

*   *   *

Rupert Murdoch and his son James, a Father Son Moment as they are questioned today . . . .

(Many Thanks to Keith Olbermann and Current and Countdown for covering this Story, reporting the facts.)

AUGUST 22, 2011, MONDAY

MY PLANNED PARENTHOOD STORY . . . .

* * *

As a young girl folks don't know this, but I moved out Early, and also fell in love early. Finding Love was easy enough in the Seventies, but finding Birth Control was not as easy. And I was not the kind of girl to talk about sex or birth control. I was shy, nerdy and a little geeky. But I also was the kind of girl to have strange goals. I was very much in love the Summer of 1976 and it was my First Love. We decided that we wanted to Celebrate Independence Day in a momentous way. So yes, I lost my Virginity on Our Country's 200th Birthday, I guess you could say that makes me rather Patriotic . . . . And to add to my patriotic Legacy, 14 years later I actually got pregnant on Independence Day . . . . Planned Parenthood is a dear part of my Reproductive History, and truth be told I would not have my son without them.

Planned Parenthood entered the scene while I was in High school. It was the first place where we could go to get Birth Control and The Pill. This was the Era where Abortion became Legal, but when also backroom abortions were still happening. So the Fear of getting pregnant was very real for young girls and women. For girls and women Sex and Birth Control and Abortion and Pregnancy were still not topics easily discussed or shared. The person who really shared and taught me was my 79 year old Aunt Elizabeth. She was Widowed and that 16th summer I got my Drivers License I would drive her to meet her "lover", and it opened up many conversations to Life Lessons I sorely needed. There are not many people that show up to their Planned Parenthood appointment with the Great

Aunt asking questions about the Newest Birth Control. (She wanted to see "The Diaphragm" and once she saw it, and held it in her hand "Well, isn't that Ingenious !" in her soft West Virginia way.)

So off I went to Planned Parenthood to learn about Birth Control and also sex and also my Period. It was finally a place where I could ask questions and learn what I needed to know. My last two years of High School I went to an All Boys School, where I quickly realized that I didn't want sex yet and that I knew nothing about my body. And for someone who is a Science geek that was a heavy realization. I also realized that I wanted to Fall in Love, but that I didn't want Sex until I fell in Love. (So much for my mother's theory that I was "sex crazed" and that was WHY I wanted to go to the Boy's School. Truth be told I wanted to go to the Boys School because they had excellent Science and Math courses that I craved. I went on a scholarship and graduated early. And to be honest at that School I learned that Boys could be my friends, and I learned that I suck at Dating.)

But for me I also learned that there were things about me that I needed to know. By the time I was almost 20 I learned thank to Planned Parenthood that I did indeed have Endometriosis. This diagnosis would change everything, it would change how I felt about Sex and my body. I thought there was Something Wrong with me, that I was not enjoying my young body or Sex. But Planned Parenthood helped me understand that all of the Pain and the Bleeding were not in my "head" and that I was not "defective". They helped me get medicine for the Pain and they would rehydrate me when I was dehydrated from the bleeding. And they even had advice about the Sexual issues that plague such a disease. And they also early on explained to me that Endometriosis must be taken seriously as it does effect the ability to have Babies and stay Pregnant.

And so over the years while in Nursing School and as a young nurse with limited income Planned Parenthood did help me cope with this Disease. And that also meant they helped me cope with 4 miscarriages before I ever was to get pregnant and have my son. Most people think of Planned Parenthood and they think of Abortion Aid, but they don't realize that Planned Parenthood helps Millions of Young Women take care of their bodies and cope with so many other reproductive issues.

For me they helped me find Hope while I coped with a disease that was indeed posing reproductive challenges. And by the time I was 29 Living in Seattle, they helped me find Doctors working with Endometriosis and Fertility Challenges and with High Risk Pregnancies. And all of those years Planned Parenthood helped me with the excessive Bleeding, the dangerous Hematocrits, the Dehydration, the Infections, and yes, the pain and loss of miscarriages.

And so by the time I was 30 and living in Seattle I still very much wanted a child. I was taking care working ER and also taking care of AIDS patients, and working at one of the first AIDS Hospices in the Country. And because I was taking care of so many that were young and dying and many that were my friends, I wanted more than ever to bring some Life into this world. And so finally in my 30th year, after coping with severe Endometriosis for over 13 yrs I finally got Pregnant and was able to have a baby. It was a complicated pregnancy and a very dangerous delivery, but my son and I both survived and I was so thankful to finally have a Baby Boy. And 5 years later I would have to have a Hysterectomy due to the damage of the Endometriosis, so truly the Clock was ticking . . . .

And this summer while so many disparaging horrific falsehoods have been spread about this fine Medical Organization, few have remembered the Truth about the Medical Care they provide to so many. Less than 3% of their services are actually spent on Abortions. And they do provide Birth Control, but they also provide reproductive care, and that includes pregnancy care and prenatal care and even postnatal care and referrals to WIC. And they are providing care to young mothers and even those that want to be mothers.

And so this is my story, just one of millions, and why I am grateful to Planned Parenthood. They were there for me, and I try to be there for them. Through the years as a young Nursing Student and as a young Nurse I have tried to always donate Time, Supplies, and funds if I have them. There is no end to my gratitude . . . . I have a Son . . . because of the Work they do.

OCTOBER 10, 2011, MONDAY

ABOUT THE DEATH PENALTY....

About Life....

I have a Bird Feeder on my back porch. It was set up lovingly for both the birds and my cats. A couple of weeks ago, things got rough at the Feeder, and a little one got pushed off the food dish and fell to the ground and died. My little neighbor who is five came to me crying, "Can't you fix him, put Life Back in him? You are a nurse, a grown up, are you going to just let him die?". Together we buried The Little Dead Bird we tried to give him some dignity as we wrapped him in Basil and Morning Glories, and put him in a spot where the Cats would not get to him. And I tried to explain to her that Life was so fragile sometimes, and that even Big People can not always "Fix Life or Save All Living things". "But you try right?" She Said with such urgency....

It was the same day that Troy Davis was executed, and her pleading voice and her Big Eyes haunted me....

* * *

About Death....

Ever since watching that GOP Debate where Perry's Record Execution Number was met with thunderous applause I have been haunted by the issue of what the Death Penalty really means to us as a People, as a Country. It was not just one person who clapped, and the clapping was not polite golf clapping, it was actual enthusiasm. And Perry smiled shyly, smugly in the warmth of the applause, not a drop of shame, not even a single moment of moral intrepidation. It was like expected applause or praise for this "Record". And I can not comprehend that he feels "pride" in his Execution Number, that he is proud to have ended other's lives. In yet another debate he proudly said that he is Pro Life, I am confused how he can honestly make that statement when he has knowingly ended more than 200 lives.

This month I tried to have discussions with people I know about the Death Penalty and the "Applause" Moment from the debate. And I was struck that others were not as concerned as I was. "Well, It is part of our Justice System." "Maybe they were only applauding Perry, not the actual number". "It is more cost Effective to execute than to have people sitting on Death Row". "Isn't it better for the Victim's Families to have the situation resolved". "Maybe the number is high because Texas is large and has more crime." "Well, it is Part of Our Justice System" "You are Buddhist and a Nurse, that is why you have a hard time accepting the Death Penalty".

I was stunned at the number of rational justifications and even placid acceptance offered to me. And some of these people are very religious and morally sound and some were and are even liberal and progressive. So I am left wondering, do I not understand my fellow Americans? Or is our Moral Courage damaged? Do we lack a Moral Compass on this Issue? Are we as a Country damaged when some Americans justify Killing Other Americans by stating it is Legally and Religiously Sound? Are we really a "Civilized" Industrial Modern Nation that values Ancient Law of "Eye for an Eye"? 139 Countries (some more developed than others) have abolished the Death Penalty since 1976, why is America not one of those Countries?

* * *

Wisdom from Others . . . .

"**Capital punishment is the most premeditated of murders.**"

-**Albert Camus, French philosopher**

"As if one crime of such nature, done by a single man, acting individually, can be expiated by a similar crime done by all men, acting collectively."

-Lewis Lawes, warden of Sing Sing prison in NY in the 1920s and 30s

"Imposition of the death penalty is arbitrary and capricious. Decision of who will live and who will die for his crime turns less on the nature of the offense and the incorrigibility of the offender and more on inappropriate and indefensible considerations: the political and personal inclinations of prosecutors; the defendant's wealth, race and intellect; the race and economic status of the victim; the quality of the defendant's counsel; and the resources allocated to defense lawyers."

-Gerald Heaney, former appellate judge

"To take a life when a life has been lost is revenge, not justice."

-Desmond Tutu

"The most glaring weakness is that no matter how efficient and fair the DP may seem in theory, in actual practice it is primarily inflicted upon the weak, the poor, the ignorant and minorities."

-Pat Brown, former CA governor

"I have yet to see a death case among the dozen coming to the Supreme Court on eve-of-execution stay applications in which the defendant was well represented at trial . . . People who are well represented at trial do not get the death penalty."

-Ruth Bader Ginsburg, U.S. Supreme Court Justice

"In the US the overwhelming majority of those executed are psychotic, alcoholic, drug addicted or mentally unstable. They frequently are raised in an impoverished and abusive environment.

Seldom are people with money or prestige convicted of capital offenses, even more seldom are they executed."

-George Ryan, former Illinois Governor

"The reality is that capital punishment in America is a lottery. It is a punishment that is shaped by the constraints of poverty, race, geography and local politics."

-Bryan Stevenson, Death Row lawyer

"It can be argued that rapists deserve to be raped, that mutilators deserve to be mutilated. Most societies, however, refrain from responding in this way because the punishment is not only degrading to those on whom it is imposed, but it is also degrading to the society that engages in the same behavior as the criminals."

-Stephen Bright, human rights attorney

"I think this country would be much better off if we did not have capital punishment . . . . We cannot ignore the fact that in recent years a disturbing number of inmates on death row have been exonerated."

-John Paul Stevens, U.S. Supreme Court Justice

"I'm of the opinion that we should eliminate capital punishment. Having been involved with justice agencies around the world, it's been somewhat embarrassing, quite frankly, that nations just as so-called civilized as ours think we're barbaric because we still have capital punishment."

-Reginald Wilkinson, was a prison director in Ohio

"Death is not only an unusually severe punishment, unusual in its pain, in its finality and in its enormity, but it serves no penal purpose more effectively than a less severe punishment; therefore the principle inherent in the clause that prohibits pointless infliction of excessive punishment when less severe punishment can adequately achieve the same purposes invalidates the punishment."

~William J. Brennan, judicial opinion, Jul. 2, 1976

"When a juvenile commits a heinous crime, the State can exact forfeiture of some of the most basic liberties, but the State cannot extinguish his life and his potential to attain a mature understanding of his own humanity."

~Anthony Kennedy, judicial opinion on Roper v. Simmons, Mar. 1, 2005

"Since I was a law student, I have been against the death penalty. It does not deter. It is severely discriminatory against minorities, especially since they're given no competent legal counsel defense in many cases. It's a system that has to be perfect. You cannot execute one innocent person. No system is perfect. And to top it off, for those of you who are interested in the economics it, it costs more to pursue a capital case toward execution than it does to have full life imprisonment without parole."

~Ralph Nader, Meet the Press interview, Jun. 25, 2000

"It's just really tragic after all the horrors of the last 1,000 years we can't leave behind something as primitive as government sponsored execution."

~Russ Feingold

* * *

Facts To Share . . . .

(1 Amnesty International has carefully researched the Cost Issue, and shown that actually the Death Penalty is not Cost Effective, far from it.
(2) And for those that say America does not execute that many, 58-92 People are still executed per year. 3300 Are at any one time on Death Row, either serving life sentences or awaiting sentencing.
(3) National Coalition to End the Death Penalty also has more on this situation, explaining that it does not cut costs, or deter crime, or "save lives". (President George Bush used to say that at Debates . . . and no one every challenged him for the Stats.)
(4) Death Penalty Information Organization (also called Death Penalty Focus) has more information and is a site that has valuable insights.

NOVEMBER 13, 2011, SUNDAY

WHEN CRIMES ARE COMMITTED AGAINST CHILDREN AND THERE ARE LIES AND A COVER UP, IT IS NOT A "SEX SCANDEL". PERIOD.

* * *

(*Originally posted Nov.10th*)

36 Hours ago the MSM began reporting that there was a "Sex Scandal Breaking Involving Penn State Football Program". This Headline that was on Tickers could not have been more Wrong Headed and Misleading. What was "Breaking" was a Horrendous Crime Cover Up was being revealed, that involved Children and Predatory Crimes against them including Rape and Sodomy. When I first saw the Headline I didn't even think of going to look it up, I thought it was some Slimy sex mess, I had no idea it was about Children that had suffered at the hands of a Pedophile or that it had been covered up by a Large University and it's powerful Leaders and Coaches. Someone emailed me the PDF link and I sat and read in horror of what the Victims, mere Children suffered.

This is the Actual Link to the PDF of the Grand Jury Report, that was made public actually over 10 Months ago, and is now just being Publicly Shared. It details not only the Crimes by Sandusky but also the Cover up by the Administration and Coaches and "Leaders" at Penn State in clear concise details. Victim #2's Rape is the case that is most horrid to read, and why Police were NEVER notified in the past nine years is mind boggling.

Pennsylvania is a State where Authorities and Police must receive reports of ALL Statutory Rape and Rapes of Children (covered in their Statutory Rape Laws link is below). McQuery an grad Assistant at the time who witnessed the Attack and Rape did report it to his Bosses at the time, but he did not stop the attack or help the child. He and all involved did NOT contact the Police or get the Child Medical Care. The ONLY consequence of this horrendous Crime was that the Locks of the Locke room were changed and Sandusky's keys were taken away.

The One 2002 case that is most haunting is of a 10 year old child's rape by Sandusky that was Witnessed by McQuery in the Penn State Locker Room, Sandusky who was no longer employed by the School, but still had access to the Facilities for his Charity Work. He had originally set up his Charity in 1977, as a way to supposedly reach out and nurture Troubled Children who had unstable Homes. It reads like a a Predatory Horror Film. He even has written a book about his work called "Touched" that is troubling and disturbing, and hopefully the Authorities will read it closely for Clues and possible other Victims. The Grand Jury report outlines Crimes against 8 Children, but that is only of the last 10 years, and even now another Victim has come forward this week. (Criminally Sandusky is already facing 40 Counts. Yet at some point there are many that Enabled him and his Crimes and and even lied for him, one has to wonder when they too will face Justice). In 1999 He was let go from the School so he could supposedly work more on Second Mile, his Children's Charity, yet one has to wonder did the Administration let him go due to Problems or reports? If so then the 2002 Witnessed Rape should not have happened? But A College where Children and Young are Nurtured and Taught and a Rape is Reported and the ONLY thing that happens is that the Locks are Changed and Keys take away? And McQuery the Witness went on to an illustrious career at PSU, how could he go to work everyday and walk by that Lockeroom ever seeing a CHILD raped and knowing he did NOTHING?

In America today we are witnessing What Broken Trust Looks Like? What happens when Power and Money and Greed and Ego Collide, are Crimes Committed? Talk to Each other about This, it is not a small issue and this unfolding Horror Story is not about Old Coaches and Broken Dreams, it is about Crimes and When Greedy Men Cover Up Crimes. America is at a Cross Roads . . . . Let us hope many find their Moral Compass . . . for the Sake of the Our Children.

> *"If we have no peace, it is because we have forgotten that we belong to each other." Mother Teresa*

* * *

MORE INFO:

(1) More Details from Mother Jones on why Coach P should have never even been coaching this season.

* * *

(2) STATUTORY RAPE REPORTING LAWS FOR PA. ALL involved were obligated to report Immediately at the time, it is now NINE years later.

* * *

(3) This is the link to Jerry Sandusky's Book that is Called "Touched", that really is a concerning book and needs further study, but it documents his "Charity" work and predatory path.

* * *

(4) And NOW it gets worse, the Original DA that was trying to Prosecute Sandusky in 2005 went MISSING. DO READ THIS . . . .

* * *

(5) More on Jerry Sandusky and his Charity and his book.

* * *

Post in Washington Post written by a Sexual Crime Survivor shows a different perspective on watching the Events unfold this week at PSU.

* * *

15 Adults KNEW of the Abuse at PENN STATE and did NOT act . . . . More From Alternet.

* * *

More Updates from the Weekend 11.11-11.13th

The Judge who set Sandusky's out on Bail is also a 2nd Mile Volunteer. (Sandusky was not viewed to be a flight risk so he was sent home without even an ankle bracelet after it was desided that an UNSECURED Bail of 100,000 dollars was sufficient. As he faces increasing Counts of Crimes against children it is not clear if Child Safety issues were considered. Does Sandusky live near any schools or in a neighborhood full of children? Over the weekend there was some damage at his home, and it was reported he was not at the Home. If he is NOT at the Home, then where is he? Isn't he supposed to be Home, being Monitored? And about the Judge who decided that he could be out on Bail, why didn't she recuse herself from his case if she has relationship with his Charity? Again more questions than answers.

* * *

The Student Press Law Center begins to explore the Issues of Reporting Issues, what are the ramifications of not reporting Sexual Crimes against Children by an Educational Institution.

* * *

NOVEMBER 16, 2011, WEDNESDAY

POLICE BRUTALITY AT SEATTLE OCCUPY EVENT 84 YR OLD DORLI RAINEY IS PEPPERSPRAYED....

Seattle PI photo by Joshua Trujillo Taken Tuesday November 15th in the Evening. (By 6th and Pine or by Westlake Center)

* * *

From the Seattle PI::: "Pepper spray was deployed only against subjects who were either refusing a lawful order to disperse or engaging in assaultive behavior toward officers," said Seattle police spokesman Jeff Kappel

* * *

When this little elderly lady was Pepper Sprayed in the Face on Tuesday Night did the Seattle Police realize who this amazing little lady was? Did they care? Is this how Elderly are to be treated peacefully marching or assembling on a Seattle Street?

Dorli Rainey is 84 Years Old, 4 feet 10 inches and full of spunk and politically active and aware. She joined in a Occupy Solidarity March in Seattle. She is not just anyone's Granma that bakes cookies, she is a real American. In 2009 she was concerned about many issues facing Seattle, including Homelessness, Tent City Dwellers needing permanent shelter, and Infrastructure and Water Quality and Sewer issues. Smart sharp little lady who loves Seattle and her country, enough to run for office at 82 years old. She withdrew from the race partly because of Bus Stop concerns and too many late evening meetings, but also because she was worried no one was taking her concerns seriously. So she withdrew in May 2009.

* * *

Tuesday Evening she was helped away from the scene, taken care of by other Protesters. Please note how tiny she really is, she surely posed no threat to any one on site.

* * *

(Photo from UK Daily Mail)

Please note the Canisters and how close they are to faces, I am still trying to get verification from others as to what type of Pepper Spray was deployed. Nurses have been actively encouraging Occupy protesters get safety goggles or even swim goggles, and to have LAW solution at the ready as well as to wear a scarf to protect face and breathing. (LAW Solution is made up of Mint Maalox and Water 50/50 and placed in a spray bottle, can cool and calm face against Pepper Spray. And according to the Arab Spring Protesters can also work fairly adequately against Tear Gas.) It is unclear if Ms.Rainey had any protection and any access to medical relief at the site. It is also unclear if she has any other medical conditions that would put her at risk, example Glaucoma or Cataracts are very sensitive to such Chemicals and Sprays.

* * *

The Story could well end with the horrific photo of her injured crying tear stained face, but it doesn't, because The Stranger reached out to her and interviewed her, And I am sharing their post with you it is quite amazing.

"Dorli Rainey, a longtime liberal activist who moved here from Austria in 1956, also sent us this email explaining how it happened:

Something funny happened on my way to a transportation meeting in Northgate. As I got off the bus at 3rd and Pine I heard helicopters above. Knowing that the problems of New York would certainly precipitate action by Occupy Seattle, I thought I better check it out. Especially since only yesterday the City Government made a grandiose gesture to protect free speech. Well free speech does have its limits as I found out as the cops shoved their bicycles into the crowd and simultaneously pepper sprayed the so captured protesters. If it had not been for my Hero (Iraq Vet Caleb) I would have been down on the ground and trampled. This is what democracy looks like. It certainly left an impression on the people who rode the No. 1 bus home with me. In the women's movement there were signs which said: "Screw us and we multiply."

Ms. Rainey, you are a civic treasure."

* * *

Indeed The Stranger got it right, Ms.Rainey is indeed a True American Treasure . . . . and Amen to what she said "Screw Us and We Mulitply." And she raises a good question, IS This really What Democracy Looks Like? And note once again an Iraq War Vet came to her Aid and Protected her. Our VETS really are protecting and serving Our Country, and we need to thank them, as we battle to find our ways in these times. And I have been haunted all day I keep thinking about MsRainey how for 10 years she worked as a Translator for our Military while she lived in Austria after WWII and how she wanted to come to America to be part of a Democracy, that is what she yearned for. So in 1956 she came to America and she came during the Cold War and the Ike Years and The Hearings for those That were Anti American, and now here we are. What kind of Democracy is she experiencing now? What kind of Democracy are we? How did this happen that an 84 yr old petite elderly woman could be treated so horribly . . . . There is Something Very Wrong in America.

* * *

Here is an amazing interview with her from August 2010, The full interview is 28 minutes, but the first 3 minutes of her explaining about surviving WWII Living in Europe, and hungering to live in a real Democracy is haunting . . . . (She also did Translation for Our American Army in Europe for 10 years, as she was born in Austria:

(1) Seattle Weekly article on Ms.Rainey's Mayoral Run.

* * *

(2) This UK Daily Mail article has more details than the Seattle PI article and better photographs, and also details how a pregnant woman and a priest were also hurt by Police Actions on Tuesday Night.

* * *

(3) Seattle PI had little up regarding this incident at 2AM, I will update this link when more info is available, especially about the Injured Pregnant woman and the priest and the total number of arrests.

* * *

(5) Ms.Rainey even started a Blog the Year she ran for Mayor, it was called Old Lady In Combat Boots, politically astute and pithy.

* * *

(6) The Late Night Post from The Stranger with her Interview.

* * *

(7) Noon Seattle PI Updates on the Pepper Spraying of Ms.Rainey and also a Priest.

SNIPPETS From Seattle PI Article:

"An elderly woman, a pregnant woman and a priest were among those who were pepper-sprayed during a protest in support of the Occupy movement on Tuesday. The demonstrators taking part in the Occupy

Seattle movement marched from their current camp at Seattle Central Community College to Westlake Park late Tuesday afternoon.

While en route, they came across police officers at several points. At the intersection of Fifth and Pine, the crowd was met by a line of several dozen police officers on bicycles who blocked the way. Tensions mounted until police deployed pepper spray in an attempt to disperse the crowd and get the protesters out of the streets. About a dozen people were hit with the stinging fume.

"Pepper spray was deployed only against subjects who were either refusing a lawful order to disperse or engaging in assaultive behavior toward officers," said Seattle police spokesman Jeff Kappel.

Police said six people were arrested during the march. A 17-year-old girl was pepper-sprayed then arrested after allegedly swinging a stick at an officer. Three others—a 17-year-old boy, a man and a women—were arrested for suspected pedestrian interference. A man was arrested after he allegedly threw an unknown liquid at an officer's face, and another man was arrested for alleged assault. By 7:30 p.m., the protesters were back at their camp at Seattle Central Community College.

The local protesters were marching in support of the Occupy Wall Street protesters who were kicked out of their camp at Zucotti Park in New York and a judge ruled that their free speech rights do not extend to pitching a tent and setting up camp for months at a time. The protesters have been camped out in the privately owned park since mid-September.

Mayor Michael Bloomberg said he ordered the sweep because health and safety conditions had become "intolerable" in the crowded plaza.

On Monday, the Seattle City Council unanimously approved a resolution in support of the growing Occupy movement."

* * *

Update The Night after the Arrests Dorli Rainey was interviewed on Countdown by Keith Olbermann, it was one of the best interviews he has ever done, and while he was interviewing her she began to trend on Twitter. I will post the Link here and post the entire interview below.

Here is Dorli Rainey's amazing interview by Keith Olbermann on the importance of Activism.

NOVEMBER 24, 2011, THURSDAY

A PROTESTER'S MOTHER WRITES A LETTER TO MAYOR BLOOMBERG ABOUT THE POLICE BRUTALITY

* * *

(Originally posted 11.21.11)

Daniel . . . Leading a March on Wall Street, November 17th, He had been arrested on Tuesday early AM at Zucotti Park, was freed and then hours later there was a March. Daniel is an Organic farmer from New England, his family lives in Japan. And In Kobe Japan his family and friends have been watching Occupy Wall street unfold. They are proud of Daniel standing up for such an important cause.

* * *

Police beating down the protesters, and clearly you can see very long weighted sticks now. (What ever happened to little 12 inch long billy clubs?) When did these huge weighted sticks become the new norm? How many people have been hurt by the Police Brutality by these new tactics. Oakland with VETS being wounded with a ruptured spleen and a Vet with a Head Injury. And the Vet that was wounded got NO Medical Care for many hours, it appears that Beatings now are encouraged and Medical Care is not to be given, regardless of the wounds.

Watergate Summer

* * *

Daniel's Parents all the way in Japan woke Friday Morning to See this on the New York Times and for many hours they had no way to check on Daniel, even though they had seen that the Police Beat peaceful Protsters. The Police would give them no information. They were not even sure he had been arrested, or merely beaten.

* * *

Today is Monday November 20th This is the Letter that Lori Vest Wrote to the Mayor and the New York Times,

From Lori Vest.

(*mom of young man in the NYT Front Page Photo*)

Nov. 20, 2011

To the editor of the NY Times, Mayor Bloomberg,
Police Commissioner Kelly, and US citizens,

I made my first trip to New York City last summer and spent a small fortune (not for you, Mr. Bloomberg, but on our school teachers' salaries) enjoying city life. We paid our share of sales tax, city fees, tourist fees, etc. Little did I realize that this would help fund the NYPD to beat my son over the head with a metal club, as he was peacefully trying to follow his convictions and help the US people. He was on the front page of this paper, the NY Times, on Friday, Nov. 18th. My son is a self-employed farmer, a small business owner, an educator in sustainable farming, and a young man who has helped build houses for Habit for Humanity in three different countries.

As a first grade teacher, I spend lots of time discussing that it is not okay to hurt others, no matter how mad you are. Lately we have all seen pictures of dictators abusing the people of their country and we are appalled. President Obama said on Jan. 28th,

2011, "The people of Egypt have rights that are universal. That includes the right to peaceful assembly and association, the right to free speech, and the ability to determine their own destiny. These are human rights. And the United States will stand up for them everywhere ". However, the same brutality is being shown to peaceful US citizens. It is time we get appalled and stop it, whether we agree with the OWS protests on all levels or not. Each one of the demonstrators is someone's son, daughter, parent, brother, sister, etc.

Sincerely,
Lori Vest

* * *

"When I see a policeman with a club beating a man on the ground, I don't have to ask whose side I'm on."

~ George Orwell

DECEMBER 10, 2011, SATURDAY

SUICIDE PREVENTION TIPS (FOR USE ON TWITTER/ INTERNET)

(originally posted 11.29.11)

(1) If you notice someone in their Timeline is Voicing Depression, Hopelessness, "Wanting To End It" Wanting Out" Etc. Do Read their Whole Page, try to see what triggered this line of thought, do see if they are talking to Anyone? Or are they talking to themselves. If they are talking to themselves, this also means that they are still willing to talk, and NEED to talk. Do Engage, but ask quietly, nicely "Are you Ok? What is going on? I am worried about you? I care."

(2) If they don't respond it is fine to send Tweets of comfort, hope, caring, let the person know they are not alone. That you are THERE, you are not going anywhere.

(3) This does especially come up at Holidays. If they tweet that they have reasons, let them talk, let them cuss, voice concerns, even get pissed. That is fine for if they are pissed off, or venting, atleast then they are talking, and not engaging in hurting or harming themselves.

(4) Offer to help, ask if there is anyone you can call for them, anyone that might be able to help. (This is also to remind them that there are others close by that care about them and that would miss them.)

(5) By looking at their page try to ascertain do they have Intent, Means, (ie weapons, alcohol, pills, drugs, razors, sharp things, even rope, hints do happen, especially on twitter). Again do keep

them talking, tweet at them, tell them they are Loved, that they matter.
(6) Do not try to deal with the Situation alone-do get help and try to work it as a team, do try to engage people that are known to the person to also help, even dig through their tweets trying to assess their followers, friends etc. If needed try to find out their name, location etc, even from the friends.
(7) If they say they want to be Dead or Dead by a certain time, and if they show photos of Plan etc. DO CALL POLICE. Be specific. If you live in another state, be emphatic when you call. Do explain why you are concerned. Do also Screen Save the Page and keep track of time called etc.
(8) As an Old ER Nurse and Old Time Blogger I have seen these situations turn out a number of ways, bottomline unless you re THERE, you don't know the facts, so you have to assume the person is in pain and needs help, so you must do what you can. If you see someone Taunting them or Bullying them, or worse Daring them Shut THAT DOWN. It is Critical, as taunting like that can literally push someone over a psychological edge. (I mention this as there are many bullies in Cyberworld and they tend to show up during crisis times, and compassion can be lacking.) Cyber Bullying is very real, and they do say things like "Oh Just do it" "Stop Whining" etc etc. So for every tweet of compassion you send, do know that there are other tweets out there that are pushing that person, doing damage.
(9) No one due to distance and Internet constrictions, No one can make assumptions or yell at the person "attention seeking" or worse, because no one knows the state of mind of the Person Tweeting. But if they are tweeting Pain, Death Wishes etc, they must be in a good amount of pain. They Need Compassion and Help. And if a Team works together, it can make a difference.

** This page was written due to concern over an Occupy Seattle Person tonight who did have a plan and was in the middle of acting on it . . . and there was a massive effort to mobilize resources and help. And Police were contacted, and even Other Media searched for this person. Please know that at the different Occupy sites that there are problems of depression,

PTSD and especially among Unemployed, VETS and homeless, these are Real Issues, and Real People in Real Pain.**

* * *

National Suicide Prevention Lifeline—With Help Comes Hope
National Suicide Prevention Lifeline 1-800-273-TALK (8255): Suicide hotline, 24/ 7 free and confidential, nationwide network of crisis centers

DECEMBER 10, 2011, SATURDAY

CYBERBULLYING . . . . AND WHY WE ON THE LEFT SHOULD BE TALKING ABOUT IT . . .

* * *

Why Talk About Bullying?

(Originally written and post December 7th)

I am bringing up this issue for two different reasons. I have been witnessing people on Twitter getting Bullied on a regular basis. I have witnessed the Insults and hurtful words that are thrown at different people. And I have witnessed it being perpetrated by people who say that they are on The Left. For many years many of us have dealt with Bullies that appear as Trolls from the Right Wing hurling insults at us on Blogs and Twitter, but never from our Own Side. I have even see good people leave Twitter due to this behavior, and people who were new to Twitter and were immediately bullied and confused and hurt they left.

I am also blogging about this because I have had to assist late at night with two suicide situations, one of which involved Twitter Bullying. I am not saying these incidents are connected, but I am trying to point out that Bullying is Dangerous and Damaging to many involved and we as a Community of Adults should be able to talk about it and Recognize it and Stop it, if it is Damaging To Our Twitter Community.

*   *   *

Look Closely at this Sign, ALL of these Bullying Behaviors have been happening on Twitter, a small group has been Bullying Other Twitter Folks on the Left, for no real reason, except that they can. ALL of the Behaviors have been seen by other people as witnesses, and yet the Bullying Continues. Why Anyone on the Left would Bully Others is beyond me, this is an Election Year when Dems and those on the Left and Liberals should be coming together. Some of us have noticed that the Bullying is happening to people who are viewed not progressive enough? Or Not Supporting Obama enough? Could they be paid Operatives? Why would they be so relentless? So heartless to others on the Left? They sometimes behave as cruelly as Right Wing Trolls (and many of them actually are paid), So it is a valid question.

*   *   *

"I've been actually really very pleased to see how much awareness was raised around bullying, and how deeply it affects everyone. You know, you don't have to be the loser kid in high school to be bullied. Bullying and being picked on comes in so many different forms."

Lady Gaga

*   *   *

Definition From Olweus.org.

The definition is below with explanation, With Asterisk*   *   *, I have elaborated how this definition corresponds to what we have been witnessing on Twitter.

*   *   *

Cyber bullying is bullying through email, instant messaging (IMing), chat room exchanges, Web site posts, or digital messages or images send to a cellular phone or personal digital assistant (PDA) (Kowalski et al. 2008). Cyber bullying, like traditional bullying, involves an

imbalance of power, aggression, and a negative action that is often repeated.

Cyber bullying has some rather unique characteristics that are different from traditional bullying:

Anonymity: As bad as the "bully" on the playground may be, he or she can be readily identified and potentially avoided. On the other hand, the child who cyber bullies is often anonymous. The victim is left wondering who the cyber "bully" is, which can cause a great deal of stress.

* * * Instead of the "Playground" let's suppose the "Battleground" is Twitter, a giant open Chatroom, or Blogs with Comment threads, or Facebook with Comment Threads. On Twitter people have Codenames or handles, their True Idenities often hidden. This gives the Bullies more power in an uneven landscape.

Accessibility: Most children who use traditional ways of bullying terrorize their victim at school, on the bus, or walking to or from school. Although bullying can happen elsewhere in the community, there is usually a standard period of time during which these children have access to their victims. Children who cyber bully can wreak havoc any time of the day or night.

* * * Please note that this site says "Children", but Adults acting like 12 year old children can also Bully other adults. Yet the Accessibility issue also is true for the Twitter landscape. On Facebook, there is a Safety division and people can be reported for behavior that is not appropriate, where as on Twitter there are no Safety Moderators to report harassing or rude behavior. So Bullies can act with abandon and no that they will not meet any fate or reprimand. No Consequences for the Bully and No Protection or course of Action for the Victim.

Punitive Fears: Victims of cyber bullying often do not report it because of: (1) fear of retribution from their tormentors, and (2) fear that their computer or phone privileges will be taken away. Often, adults' responses to cyber bullying are to remove the technology from a victim—which in their eyes can be seen as punishment.

* * *On Twitter there is No Authority for the Victims to report the Bullying. Yet an interesting pattern that has occurred on Twitter that people that face off with the Bully are often later suffering Hacking or computer virus problems, which could just be an ugly coincidence that happens more often than not.

Bystanders: Most traditional bullying episodes occur in the presence of other people who assume the role of bystanders or witnesses. The phenomenon of being a bystander in the cyber world is different in that they may receive and forward emails, view web pages, forward images sent to cell phones, etc. The number of bystanders in the cyber world can reach into the millions.

* * *Witnesses and Bystanders who witness Bullying on Twitter are often left trying to ascertain what to do, how to help and how to stop the Bullying.

Disinhibition: The anonymity afforded by the Internet can lead children to engage in behaviors that they might not do face-to-face. Ironically, it is their very anonymity that allows some individuals to bully at all.

* * *The Cyber Bully is empowered because he/she does not have to show his/her face or reveal his name, it is like being slugged in the Dark Alley by someone wearing a Mask in the dead of Night.

* * *

I have been trying to Tweet Solidarity to the Person(s) being attacked. I have been trying to change the dialogue, to provide support to the person suffering. I have at times also been at the Brunt of this small little gang on Twitter, so I do understand how horrible it can be and how it can hurt some many involved. I don't have any solutions or answers, but I have concerns, and I can no longer be silent watching good people getting Hurt. Something has to stop this behavior on Twitter.

Allie McNeil

* * *

From Twitter This Tweet Was Posted tonight . . . From John Dean: "I'm writing on CYBERBULLYING: If you have experience(s) to share, on or off-the-record, send me a note: jwd.re.cyberbullying@gmail.com"

99 REPORT AWOPRADIO SUNDAY DECEMBER 11TH: FORECLOSURE STATS

* * *

(1) First I am going to highlight the Numbers from Last week Poverty Numbers and UnEmployment Numbers as combined with the FoodStamp Numbers they tell the story of America and the 99 Percent and why OWS is fighting for the 99 Percent. There are huge numbers of People Impacted. I watch these GOP debates and they talk of their God given rights and family values and I would just like to ask them, even one Why they think it is Acceptable for them to let their neighbors live like this?

And if someone has lost their job, you can bet that they are either on Foodstamps or living in their car, or buying Catfood for dinner or having to send their Kids to School Hungry. And While Real Americans, Millions of them are facing these Living Conditions GOP is Gutting Medicaid, Medicare, Food Stamps, Planned Parenthood. And I have seen these Republican Candidates say well let them seek Charity and Churches for help. Well news to them, in many of the poorer Cities the Churches are even closing due to lack of funds. All of these folks are our Brothers and Sisters, they are Americans and they are the 99 Percent. So I say give what you can and Occupy The Vote and do what you can to help: Salvation Army and Feeding America do stellar work and do Support the Occupy Movement.

The Stats that Tell The Story of the 99 Percent

29 Million UnderEmployed and UnEmployed

46 Million Living in Poverty

49 Million as of this Month on Food Stamps and SNAP

22 Million (or 12 Million depending on sources) Of our Elderly living in Poverty or eating catfood

On In Four Children going to bed hungry

22 Millon Children living in Poverty, this includes living in shelters,or hotels, and Hunger Issues

8 Million Foreclosed Homes 2008-2010, 4 Million More so far for 2011, and 2 Million facing foreclosure next 90 days

(Example for Cleveland that is 25,000 Empty Homes. Water Depts. have the Best Records on this)

Commercial buildings the Foreclosure Rate is even higher over 9 Percent (which explains the empty buildings downtown)

*   *   *THIS NPR MAP has imagery that shows the Economic Mapping, so you can examine your area and see UnEmployment and Foreclosure Issues Mapped.Really raises questions were the Banks Targeting Certain Neighborhoods and areas?

*   *   * Meanwhile here in Cleveland where there are 25,000 Empty Homes, The City Council Here passed an Emergency Resolution in support of the Occupy Movement, it is four pages long and beautifully written and describes the movement as related to the Economic Distress of our times, it was passed 18 to one. You can read more here, and see the Resolution.

- (2) Occupy Is moving their focus to Homes and Empty Buildings, trying to save Homes from Eviction, as well as reclaim homes for homeless families and also reclaim Empty Structures for use for shelters.

(Some folks would say that this is encouraging "Squatting", I would like to point out in parts of Europe Squatting is actually legal and that folks are allowed to squat as long as they keep structures clean, don't burn anything, or mis use fuel, and they leave the Water on so that people can keep themselves and the structures clean).

(3) Residential Foreclosures 2008 to 2010 = Over 8 Million (yet not all the numbers have been fully disclosed). This year 4 Million so far and another 2 Million are facing it in the upcoming 90 Days. Commercial Real Estate is over 9.1% which explains many of the empty urban regions. What I did start examining are Regional Maps (from NPR) that I am including in the Post on Foreclosures that clearly show that only certain areas of larger cities had Foreclosure Issues, and the neighborhoods with certain middle class jobs and incomes were indeed targeted, and the JD should be investigating those banks that targeted those Hoods. (IE. In Washington State Washington Mutual which sold their debts to Bank of America should be scrutinized). And another article also explained that the FDIC did know that 1: 200 Homes were starting to face Foreclosure in 2005. (Some articles also pointed out that some of these homes were VA Loans and possibly related to change of employment due to war Serving). So even in 2005 the Foreclosure rate was rising to 250,000 per quarter, and it kept rising per year.

* * *Here are some of the Stats: from the FDIC.

(4) The Occupy Stats are explained more here in the Thanksgiving 99 Report, and are great for explaining the 99 Movement to folks.
(5) The Post On Poverty and Children in America from last Sunday is a Must Read and has more information.

* * *

To Folks who say "I Don't Understand the 99 Percent Issue, or the Occupy Movement" I say "Which Side Are You On?"

Allie McNeil

It's about Americans being being Attacked by the GOP under 8 Years of Bush and the Current Congress, So Do Occupy the VOTE, but also do talk to your Neighbors, Know your Neighbors. And to President Obama I say, you do need to Acknowledge the 99 Percent, many of us Voted and helped get you to the Whitehouse, and are now facing Homelessness, Hungry Kids and Joblessness, and yeah, Millions of Us VOTE. The Occupy Movement is truly about the Middles Class being destroyed, and the Republicans and Tea party continue to be hell bent on destroying working class jobs and also taking away any efforts to help the Economic recovery.

DECEMBER 14, 2011, WEDNESDAY

HOW TO EXPLAIN OWS TO CONFUSED RELATIVES... #WHYWEOCCUPY THE #STATS

(Originally Posted For Thanksgiving Nov24th)

So this Thanksgiving I am going down to visit Occupy, take them some hot Turkey Sandwiches, and some winter goodies.(Many thanks to Bonni in Mass. who made incredible warm scarves for them...) and some mittens and gloves, cold medicine and I will be checking the medical bag. But it occurs to me that Thanksgiving is about families gathering and many won't get it, don't understand how many are damaged by this Economy and how it got this way. There is true economic pain that can be measured in Numbers. So here are some to share as you pass the gravy. (If you follow me on Twitter you know I do this #WhyWeOccupy hashtag every couple of days to educate folks.) So here are some of the Facts.

The STATS: #WhyWeOccupy.... in America:

(1) 50 Million are still without Healthcare (due to loss of jobs, States HighRisk Pools pricing folks out)
(2) 46 Million Living in Poverty (this Number includes Working Poor)
(3) 49 Million On Food Stamps
(4) 22 Million Children living in Poverty
(5) One in four Children going to bed hungry every night
(6) 29 Million UnEmployed and UnderEmployed
(7) 14 Million of our Elderly Living in Poverty

(8) 47,000 Dying Without Healthcare per year
(9) 235,000 Vets returning from Warzones to NO Job
(10) Vet Unemployment rate consistantly at 29%
(11) 600,000 Vets Sleeping on the Streets each night
(12) 26,000 Vets Lost Homes 2010 (some while serving overseas)
(13) 18 Vets commit suicide per day
(14) 8 Million Homes Lost In Foreclosure in past 3 years
(15) 62% of All Home Loss in Foreclosure due to Medical Debt

DECEMBER 20, 2011, TUESDAY

SOLSTICE POST . . . . AND SOME THOUGHTS ABOUT COURAGE AND WHO MATTERS . . .

* * *

"Courage is not the absence of fear, but rather the judgement that something else is more important than fear."- Ambrose Redmoon

About Courage . . . . And Why It Matters . . . .

Courage matters in so many ways, large and small and sometimes even silently. I am mentioning this issue because I am tired of watching a Smear Campaign unfold day after day over on Twitter. There is someone there who is attacking really good people, I am not even sure why, maybe it makes him feel good or "Bigger", or maybe it is for attention. But this I do know most people are having a hard time this Christmas, his attacks are cruel and baseless, and unwarranted. So many people are dealing with illness, and job issues and economic issues, his attacks could seem Petty and small minded. But they are damaging and hurting the Fabric of the Left. I have lost friends because of his attacks and lies and smearing. I have lost Followers on Twitter and Facebook and even gotten emails that were hate filled and senseless. I am and was a whistleblower, I know a thing or two about attacks, trolls and hate. Yet I have to say there is nothing worse than Hate on Our Own Side that is spun into a frenzy and fueled by people acting like Children. It is why I wrote the Cyberbullying Post, because I don't think Silence helps anyone. (The post I wrote on Cyberbullying is here that I wrote earlier this month.)

I share here and on Twitter and Facebook. I share my life, my home, my political thoughts. And yes, I post my Home, because in many ways I open up my heart and my home to all, I share. And yes, if you are rude to me, or my friends . . . I shut the door, I have to . . . . (On Twitter or Facebook that means you are Blocked . . .)

So I am just saying it right here, right now. I stand by my friends, and I say what I mean and mean what I say . . . . And there are certain people I value, not all of them get along or are even friends . . . but I love them all and value them . . . very very much and I have told them Publicly and Privately. The past two years working on the Book there were certain people who really were a Rock . . . . and I am grateful . . . very. So as this Solstice reveals and unfolds this year, I value those in my life and also those who have been there for me . . . . I honor Who and What you are, and I KNOW you . . .

Is it Wrong to want Peace here and in Twitterland? Is It Wrong to not want to be gossiped and slammed like a Highschool nerd? Is it wrong to want Peace for dear Friends? (seriously I had enough of that so many years ago) Is it wrong to want Solidarity on the Left? Is it wrong to expect and hope that People will act like adults and have Compassion?

Signed . . .
Praying for Peace . . . We Need It.

* * *

A Video for Solstice . . .

* * *

> *"Every day you either see a scar or courage. Where you dwell will define your struggle."*